THE ADVENTURER'S GUIDE

THE
ADVENTURER'S
GUIDE

JACK WHEELER

*Illustrated with photographs
taken by the author*

DAVID McKAY COMPANY, INC., NEW YORK

Library of Congress Cataloging in Publication Data

Wheeler, Jack, 1943-
    The adventurer's guide.

    Includes bibliographical references.
    SUMMARY: While relating five experiences such as
climbing the Matterhorn or living with the headhunters, the author offers hints for striking out on
one's own.
    1.   Adventure and adventurers—Juvenile liter-
ature.   2.   Voyages and travels—Guide-Books—Ju-
venile literature.   [1.   Adventure and adventurers.
2.   Voyages and travels]   I.   Title.
G525.W44   910'.453   75-43032
ISBN 0-679-20312-5

To My Dad

ACKNOWLEDGMENTS

This is a happy custom—taking time to thank those friends who have helped and assisted you to write a book and see it published. A book is a precious thing to an author, and those who have given their advice, expertise, enthusiasm, and encouragement become uniquely endeared to him.

My first debt of gratitude is owed to Mrs. Vera Webster, a woman of strength and intelligence. It was she who presented my manuscript to the good people at McKay. Thank you, Vera.

Deep thanks are also due to an old and dear friend of my family's, Mark Swain.

Charles Braly financially enabled me to start writing my book, and Dennis Turner enabled me to finish it. Thank you, Charles, especially for your patience, and thank you, Dennis, particularly just for being who you are.

I'm quite appreciative of the valuable advice on big-game hunting that C.J. McElroy was kind enough to give me, and of the time that Roy Weatherby took to read the Tiger Briefing chapter and offer his acute comments. Thanks also to my good friend Drake Morton for his suggestions on cameras and photography in that same chapter.

The two people to whom I owe the most, however, are my wonderful parents. Both my Mother and Father never ceased in their encouragement, always maintaining their conviction regarding my book's worth, even in those dark moments when I despaired of ever finding a publisher. It is a sad and contemptible fact that it has become old-fashioned for someone in our culture to say that he loves his parents. Well, I do, very much, and I am damn proud of it.

And, lastly, I would like to thank a beautiful woman, who has helped me in many ways, in some more than she knows, but who prefers that her name not be mentioned.

"Character Is Destiny"

—HERACLITUS

CONTENTS

Author on top of Kilimanjaro

I have climbed the great and holy mountains of this earth, and each time I have performed a ceremony that is mine alone, a small thing but a search unending. I place my hand upon its body. The Matterhorn remains the only one who answered.

INTRODUCTION
BEING AN ADVENTURER

All that life means to me is expressed in the picture on the facing page. Excitement, struggle, achievement, victory, joy. And living at home with these emotions . . . that is perhaps most important of all.

I get tired of hearing self-proclaimed intellectuals announcing in a tone of petulant arrogance that to be concerned with these things, to be excited about what one can achieve in life, is to be shallow and superficial. To be in touch with reality, according to them, is to assume the look of a mortician and constantly bemoan the poverty, suffering, and misery there is in the world. To err is to be human, they say, but to be right is not. To fail is human, but to succeed is not. To beg is human, but to produce what you consume is not. To suffer is to be human, they say, but to be happy is not.

I teach philosophy. For years now I have looked into the faces of young America. In some of them I see, with both horror and sadness —boredom. Bored with life at eighteen! Flowing from every pore— resignation, despair, fear, bewilderment. And above all, that most deadly destroyer of the human soul: cynicism. At eighteen. Tragically, they have accepted the black gospel of those against whom Nietzsche warned us in his *Genealogy of Morals*:

> All men of resentment are these physiologically distorted and worm-riddled persons, a whole quivering kingdom of burrowing revenge, indefatigable and insatiable in its outbursts against the happy, and equally so in disguises for revenge, in pretexts for revenge: when will they really reach their final, fondest, most sublime triumph of revenge? At that time, doubtless, when they succeed in pushing their own misery, indeed all misery there is, into the *consciousness* of the happy; so that the latter begin one day to be ashamed of their happiness, and perchance say to themselves when they meet, "It is a shame to be happy! *There is too much misery!*"

It is only by accepting such mind poison that the faces of these young people can be flushed with such tragedy. But in the faces of others—yes, in the faces of *others*—I see anticipation. I see the expectation and conviction that life is full of adventure and challenge, that the world does indeed hold an infinite potential for achievement, that happiness, their *own* happiness, is something enormously important, and is to be treated with unrestricted seriousness.

Pain . . . suffering . . . calamity . . . tragedy . . . misery . . . holocaust . . . all are *irrelevant*, irrelevant to what man *is* in this world, irrelevant to *what we live for*: We live *for* accomplishment, victory, happiness, and creation, not *for* defeat and pain—and if pain and defeat come, and they must, at some time, come to all men, we can't combat them by bewailing the "fact" that the universe is malevolent, that man was meant to suffer, that life is meaningless.

This is philosophical garbage, but it is polluting the minds of more and more of our youth, feeding the middle-aged tumor born of this so-called Age of Anxiety, and infecting the autumn years.

Man is a unique living organism. He m st *choose* to live, *choose* his goals, and *choose* to achieve them. Only you, an individual human being, can select your objectives and values—and only you can achieve them. In other words, life, *your* life, is as dull or exciting, as happy or painful, as meaningful or meaningless, as you make it. The world is a place of *unlimited* potential for human greatness, achievement, and happiness. But no one can experience it for you. No one can live for you. You just can't live life second hand.

Adventure! What a magnificent ring to that magic word. In its purest and truest sense, there are few to equal it in any language on earth. The man who lifts himself above the crowd, fixes his eyes upon the horizon, takes that all-important first step, *and does not stop*, will not go to his grave with a sterile heart and empty hands. A man of high spirit and rock-hard determination, he stands atop mighty Kilimanjaro. It took him four days to reach that fabled peak. The last few vital hours? Fighting to breathe, forcing strength-drained legs to take just one more step, then another, then another. His whole being condensed into *willing* one foot to pass the other, higher and higher, slower and slower. Altitude sickness has blurred his vision and nausea grips him with dry retchings that cut and burn. Three words consume him. His brain repeats them over and over and over again, his voice cannot: "I'll make it . . . I'll make it . . . I'll make it." One labored, dragging step more—and he does. He has reached the top. He pulls himself upright, his brain and vision clear, and in some miraculous fashion, strength flows through his body. He takes one great shuddering breath and looks down at Africa spread beneath him. A moment of such pristine exultation that he is screaming at the top of his lungs and not a sound is heard. Giant shivers are racing through his body and his scalp is on fire. "*I* made it . . . *I* made it . . . *I made it!*"

That person is *you*. And he is a hundred different men and women. He or she is a student, a teacher, a lawyer, a bank clerk, an executive, a salesman, a secretary, a truck driver, and ninety-two more.

Is he the same person who a few days before had laid down his tools, or his books? Never in this world—and he never will be again. He has won a *personal* victory; he accepted a difficult challenge and he met it. As an individual human being he found himself a far better person than he ever dreamed he was. When he returns to his classes, or courtroom, or workbench, there will be a new confidence, a deeper happiness, and above all else, a satisfaction with life and all about him that is beyond measurement. To conquer a mountain such as Kilimanjaro is to assert a mastery over life itself, and to experience that soaring freedom that comes with victory in the sky. There is nothing now that this man cannot face. He has proven himself to the most important person in his life—himself.

This is why I am writing this book. This is my goal. I want adventure to reach out and touch the heart and mind and soul and body of every man and woman, boy and girl. I want *you* to stand atop Kilimanjaro.

We get only one crack at life. It lasts but a snap of the finger. What a waste, what a *damned* shame, if you are lowered away, for all eternity, without once having your mortal soul purged with the emetic of High Adventure.

Put another way, I want you to be a hero to yourself. Being a hero means to strive for the best within you, to strive for unalloyed pride of oneself. It means to do one of those rare things that enables one to thrust aside all the self-doubts, all the appeals to duty, sacrifice, and unimportance made by the envious and self-hating, so that one can look at oneself in the mirror, right in the eye, and say, *"Damn, am I proud of you!"*—and mean it, right to the bottom of your soul.

Such a moment does not come often. It cannot be faked—for pride, to exist at all, must be honest and genuine. One may put up a front of false pride, or conceit, to fool others—but conceit cannot fool oneself. TANSTAAFL: "There Ain't No Such Thing As A Free Lunch"—in matter *or* in spirit.

We must, however, strive for such moments, with everything we have within us, for that is the only way they may be gained. And if we strive for them long enough, and achieve them often enough, thrusting aside those self-made or self-accepted barriers each time, we may find one day that they no longer exist, and that purity of pride, that pride in being proud, we felt in those extreme moments now exists within us naturally, as our normal, everyday attitude towards ourselves.

3

Every human being should be a hero to himself. We should all strive to live up to our genuinely own heroic ideals. Be a hero to yourself. Never treat yourself, your values, or your happiness lightly. And treat anyone who sneers at the heroic with nothing but contempt.

Take your dreams seriously. I am convinced that within almost everyone is a dream of adventure—of excitement and challenge, of the remote and exotic. This book exists to help those dreams come true. *The Adventurer's Guide* is against the idea of Don Quixote: the idealist fighting windmills. Don't dream about the stars, about fighting2the unconquerable. *To hell with the impossible dream!* The *AG* is here to show you how you *actually can* achieve dreams of adventure, adventure-in-reality. One may admire Don Quixote's idealism but its *effect* on the reader is for him to consider his dreams as unrealistic as Quixote's. The *AG* will show you they are not.

We live in a time in history called by defeatists the Age of Anxiety, an age characterized by despair, resignation, guilt, fear, and insousciance. Why in the Holy Cheendon's name do people allow these rabbits to nibble them to death? The average person is able to see, and go, and do, far more today than at any other period in human existence—more than the richest of the rich but fifty years ago. Age is no barrier to walk the highway of High Adventure. Nor is the fatness of your bank account. Added zeroes to a bank statement never placed strong feet upon the crest of Mt. Olympus.

In fact, you should dispel right now any thoughts that you have to have a family that's loaded, or a fixed income that's as steady as Greenwich Mean Time, to seek adventure. (That's fortunate for me, as I possess neither of these myself.) To live with a tribe of Amazon headhunters, or join a trans-Sahara expedition, for example, is far, far cheaper than a vacation in some famous resort, like Hawaii or Acapulco. There are no Hiltons in the Amazon or Sahara!

There is no problem, business or personal, no school standing or grade, no public fear or private worry that cannot be helped by a fourteen-day recharging of your soul and hypo to your character. Take a train across Siberia, a bus through the Sahara, a steamer down the Amazon. Explore a massive iceberg in the Antarctic, live with the Bambuti Pygmies deep in the Ituri forest, sail a dhow down the Ganges River, share a meal with a *real* cannibal, shake hands with the long-lost people of Easter Island, spend an afternoon on the North Pole, hunt a man-killing tiger in Asia, visit hidden kingdoms in the Himalayas, join a caravan of forty camels to explore unknown country leading to the Jade Sea, trek with Bushmen in the Kalahari Desert, enter an unknown and uninhabited forest in Nepal to discover and photograph snow leopards, ibex, bearded vultures, langur and macaque monkeys, marbled cats, sun birds, strange wolves, and giant bears. This amazing forest has been undisturbed for millions of years. Be a member of an underwater expedition to excavate a sunken sixteenth-century galleon, live with the Turcoman tribes of northern Afghanistan, bush trek in New Guinea, armed with blow gun and poisoned darts, be a member of a hunting party of head-shrinking Jivaros, swim naked—as did Leander—the fabled Hellespont, and, above all else: Stand atop the Queen of all mountains—the Matterhorn!

So you're a jaded traveler? Thought the world was a crossroads for all humanity? That adventure was dead? Nothing new to explore or do? No new sights to see or wonders to behold?

My job is to prove to you how false these notions are—to search the earth for you and demonstrate just how much adventure there still is in this world. And I don't mean group-tour, travel-club "adventure" either. I mean the real thing: first-rate, genuine, High Adventure. My next job is to convince you that you really *can* achieve your dreams. The best way I know how to do this is to tell you about some of my adventures, and then show you how you can do these very things yourself.

Most of the adventures we'll talk about I did when I was pretty young. That's to show you how *possible* they are. The Matterhorn was the first real mountain I ever climbed. I did it with no previous rock-climbing or mountaineering training, just Boy Scout hikes and scrambles around rocks and mountains myself. Now if an inexperienced fourteen-year-old boy can climb the Matterhorn, so can you! If a sixteen-year-old kid can saunter off alone to live with a tribe of Amazon headhunters, damn it, *so can you!*

I am no superman. Far from it. My physical abilities are really quite ordinary. After I swam the Hellespont, people asked me, "Are you going to be in the Olympics?" The question floored me—I was light-years away from being an Olympic-class swimmer. I just wanted to swim the Hellespont.

After each tale of mine will come a *Briefing*, which gives you every condition, physical and mental, required for that adventure—plus information on guides, equipment, costs,* etc., every detail on how

*Inflation has forced me to delete many prices and costs that in less mercurial times I could count on lasting for a couple of years at least, instead of barely beyond next week. Those that are listed should be good through 1976. How long all the specific information contained in the Particulars section of each *Briefing* will remain current, I have no way of knowing. But the main function of each adventure we'll talk about is, as I stress above, to serve as an *example*, illustrating the fact that real adventure is indeed possible in this world today. Thus, even if certain information becomes dated, its principal function will remain. It is extremely unlikely, however, that all, or even anywhere near a substantial amount, of this specific data will cease to be up to date during the next several years. Most of the people or organizations, for example, I recommend have been established for some time, and intend to remain that way. *However*: If you have your heart set on a particular adventure I do talk about, and the information on it does become dated, write to me, c/o David McKay Publishers, and I'll see what I can do.

you can have that adventure for your very own. (Note: There is no Briefing on Mongolia, per se, as Mongolia here is rather symbolic of the wild and remote. In the Mongolia chapter you will find out how you can join an expedition—or head up your own—to many of the remotest and most exotic places on earth: across the Sahara, overland to India, trekking in the Himalayas, diving for sunken treasure, going to the North Pole, living with cannibals in New Guinea, exploring Outer Mongolia, sailing to forgotten islands in the South Pacific, and many more.) And, by the way, I assume no experience or familiarity on your part with whatever each adventure requires. We start from scratch, just as I did.

Now I realize that your dreams of adventure may not be the same as mine. That's fine with me—for the ones I have picked are but examples, examples only, out of all there is that is truly adventurous. I do expect, however, that by reading how I achieved some of my dreams, and being shown how you can achieve those very things as well, you will become convinced that you can indeed accomplish your own special goals of adventure.

Besides, what we'll discuss in the *Briefings* will prepare you for climbing a great many mountains, not just the Matterhorn, or for living in most any jungle, not just the Oriente of Ecuador. I followed my own advice just recently, tramping through the jungles on Malekula and Pentecost Islands (in the New Hebrides, South Pacific) visiting Namba villages, and everything worked fine.

The primary purpose of *The Adventurer's Guide* is, then, not to teach you how to be an adventurer—although it certainly will try— for that must be learned in the doing. It is, rather, to engender within you an *attitude*, an attitude towards yourself and your life: the adventurous attitude.

With it, you'll never settle for the ordinary, the dull, the common ever again. You'll demand and strive for the exciting, the remote, the challenging. And in the doing and the striving, you will also learn things of precious value about yourself and your way of life. As Hegel said:

> Inherent in the strange and remote is a powerful interest . . . the attractiveness of which is in inverse proportion to its familiari-ty. . . . Initially it is in that remoteness that depth must be sought. But the depth and strength which we attain can be measured only by the distance to which we have fled the familiar center where we first found ourselves embedded, and to which we then strive to return.

Living within a culture that is very much removed from ours, like the Jivaros in the Amazon, the Sherpas in Nepal, or the Khalkhas in Mongolia, provides a unique and valuable perspective on our own way of life. And reaching for, and being on, what W.W. Sayre calls the "feather edge" of challenge gives one a pride in and understanding of oneself that can come in no other way.

And how to take that first step towards being an adventurer? Stop trying not to! That's the secret. Don't ever tell yourself that the heroic, the adventurous, is the not-realistic, the not-to-be-striven-for, the *not-to-be-accomplished-by-you*. High Adventure does not belong to the person who spends his time figuring out, very carefully, all the reasons why he is unable to do what he dreams of, but to the man who sits down and decides what he wants, decides how to achieve it—and then *does it*.

The easiest thing in the world to do is to figure out an excuse not to do something. I tell you, your brilliance at coming up with an almost inexhaustible number of incredibly persuasive excuses will astound you. Try it and see. Write down all the reasons you can think of why you shouldn't take a dugout canoe down the Pastaza River in the Atshuara headhunting country through the jungle to the mighty Amazon, or join a Mongol caravan deep in the mysterious Gobi Desert in Mongolia. Fine. All done? Right. Now take that paper and throw it in the wastebasket. You've taken that vital first step to being an Adventurer. You've stopped trying not to be one.

1
CLIMBING
THE MATTERHORN

I was looking up at the sky. The time was 4:00 p.m. on the fourteenth day of September 1958. I was fourteen years old. All about me, on the small platform of the famous Alpine railroad station, there was a great clutching of hands, a fervent embracing of bodies. The nibbling air was saturated with a babble of voices that few interpreters could translate: a high-keyed *good afternoon* in French; a low-keyed *how do you do* in British; an affectionate *I am glad to see you* in Swiss; a tenor-pitched *I thought you'd missed the train* in Italian; a booming, jovial *where the hell have you been* in American; *I am honored to greet you* in Japanese; an unbelieving *I am so cold* in Swahili; *I thought you'd never get here* in Israeli; and a dozen more, serving up a linguistic chop suey that could not be ordered in any vehicular terminal, stepladdered a mile high in the sky, anywhere, anytime.

It was exciting, exhilarating. It grabbed at your innards like a double shot of day-old moonshine on an empty stomach.

The feathered hats, the heavy boots, the bright jackets and glowing sweaters, the bulging plus-fours of weighty wool and stout corduroy, the full-faced smiles and overlapping laughs, the shrill and the deep, the tinkling ones of the distaff side, primed and eager. The ages? From May to September, and the white crowns and the hairless move as if one with the black and the red and the gold.

It was this constant *movement*, this *coursing*, no one still, no one anchored, that turned you on. And no one sad. Mental martinis by the magnum. For these were climbers all—not of hills nor small

8

mountains mortgaged to the earth, but of the great peaks, the towering ones: the Alps. And supreme amongst them all, the embodiment of their dreams, the high water mark of their climbing lives, was at that very moment before their eyes: the *Matterhorn*. And the strangest thing happened, yet it was not strange: Their greetings over, each one turned his eyes to that awesome giant stretching and stretching up into the sky, and fell silent. It was a little unnerving, that sudden quiet.

Then, as if embarrassed, all talked at once, a little faster, a little shriller.

This was the moment of their arrival at Zermatt. Tomorrow, or the next day, or the next week, they would challenge *the* Mountain. But while they slept this night, some quiet, some tossing and turning, but all dreaming of their moment to come, one of them would be scrambling his way up that magnificent face in the blue-black darkness. My long-prayed-for hour had arrived. I turned to look at my mother and sisters. They too had been arrivals on this train and were meeting my Bergfeuhrer for the first time. I myself had shaken his hand for the first time a mere ninety minutes ago. I watched them talk, close-faced and low-toned. Let them be reassured a few minutes longer; our deadline for boarding the tram to take us to the base of the Matterhorn was not till 4:30. I turned my head to stare up at *my* mountain once again.

When *you* arrive at Zermatt, I tell you this: You will lift your eyes, as I did at that moment, and simply not believe what you see, and feel, straight to the depths of your soul.

It is a living rock, an obelisk of enormous height, that by its very purity of shape personifies the imperishable, and engenders in oneself an almost awesome respect for a genuine miracle. Millions have caught their breath at the sight of her and thousands have met her challenge, yet nothing has changed. The spell she casts upon humans is uncanny. The Matterhorn is not a mountain, it is a presence. She lives alone, neither flanked nor protected by other mountains. No one shares the air she breathes. There is an emptiness all about her. All other mountains have been swept away. There are no towers, no spires, no spurs, to disturb her elegance and simple dignity. Where are the masses of debris that fell about her when she was being chiseled by millions of years of countless glaciers? Gone, for her flanks are clean and bare. She is a wonder of construction who lives alone in isolated integrity and harmony. You look from the north, the south, the west, and the east—and you see nothing. The Matterhorn reigns and governs like no mountain in the world. The vast waves of Alpine peaks that stretch in all directions carefully keep their distance. She is not cold and forbidding, the

10

hallmarks of nobility. There is a shimmering passion within her that feeds you every step as you climb to her long, knife-like crest in the sky.

The Matterhorn is the Classic Mountain of this earth. Her mold was shattered. There are no copies, and the soul of every man who challenges her is enriched beyond mortal measurement. She is unique. She is the Matterhorn.

I jumped! It was the sudden hand on my shoulder that did it. I had been watching myself climb magnificently, scaling each crag with the ease and agility of the reigning king of the mountain goats. What a dreamer. "Jack, it is time. We go." The voice of my guide, Alfons Franzen, Bergfeuhrer of the Matterhorn. No slave ever looked at his master with a greater appeal for sympathy or, failing that, encouragement of any nature, any amount. I received neither. A warm smile that I instantly decided was genuine, a matter-of-fact directness, and I was a slave no more. By magic of his own he had made me an equal, a climber.

I embraced the trembling distaff side of my family, reaffirmed an agreement—no, more than that, a pledge—with my father, and with shoulders painfully squared and pulse running wild, I strode away, taking a hasty quick-step to get in stride with the blond god beside me.

We were in the train, and there were other climbers with us. They too, would make their run at the great peak that night and the following day. Few spoke English. Once again, the Matterhorn had called to order a meeting of nations.

Alfons was silent. He had no need to speak. I had arrived by helicopter an hour and a half before my mother and sisters, my father being with me. Karl Franzen, Alfons' brother, had done a very decent thing. He had met us in Geneva the night before as we were arriving from Russia, and his greeting was short. "You must climb tomorrow, Jack. The weather will hold for seventy-two hours. I have arranged for my old friend, Herman Geiger, to fly us tomorrow to Zermatt. Your mother and sisters will take the Orient Express to Brig, where they will transfer to our Zermatt train, and will arrive just in time to see you off. We will arrive ninety minutes before they do. That hour and a half is all-important, Jack. You must be completely outfitted and briefed in that time. My brother will meet you and take care of everything. Our weather reports indicate that a storm will envelop the Matterhorn in less than seventy-two hours, therefore you will not have your week of practice to condition yourself to our altitude. It is to be regretted, but there it is!"

We had raced at Grand Prix speeds beside Lake Geneva, dipped into France, swerved back into Switzerland to arrive at Sion and board the red and white helicopter. Up the Val d' Herens to set down in a pasture in Zermatt. And there, my first sight of Alfons Franzen: six feet, 180 pounds, blond, muscular, deeply tanned. Type casting, I said to myself. Charming, quiet, with an air of confidence and stability, his blue eyes smiled when his face did. After three minutes flat, I was ready to climb in shorts and tennis shoes.

The tram rose higher and higher. All were quiet now, staring down, but then always turning their eyes upwards to the mountain, now looming larger and larger by the second. I had time to think again. The weather; the key to success on the Matterhorn.

The weather is the implacable foe of the transgressor on the vertical flanks of the world's most superb mountain. A sudden embrace of massive, enveloping clouds, and the climber is gone.

This perpetually reigning Queen of the world's peaks is a lightning rod beyond mortal compare. The earth's electrical charges are born at her feet and travel with inspiration up her sharply carved ridges, and marry their mates in the clouds at her summit. The resulting bolts that envelop the Matterhorn are without equal on earth. The blasts of thunder originate at her peak, and rattle the windows of chalets two miles below. A sudden snowfall, a freezing rain, and the pyramid of rock is transformed in minutes to a never-ending tower of blue-white ice. With a single snap of ruling Nature's finger, winds howl with a force and fury that tear a multitude of rocks from her sides to fall with blinding speed from which there is no escape. Avalanches of snow may at any moment sweep downwards, burying all beneath.

My thoughts kept switching almost in tempo with the cable car's swaying. To correct this haphazard thinking, I reverted to habit: a private conversation with myself. I suspect the reason for these frequent get-togethers is the fact that I have spent so much of my life alone in strange places around the world. I hasten to add that my lips do not move, neither does my head nod up or down, nor shake sideways, nor do my eyes become those of a hooded falcon in heat. But whenever I begin to feel like Diomedes facing the onslaught of the Trojans, I "take counsel with my *thumos*."

". . . two mistakes you've made already, my boy. You hear me? Two. You let yourself go to seed with your weeks of sightseeing in Russia—okay, okay, I take that back. You helped Dad with

12

his photography, but you still went to pot. On top of that, you've only got one pair of glasses. I don't know about you—you were going to get a full week, a fat seven days, here in Zermatt, before your climb. To get set, right? Double up on your daily exercises, climb a few normal practice mountains, run up and down some dumb hills to get this mountain air on your side, eat a lot of *good* food for a change, get a lot of sleep, eh? Sure you were. So the weather double-crossed you? Poor boy. If you'd stayed in shape in Russia it might be a different story. Why, you didn't even do your exercises! And how about all that work in the Sierras? Months of climbing and hiking—to no avail now. You honestly didn't think just a few weeks would louse you up, did you? And another thing, you covered up real good last night with Dad in Geneva, didn't you? Sure, you said, I feel great, Dad. Then you got off *that* subject fast. You then put the clincher on the old man, right? The funny thing about it, you meant every word of it. Even I believed you, and that's a miracle. Dad, you said, I've worked and planned a long time for this climb; I may never get another chance. Look at all the letters back and forth to the Franzens, Karl coming here tonight, all the work that's been done. That old friend of Karl's who's got the helicopter waiting. All of us here together, even Judy and Janine. When will that ever happen again in Switzerland? Yeah, that's just what you said, my friend. All the time he just kept looking at you, and then—will you ever forget it?—he asked one question, that's all, just four little words. Can you make it? And you answered, yes, sir! He nodded, you shook hands, and that did it. All right, big man, you're *going* to make it.

"Hey, we're here! Now, have I forgotten anything? Yes, yes. And listen very closely. Concentrate, if you're not too weak. I think Alfons is going to watch you real close on this first climb to the Hut. I think it's a test: From the Hut you can always walk down tomorrow morning. But it *won't happen*. Okay, pardner, it's up to you. You're on your own."

It was a long, hard hike. That's all, that trip to the Hornli Hut. A well-defined route; the higher we walked, the narrower it grew. The passage was cut sharply into the side of the great mountain, and by the minute the trail became steeper and the straight drop to my left more vertical. It was the pace that began to exact its toll. Alfons, ahead of me, his red jacket a beacon to follow, was striding upwards as if jet propelled. This is it, I said to myself, my climb is up for grabs. Why else had we strode off from the cable car terminus ahead of what I was convinced was the most experienced group of mountaineers on earth? Their ax heads gleamed from countless sharpenings and the handles were smooth from a thousand palms. Their ropes could have towed the Queen Mary.

It was a zig-zag ribbon we followed, and the pace, if anything, grew brisker. Silence was our third companion. The sun had disappeared behind the giant above us, and the first faint tinges of dusk appeared about us, all purple and gold. I learned to time my leader: 250 steps and he would turn, "You alright, Jack?" At the first crinkling of the red target above me I would summon a pleased expression, and, lifting my knees up high, sing out, "You bet!" No rope bound us; it remained, coiled and ready, looped over the broad, red splash in front of me.

We stopped at a promontory finally and stood looking down at a canyon far below us. It was still daylight to a degree, but the lights of Zermatt were already flickering on, one by one. Honesty, born of necessity, gave birth to my first, wholly individual act of this historic day. It was my own thing, and I recall doing it with a certain flair. I sat down. For ten seconds. "Jack, we have twenty-five hundred feet to go. Do you like meat and potatoes?"

I was reborn. The taste of what this psychologist and/or guide had just said rolled around in my mouth, and I was crowding his heels as off we went. You noted that I used the word "walk" a paragraph ago? I shall never mislead you knowingly, even when I am caught up in the joy or the pain of an adventure. The use of the word is literally correct: it *is* a walk, or, if you prefer, a hike, this first trek to the Hornli Hut. It will be a good shakedown for you. Strenuous, yes. Difficult, no. You must be in good condition, having done considerable trekking up hills for long distances, or you will wallow like a speared hippo.

We reached the Hut, and I was tired. My muscles ached and I was breathing heavily. That last half mile had been steep. We stood at the entrance, and I tell you this: It was a setting once seen, never forgotten. For this building—it is not a hut by a long shot—literally clings, hangs on, to the Matterhorn. Our evening was a quiet, still one as I stood behind Alfons and looked beneath me. The light was holding, and far below me I saw a twisting, rushing thread of silver. All about me, like a giant circle of Olympian sentries, were snow-encrusted peaks. And my goal? I stretched my neck back till it cramped my head to see the top of that overhanging crest, and for the first time in that grueling but dispassionate trek into the sky I felt a great surge of feeling.

Then I did something that to this day I cannot fully explain: I walked over to the very edge of that little platform upon which the hut was perched and laid my hand upon the rock wall that held it fast for a very long minute. It was a gentle touch; the sharp, small edges made no impression on my palm or my fingers. And then it came. A feeling, a vibration, then a throbbing that flowed up my arm, through my head and shoulders, and then downwards through my body. My imagination? Let me share something with you that I never talk about. I'll do it here, in these pages, for I shall hold nothing back, nor stop at anything, that will enable *you* to join me in this splendid world of adventure. Since that evening on the side of the Matterhorn, I have climbed several great and holy mountains of this earth. In each, I have found excitement and reward; in one, I discovered sheer and complete exultation—Kilimanjaro. But at every mountain, I have performed a little ceremony that is mine alone, a small thing, but a search unending. I place my hand upon its body. The Matterhorn remains the only one who answered.

We entered the Hut. Smoking candles and rough-hewn timbers. A handful of men, bearded and shaven; a sprinkling of women. Tall and short, thin and stocky, but a fat one there was not. In their twenties to their fifties, and every one of them young. When you call upon this Lady, there is no request for your birth date; she weighs only your heart and measures your spirit. We all shook hands and the smiles we got are the kind you store away.

It was a beat hiker that walked into that hut, and if in eight hours a fresh climber walked out it would be something of a miracle. And in five minutes I actually began to feel one coming my way. Wait till you sit down in that suspended room in the sky, surrounded by men who are members of that exclusive fraternity—the scramblers to the top of the world. It takes guts and heart, and Howard Hughes himself didn't have the money to buy their spirit and their rewards. English, German, French, Italian—it flowed about us. I was saturated with the feeling of companionship; not one comment about my age, not one dubious look. They were paying me the highest possible compliment: They were accepting me as one of them. I was just another place at the dinner table; the mere proof of my being there was enough for them. With one important extra—Alfons Franzen. He is a legend, and he was my guide. And what of my fearless leader in those moments of partial recovery? Moving easily about, a smile here, a laugh there, seeming vastly interested in what the other man was saying—and I'm sure he was. I was reminded, as I watched him, of what a man of position and worth to his country had told me two years earlier: "If you desire a reputation as an excellent conversationalist, Jack, you must first train yourself to be an excellent listener." I was equating Alfons with that wise philosophy when another memory of this same man came back to me in the form of a story that he told me with great, good humor. More than that, he had told the anecdote with out-and-out self-satisfaction, as if it were one of the great accomplishments of his life.

> . . . .and the day finally arrived, Jack, when my son had to make that long hike to receive his Scouting award. He had trained well, and would make it, but we had cooked up a surprise for him. The night before his mother had filled a basket with sandwiches, milk, tea, soft drinks, cake, candy, and a lot more, I can tell you that. Well, we said good-bye to him very early that morning and off he went. And off *we* went, straight to the garage, put our feast for at least ten starving people on the back seat, jumped into the car, and I do mean jumped, and took off to follow him. And son, that's just what we did, mile after mile, up hill and down hill, always keeping a safe distance behind so he wouldn't spot us. His mother, who had been sitting transfixed beside me, watching that boy of ours ahead as if he were marching into battle, suddenly announced, "It's time, dear, and I recall that when I asked her how she knew that this was the moment, her reply was, "When I'm hungry, he's hungry!"

If John Eisenhower reads these words, and I hope he does, he will remember this incident in his life, and will appreciate anew the heritage he received.

Of course, the association was there, hikes and good talk, but nevertheless it was a little unnerving to remember *that* story when my own father was doing *his* watching of his son, and I got the feeling that at that very moment he might be looking up through the moonlight. (And he was.)

Steaming broth, orangeade, and the promised meat and potatoes. Unbelievable—high in the Alps! What hero packed this epicurean's feast to our eagle's nest? I dedicated my seconds to him. At half-past eight I was sitting on the side of a well-rounded, feather-filled bed, with a candle flickering beside me. Alone now, I was unsupported by the buoyancy of new born companions. My temporary state of euphoria was being rapidly replaced by one hundred percent exhaustion.

I dared not climb into bed—instant blackout. No, I simply had to force myself to stay awake for one minute, make that two minutes, for my thoughts were racing: figure potentials, project contingencies, chart a course. Do these things quickly and your brain will clear and stop fighting you. A meeting. Not a General Conversation No. 1 like on the tram; no, this calls for Question and Answer No. 2.

Q. Okay, Jack. Concentrate. The last two hours of the hike: You were putting on an act for Alfons? Of not being tired?
A. Yes.
Q. Did it fool him?
A. I don't know.
Q. When he said good night to you three minutes ago in this room, didn't he say, "Until three o'clock, Jack"?
A. Yes.
Q. Isn't that a good sign?
A. No. He studied me for a whole minute before he said it.
Q. If he knocks at the door at three, haven't you got it made?
A. It depends on how I react when he awakens me.
Q. If he okays you, will six hours of sleep do the job?
A. I'll make it do. Believe me.
Q. I do. You worried about holding up climbers behind you?
A. No. I won't let them get that close. I'll keep up with Alfons. I won't slow him up.
Q. Pretty confident, aren't you?
A. The word is determined.
Q. You have to be at the top by eleven o'clock?
A. Yes, and you know why.
Q. Be specific: What's your plan of climb?
A. One, do exactly what Alfons tells me to do. Every second. Two, place my feet right in his steps where he has placed them ahead of me. To the inch. Three, never give up.
Q. Do you know that the toughest part of the climb is coming down? That you go first?
A. I know that. But reaching the top, and what happens there, will double my strength.
Q. You know something? You're gonna make it. Now go to sleep.

I carefully folded my rented outfit, slid into bed in my underwear, and blew out the candle.

If it was the first knock or the tenth I had no idea, but the last one did it. As of an instant I had thrown off the heavy quilt, swung my legs around and lunged forward. My feet hit the boards, and in total blackness I leaped for the door. A new bed-exit record had been set in the Alps.

The next ten seconds were a blur to me then, and they are to me now. My take-off was poorly executed, that I know, for at the instant of full power the door had opened and a flashlight had swiveled around and impaled me in mid-flight. God, what a horrible picture! Airborne, with eyes flaring, arms beating, legs churning, I tried desperately to arrest my flight and come in for a landing, but I stalled. The resulting touchdown was a one point disaster, for with all controls crossed I skidded off the spotlighted runway and totaled myself on the wall.

Silence. Dead silence. The spotlight beam that had lost me in flight and then swung to cover my landing was quivering madly, no longer steady. Again speared in its glare, I was unable to move. A candle held high aloft, and then another, suddenly illuminated the ghastly scene. And then, four immortal words issued from the dry lips of the downed bird, never to be forgotten, always to be remembered in Zermatt, Switzerland: "I'm ready, Mr. Franzen!"

Silence. Dead silence. The spotlight dulled and died. Its owner turned and lit the candle on the table. The two candlebearers retreated, and Alfons Franzen turned full square to me. His expression was now serene and composed. God knows what it *had* been. And then this man did something that must rank among the kindest acts of mankind directed to a single fellow human being.

He moved, he stumbled, he staggered to where I was frozen against the wall and, breathing heavily, looked me straight in the eye and said: "I'm ready, too!"

Alfons Franzen is some kind of man.

"One minute to get dressed, Jack. Your hot breakfast is waiting for you."

I stood outside waiting for Alfons. The moon was half-full and pale. It did not shine on the crags and peaks surrounding me; it simply set them glowing in a soft, eerie sort of way. The night was not black, it was dark blue, and the total absence of the slightest sound made the silence almost a living thing. I had never *felt* silence before; it pressed against me, and I had the sudden thought that this was the first time in my life that I knew the ultimate quiet. I believed at the time, and I still do, that this impression was created by a vastness—unlimited stretches of sheer unending distance, all deathly still, that made this total absence of sound a living thing, something that you wanted to reach out and touch. The poetic silence of the tomb is meaningless, for there is no one to report the quiet.

I listened for the wind to break this spell. There was not a single breath of air, not even a sigh. I strained for the sharp, continual cracking of a falling rock, close or far away, as it bounced from crag to crag. But not a sound. They were waiting for the sun to warm the surface and loosen them. And I remembered Alfons' warning to spread-eagle against the wall if above me came the string of explosions that signaled their approach. I took a series of deep breaths to remind myself, when the going became very steep and the altitude very high with the air so thin that my lungs would be laboring, to take a chest-filling inhalation every seventh step.

It was cold, but not overly so; the air did not pinch my nostrils nor put vapor before my lips. The stars were in the billions, but, strangely, they too did not sparkle and shine but glowed and fused in the navy-blue dome over me. It was the *glowing* of everything in this night that got to me; it was as if a razor-thin coating of silver fluorescent paint had been carefully sprayed over every inch of this vast, crag-studded world, with a second coat on each of the myriad number of peaks. For there the glow was brighter because of the capping of snow and ice, and the snow remaining beneath them in September was in long silver streaks and rivers that wound down to earth far below.

At last I looked beyond and above me to the Matterhorn. I had carefully avoided her until the last possible moment. A rule of mine—then and now. If I am faced with a challenge involving a degree of risk and hardship beyond the norm, I set myself to the task at hand to the exclusion of everything else in my life, bar nothing. Up to the second of the crouching at the starting line, I appreciate every molecule of the atmosphere around me. I taste it, I swallow it, I breathe it, I absorb it—and it never leaves me. But with the first look comes the first step, and from that moment on it is a completely personal matter between that challenge and me.

She was waiting. It was as simple as that. The steeply sloped ridge, appearing vertical from where I stood, was never-ending in length as it held steady in its upward march to the summit. It was to be the route of our climb. Certainly this mountain didn't need to add to her act, but she did. Six sharp, tiny but brilliant lights were appearing, disappearing, then suddenly winking again as they traveled upwards slowly but inexorably—flashlights of climbers who had jumped the gun. In the moonglow she was pure magic, and I really understood for the first time the deep-rooted conviction that men had held for centuries that she was impregnable. This feeling, basted by superstition and undiluted awe, had kept men from reaching her summit until every other major mountain in Europe had been conquered. The Matterhorn had held out to the last.

I was not aware of Alfons being beside me until the rope was pulled tightly and knotted around my waist. Not a word was said. I had received my last briefing over the biting of the hot rolls heaped with rich jelly, and the gulping of scalding tea thick with sugar. By yellow, smoking candlelight, large moving shadows become grotesque, and the four walls of that small room were alive with them as men carefully hung axes and pulled rope through their hands very slowly, feeling every inch. Careful study of shoes and their heavy soles, the fit of crampons, the last checklist of equipment and the stowing of packs. Only a quiet word here or there, these mountaineers were absorbed with their own thoughts and preparations. No man intruded upon the other. No order of climb. When each pair or foursome was ready, there would be a firm shaking of hands all around, a quick or a slow smile, and, in all the varied languages, the parting was the same: "Have a good climb!" I heard not one mention of luck. Not once.

Ready at last, inside and out, I left Alfons as he was talking quietly to the party that was to follow us, for I wanted above all else to have the moments alone that I have just shared with you.

Alfons was ten feet ahead of me. The rope was not tight between us. In sixty seconds I had made my first vow: For as long as possible, keep that rope loose—don't let it grow taut. I could see him clearly as his flashlight's beam kept probing and stabbing about him. In five minutes I had made my first discovery: I was not climbing but crawling, pulling myself up rock by rock (my first mistake). After a mere 500 feet I placed my first word in my mental handbook on mountain rock climbing: scramble. At this low level I was not walking, I was not climbing, I was scrambling: my arms outstretched high above me (I was making my second mistake), finding a finger hold, my legs getting a purchase on a ripple or a crack, lifting myself up (my third one). Time after time, rock after rock, each growing larger and steeper, my eyes never once leaving the beam of light on the mountain above me, for in its white glare I would see where Alfons placed his feet and extended his arms. With their motion, the light would dart about for a second or so, then zero in on the next rock above. At the instant of his arrival there, my fingers would be feeling for a handhold on the wall, and my left leg would be moving upwards seeking a toehold in the exact position that Alfons had just vacated. I thought of absolutely nothing else but the rock above me and the coordinates in my mental map. It was simply a case of one rock at a time. No thought of how many more, do they get bigger and more vertical, am I getting tired—just the next rock.

I was aware at the start that it was an extremely narrow ridge that we would be following upwards and that with each passing minute the drop straight down would increase, but I had not known how exquisitely thin was the leeway allowed me on either side. There was Alfons above me, and to his right and left— nothing. Scramble and pry. Grip and lift (that mistake again!). On and on, higher and higher. And then, with yet another rock under my belt, the easy introduction to the ascent was over. Alfons had stopped above me.

"Jack, we must leave the ridge. We shall be climbing the first cliffs I told you about. At the start they will not be difficult, but they will become higher and more difficult. They will continue for a thousand feet, then we shall return to the ridge. As we planned, I shall climb each one first. You will wait in a crevice below. At my signal, you will commence to climb and my rope will assist you. Understood? Good. Now we rest for exactly two minutes."

False dawn. The navy blues and the glowings were fading, blurs were sharpening into focus. I could now see clearly the near vertical drops so close beside me on either side. Giant bodies all about me in the distance were taking shape. I looked above Alfons, standing so still. The mountain was growing before my eyes, taller and straighter. Still working its magic.

I climbed to stand beside my guide with inches to spare on either side. Standing in space.

He carefully checked the rope again, inch by inch. He had me slowly lean down, tighten my laces, and check the soles of my shoes. As I was doing so, I was reminded of his stopping our hike to graphically illustrate a point on the day before, on the way up to the Hut. Walking to the very edge of the trail, where the drop at that particular spot was vertical to the canyon floor several thousand feet below, he had placed his right foot on an outcropping that extended over the edge. He had then balanced his body on the very toe of his shoe, with all the weight of his body on that forward portion of the heavy sole, and slowly and gently had rocked back and forth. While in motion he said, "Jack, always trust your equipment. Pay close attention to the shoes: the perfect fit, the strongest, the most pliable. Your shoes are the same as this one and they are most important to the rock climber. Pay the same attention to your ropes. Get the best—and then trust them." It was an effective demonstration, and one calculated to stick with you to the grave.

Alfons checked the knot that secured the line to my waist with his deft hands. He called it his "climber's hitch." And then, "We go, Jack."

We inched our way across the enormous face. As we arrived at the first sheer cliff, Alfons quickly scaled the wall, for this was but ten feet or so. Anchoring himself, he called out, "Now, Jack!" Up I went, now seeing in the growing light the cracks and footholds above me. The cliffs grew in number and in height. Now every part of my body came into play, for the first of the twenty-footers faced me. Alfons had already disappeared above me. His voice came from space, "Now, Jack!" Elbows, fingers, knees, feet, toes, legs for steadying and pushing, head for balance, eyes for searching, neck for arching, hips and shoulders, everything. The rope was taut and firm about me; the sense of security it gave me was incalculable. The cliffs grew higher, and as with the rocks far below I lived now for each single cliff. I said to myself, "If you never climb a single vertical cliff again in your life, alright: But make *this* one!" And I would find myself at the top.

We crossed the face again in our return to the ridge. And then Alfons stopped. The second time. He told me to lift my eyes and look above. The sun, rising from the East behind and far to our left as we climbed, had at that moment touched the very summit of the Matterhorn. A crest of pure gold on sparkling silver. And all below, reaching far down to us, her body was still in deep purple shade. It was the most magnificent picture I had ever seen. As we both stared upwards, the burnished triangle of the great mountain grew greater and greater in size as the purple veil was lowered by the rising sun. The Matterhorn was revealing herself, foot by foot, against a background of blue, virgin-fresh sky.

There was not a word spoken by my guide as he shortened the length of rope that bound us. I respected that silence for I too had been profoundly moved, and no words were needed. We began to climb again, to meet that descending curtain of gold.

The ridge had become a balancing wire 1,000 stories high, and our Lady supplied no nets at her feet. Automatically my inviolate rule of climb took over again. The next hundred feet—make it! Done. The next hundred feet—make it! Done. And still another rule of almost equal importance that I knew by instinct then, and by experience now, applied itself. Not once in the next five hours would I look to the summit, not once would I look up and ask myself, or Alfons, how much farther to the top.

We at last reached the Shoulder, the first of the only two extreme challenges that face the climber of the Matterhorn. It is a great bulge. You must surmount it by climbing, hand over hand, a fixed rope held firm at the top by a heavy iron spike driven deep into the rock. We stood at its base. We were now 1,300 stories high above the ground, and the wind had joined us; not a vicious coming, not a shrieking thing intent upon sweeping us off the ridge, but a gentle companion come to share our climb. We looked down to check the closeness of our rear guard. Close. The depths below us were staggering and exhilarating. "Jack, attend me closely. I will reach the top of the Shoulder. You will see me, you will hear me. Hand over hand use the fixed rope. Employ your legs against the wall. Do not stop, for it will weaken you, not give you strength. As you can see, I have lengthened our rope. You will be secure to me every second." The vibrations and in-and-out pulsations that had been keeping my muscles occupied for the last several hours had lessened, but in their place a deep aching had taken charge; each minute of the last hour had seen the increasing altitude take its toll. My breathing was quicker, thinner. I wasn't about to admit it to Old Faithful up there, but I was getting a bit weary.

"Now, Jack!" The words were faint in the distance above me, our new member weakening the call. Hand over hand I began the ascent. Ten, twenty, thirty pullups and I lost count. My rule of rules took charge. One more. . .one more. . .one more. . .and I was at the top and Alfons was coiling his rope. I got a smile but it was more than I deserved—it had been slow, that beating of the Shoulder. I would do better at the Hang-Over.

Up, up the ridge. A thousand feet, another thousand. The air got thinner, the wind blew stronger. Our new companion is getting restless. Move it up! One hundred more feet. Attaboy. One hundred more feet. Good goin', Jack.

Without warning the moving red sweater above and beyond me went out of focus. I bumped into it, and two strong hands steadied me. It was a good thing, for my flight would have lasted two miles plus. "We rest a minute, friend Jack." I could not sit down, there was no room. There never is on the Matterhorn. That is why you must climb to the Hut in the late afternoon, leave it in the dead of night, and reach the top by high noon. For to return to earth before nightfall is to insure your life. There is no haven of rest at the top of the Queen of Mountains. Her summit is not what it appears to be from the ground—far, far from it. Her best kept secret is reserved for those who reach the top.

One hundred more feet. Great care now to maintain my balance. Higher and higher. A quiet, "Jack, there it is," brought me up short—to stare in honest-to-goodness astonishment at the justly famous and deservedly notorious Hang-Over. A massive, five-story-high cliff with the top extending out into space *over* its base. I looked quickly down beneath it and judged the straight fall to be over a mile. The fixed rope snaked over the very center of that thrust-out lip and was dangling and swaying back and forth.

This was the scene of the most horrible of all Alpine tragedies. On a pretty summer's day in 1865, four men plunged off the top of this cliff, one dragging the other, as the remaining three in the group braced themselves, hoping the rope would hold. It did not. Thus the first conquest of the Matterhorn, and the rest of Edward Whymper's life,* was stained with death.

I waited, pressed against the almost vertical wall. And still once more I was forcing myself to think only of the job directly ahead. But this time it was hard going. Questions, like rapier thrusts, were penetrating my defenses with ease. When was this free-hanging line checked? When was it last replaced? Why does not the sharp edge above fray the rope as it is rubbed fiercely by the climber? Will the spike above pull out? Above all, have I the strength left, after all these hours of continual and never-ending strain and all-out effort, to pull myself up that *damned* rope? No time for answers. Two words rang out loud and clear, "Now, Jack!"

*Whymper was the leader and one of the survivors. The others were Peter Taugwalder and his father, both Swiss guides. The victims were Michel-Auguste Croz, a French guide; Charles Hudson and Francis Douglas, both experienced climbers; and a friend of Douglas', the inexperienced Donald Hadow, whose slip caused the accident.

I took two steps, placed my left hand above my right on the thick hemp, pulled myself into the air, thrust my legs out from me to plant them against the wall of the Hang-Over. With every bit of concentration left in me I set myself the goal of one hand over the other, lift my body, one hand over the other, lift my body. I willed my legs to work in unison with my hands. Don't lose the wall, I kept repeating. Now the next. Good. Now the next. Good. Upwards I rose. Now the next. Good. Halfway up—my feet slipped off the face in a downward skid and the result was instantly catastrophic. Out swung my body over space like pendulum over pit. My legs moved up with an arching of my back to cushion the impact of whamming against the wall, but it was purely a reflex action. For the first time in my life, fear hit me like a sniper's bullet. A searing, encircling pain flashed through me and averted what surely must have been sheer panic on its way. Alfons' rope! And the calm words that floated down from above, "Stop the playing around, Jack. Up you come."

There were still hours to climb. Going by my rule book again I never searched for the summit, but covered each rapidly rising 100 feet a block at a time. The sun was now brilliant at the first-quarter pole, and plainly visible above us were the French and German climbers who had departed first—that was a good sign. The Italians and the English behind were not gaining—another plus. Alfons, by his very silence, was affording me the supreme compliment. All was going well, except for one alarming development: I was running out of gas. A quick look now and then in my direction by the Prince of Guides in red—dead ahead—led me to believe that his confidence in my superb physical condition was on the wane. As before, I tried to time a high knee kick and a pleased expression with the turning of the golden head above me, but at this stage of the game the spirit was willing but the body passed.

I was saved from ignoble defeat by an invitation from my guide to sit down. This in itself was a display of respect for a fallen sparrow, for the seat so graciously offered was a full one foot square in diameter. One heavy sigh and I would take off with a new glider record for sustained free flight that my heirs would cherish for at least a week. "Jack, how do you feel?" "Alfons, I am very tired. In a word, sir, I am exhausted."

A smile, and, "My young friend, I have watched you. You have set yourself a plan, no? In it you never look ahead. Not once have you asked, 'Alfons, how far do we have to go? Can't we stop now? How far to the top?' This is very good. Now, Jack, I ask a favor of you. Will you oblige me? Now, right now, Jack, look up over my shoulder. That's right. See? The summit, Jack. You are one hundred yards from the top."

In all the affairs that I have been concerned with since that moment on the Matterhorn, I have never, *never*, felt such an uplifting of spirit, such a physical rebirth, as when I looked up and there it was. I rose to my feet weighing ten pounds, six ounces. "Alfons, let's go!" It's tough going, that last stretch, but I was hardly conscious of it. Three thoughts I had tumbling around in my numbed brain those last, long minutes, not in the orderly fashion that I count upon but one over the other and back again: "How smart of Alfons to stop, let me rest, and then fire me up to reach the top with a clear head and great spirit so that I could *really* appreciate the moment and the sensation. . . . I'm going to make it. . . . I'm going to make it. . . . how smart of Alfons to stop, let me. . . . will it happen at the top? . . . will it happen? . . ."

At last. *At last.* I stood upon the summit. The most famous and revered mountain in the world: the Matterhorn.

And instant bewilderment. That's right—instant bewilderment. Even at a moment like this, the culmination of an afternoon, a night, and a day of tortured muscles, flashing fear, and god-like inspirations, I must report accurately. It would be so easy to follow the normal path of literary build-up and type the expected words of ecstasy, of joy sublime, of great pride, and unbridled enthusiasm, but they would not be correctly timed. Oh, they came, indeed they did, but not at the second of ascension. The first thought of your boy climber as he stepped upon the ground trod by immortals was, "It's not a peak. It's a football field two feet wide!" And that's exactly what it was: a long bowie knife, twenty-eight inches wide, its polished cutting edge extending from the hilt upon which I stood, straight out into empty space 300 feet, the great surprise that I promised you that this most honored crag in the world keeps for only those who conquer her.

Now I looked around me. Unbelievable. A perfectly clear day, cloudless, radiant, a vast unending panorama of peaked crags, glaciers, and snowfields, all proud and glittering. There was the immense shining dome of Mont Blanc far to the west, the marching away of the crested legions of the Pennines and the Oberland to the east and north. "See, Monta Rosa, Jack." And again, even though he had relished it 150 times, "Monte Viso, Jack. She is one hundred miles from us!" Incredibly white, with a burning vividness against an unending cobalt sky, the phalanxes of soaring rock-fangs literally stole your breath. I was standing on top of the world, and there was nothing around me to dispute my rule. That is the uncanny feeling that the Matterhorn grants you at her top. You stand alone in the sky.

We sighed, Alfons and I. Almost at the same instant, suspended up there in space, we happened to take a great intake of cold, thin air. And then as if by signal, our heads turned and we looked down upon Italy. All that I have so inadequately described above took but fifteen seconds. My eyes had been a camera clicking off shots for future viewing, but my mind was on the depths below. Alfons and I were searching for something, though not once had we mentioned it during the long journey to the top. Side by side, looking down, there was no sound on the top of that peak from the two solitary figures standing there, balanced on a tightrope—only the wind, which had lowered its voice as if its task in helping us to the top was finished.

"Alfons, there he is." A small plane was a thousand feet below us, banking sharply as it climbed. Its wings were a hundred feet from our mountain's side. And then the whining of the engine; we heard it together, at the same insant. Alfons quickly placed his right arm around my shoulder and took up the slack in the rope that bound us so tightly that I gasped. I was in danger of falling off for I was jumping, yes, jumping on top of the Matterhorn. I was yelling at the top of my voice, "Come on, Dad. Come on!"

Yes, it was my father coming to meet me. He was keeping his promise.

As I write these words now, in describing this strangest of rendezvous, even after sixteen years, the emotion that I feel is very difficult to control. The plane was twisting badly beneath us as vicious downdrafts were attacking it, and, as if it were this very second, I can hear Alfons shouting, "You're too close, you're too close to the wall." Our heads and shoulders were extending over the sides of the vertical wall beneath us when suddenly the tightly banking plane disappeared from the Italian side below us. As one we turned around, looked straight down on the Swiss side and waited for it to come around. There it was. Higher now. Its engine louder, screaming in the thin air. Suddenly, it banked sharply and flew away to the east. Alfons and I were aghast. We said not a word. We watched it grow smaller and smaller—and then it began to climb. "He's gaining altitude, he's getting higher so he can reach us," I yelled to Alfons, who was standing one foot from me. "Right," he shouted back.

I simply cannot express my feelings, *our* feelings, as we watched it go higher and higher, bank almost vertically, and head directly towards us. Closer and closer. The engine was louder and louder. "There he is, Alfons." My father, with the door of his plane removed for us to see each other clearly, was waving. He was a hundred feet away. It was unbelievable. I am standing on the top of the Matterhorn and my Dad is right out there. He circled us three times; we could almost reach out and touch him in space. Never in the history of that great mountain had such a thing happened. And perhaps, for the first time, a Bergfeuhrer was crying at the top of the Matterhorn.

I am proud of the fact that I can still feel the tears that streamed down my face. It was the most glorious moment of my life, and the most moving. To this day, it still is. With a rocking motion of his wings saying "Good-bye," my father's plane went into a flat dive and disappeared below. I was not to know for several hours that, across the great abyss that separated us for many, many miles, my mother and sisters had watched us through a giant telescope from atop the Gornergrat.

Two minutes later we were spraddle-legged over the Matterhorn. Now *that's* something, eh? To complete the picture, we were munching goat's milk cheese and sipping jasmine tea. To speed our recovery from our emotional letdown, we had carefully selected the finest honed edge of the bowie knife in the Alpine sky for our luncheon table. With one leg over Italy and the other over Switzerland, if you ever hear of a more far-out picnic, let me know, will you?

With the last bite and swallow it was all business again. "Jack, attend me. You have climbed the Matterhorn, but now you must climb down. You perhaps think it will be easier? Ah, you don't. Good. I will not alarm yo ι, but most accidents occur on the *descent*. You must go first. You will not see your handholds and footholds. You will *feel* them. I have noted with pleasure that you, how do you say, glory in heights? That is very good indeed. Now listen very carefully. Going down, *stretch* out and use the *lowest* hand-hold. Remember your *three-point hold*. Both feet and one hand in hold, the other to search. Okay? Again I tell you, do not stay in one position too long; tension, she will weaken your muscles. You do not forget this on ascent. I am happy with that. On the Hang-Over—and do not play the games again!—and the Shoulder, face in. All other times, except when I tell you, face outward. You understand? Good. If you get tired, call to me and we stop. Fatigue has been my climbers' worst enemy. Very bad. You call out to me. Remember: You are *not to worry*, Jack. I am above you and [a quick, warm smile], I am the best!"

We stood up very carefully (muscles get tight after great exertion for a long period, and sitting down for even a few minutes can result in a stagger or lurch when you arise quickly; it happens on mountains fairly often with unpleasant results) and Alfons quickly wound the rope around my waist two more turns. Answering my obvious question, he said, "It is more comfortable for you if you fall and I must hold you." He then asked me to grip his shoulders hard with both hands. (The wind had increased and was now quite strong.) With fingers flying, he untied his "climber's knot," fashioned a new one, and, pulling it firm, moved his fingers over it once again, slowly and carefully, just as he had the entire length (120 feet) of our rope a moment ago. "At the spot where I surprised you with the summit, Jack, we'll stop and remove our crampons." It was there that we had placed them on our shoes, and I now fully appreciated them; they had done wonders for my footing on the summit. (Crampons have ten or twelve extremely sharp steel points. These spikes bite deep into snow or ice and are absolutely essential for all snow climbing or on a dangerous summit. They must fit perfectly and Alfons had instructed me to shake my feet after they had been placed on my shoes and *before* I strapped them on. They had not come off. It is a must practice to follow.) We walked down the snow-covered knife blade and, just before starting down, stopped and swept our eyes across that vast separate world around and beneath us for the last time.

The descent was tremendous. It was, of course, completely different from going up and considerably harder. It was great fun and I enjoyed every single minute of it, even with enduring the intense mental strain from the concentration demanded by Alfons. I was the leader now (well, I *was* going first, wasn't I?) as like a new-born bat I clung to a vertical wall, staring out at the world beneath me, my heels wedged into a horizontal crack, my back arched slightly to put my body weight over my feet, my arms extended sideways with my hands supplying the holding power to my fingertips, which were inserted backwards into holes discovered by Alfons above me. There was nothing directly beneath me for a mile or so—I was almost literally standing in space, defying the law of gravity. It was a magnificent moment, and I was to enjoy many more before I grounded. The taut rope about me not only supplied balance but a sense of security that was almost holy.

Remember on the way up, to the Hut? Trust your equipment. And your guide. *You* will have no problems either.

Life on the descent was a constant, never-stopping series of instructions from Alfons. Above me, he would direct every placement of my legs, arms, hands and fingers. Every foothold, every handhold was selected by him, and then its exact location would be painstakingly described as he steered first my left foot, then my right, then my left arm, then my right, then my left hand, then my right. Then the fun began; it was like a highly refined game of blindman's buff. Much of the time I couldn't see. Alfons at the top had been right on course once again. I had to *feel* constantly, seeking that particular foothold or handhold by touch alone. Body balance was a must; this was especially true when I was facing *in*, for I did not have the perfect center of gravity that is nearest to the wall when you are facing *out*.

It was meticulous, mind-exhausting work, and if it hadn't been for the fact that most of this inch-by-inch blind searching was in almost pure vertical position, with straight down drops of considerable distance, it would have been a real drag. Even this exhilarating feeling began to pale as the procedure kept going on and on. It was the *slowness* that got to me, the exquisite care that you had to employ every second. Then and there I decided that the words patience and self-control led all the rest in the mountaineer's lexicon. And I added a new one to my own mental manual: *fingernail* holds. At times I was using such tiny cracks and ledges that even if I had been able to *look* for them I would not have found them. I had made a mistake early in the ascent of reaching too far up for holds (remember?), which Alfons had soon corrected by having me find one that required only the reaching to my chest or neck level. This procedure kept my body *out* from the wall so there was less chance of falling. It kept me from *pulling* myself up (remember?) mostly with my arms which is the last thing a climber should do, for it ties up the muscles quickly, regardless of how they are developed, and it forced my legs to do the job for which they are intended in rock climbing with rope ascents: *pushing* your body up. They are your workhorses. In a descent—turnaround. My legs were *not* the chief instruments. I was stretching out constantly, searching for the holds and, once found, my arms had to supply my hands. They in turn had to deliver the holding power to my fingers: *They* were the holder-uppers, with the legs as balancers and supporters.

Time after time, the taut rope of my friend above came to my aid. Instruction after instruction. No letup. I could not permit myself to stop for long, nor would Alfons have permitted it had I asked, for if I did the tension on my muscles would have set them to trembling and jumping (another new rule I had learned the hard way on the ascension).

As in going up, my number one rule took me down. One lowering at a time. Then the next. Never think how many more, or how far to go. One at a time; it got harder and harder to abide by it, but the very nature of that complex mental and physical combination kept me occupied, to say the least. And yet, with all of this, I was enjoying the descent tremendously.

Lower and lower we came. The traverse. The cliffs. Across to the ridge again. Far, far above us now was the Hang-Over. Now that had been *really* fun, a sheer delight. The going down backwards, out, over, and under, and down again. Right at the center of that monster, I had said to myself, "Tarzan *kreegah, yo bundolo!*" but you can lay it on the line that I didn't say it too loud. I sure as fate would have gotten that "playing around" bit again.

Now the rocks. In daylight, these first encounters of mine in the dark now looked enormous, and when we made our way down them one after the other, the ridge falling off so steeply on either side was a sight to behold.

The Hut. At long last. The minutes we spent there were unforgettable. My new friends of the night before were now my comrades, and at least half of them were in that small room with me again. We had all reached the top, each of us had drunk his fill of the exclusive elixir that *only* the Matterhorn serves to her climbers at the summit. For the first time, I knew the meaning of *youth* in life. I know now that it is in all men if they will only seek it out.

The long hike down. We said not a word to each other for the first hour. My thoughts you can well imagine. But then my guide spoke up behind me. He was making conversation, I thought, to ward off a letdown; he wants nothing to mar my reunion with my family below, and wants to deliver me fresh and triumphant. He was thinking out loud behind me of a strange meeting on the climb that morning. It had been all of that, and it has been one of the memories of the Matterhorn that I shall always cherish.

Halfway up the mountain we had overtaken a climbing couple that I had not seen the night before at the Hut; obviously they had started off before us. It was a narrow passage, and extreme care had to be taken in order to pass. There was time for a greeting and that was all. But I stopped, flattened against the wall, for sweet smiles of senior citizens, and apparent long years of union are not the order of the day on the Matterhorn. I was genuinely surprised, for it was the instant association with them of my parents far down in Zermatt that did the stopping. Three things on that mountain I shall never forget: This was the second.

·"We made a pledge to each other, my wife and I, that on our silver wedding anniversary we would climb the Matterhorn together. We are keeping that promise: We were married twenty-five years ago today."

This was the first of our thoughts together on the long march home. Alfons talked again of a man who had spent his life dreaming of climbing this great crag. And the day had come, late in his life, when he had come to Zermatt to make his dream come true. He had been successful for he had reached the summit and had been fulfilled. He had finally come to earth again, and looking upwards at its shining, horned crest, had said, "I have climbed my mountain. I have seen the Matterhorn." And the blind man turned and was led away by his guide.

We had entered the last stretch that curves around the mountain's lower level; for the first time I could see in the distance, still far below, the tram terminus where surely my family would be waiting. We had not said a word now. I was still leading, an honor Alfons had insisted upon, and exultation and pure joy speeded my every step. Suddenly, a sharp, "Jack, look."

There is a long stretch of gradual rise, flat and wide, leading from the station to the trail upwards—it is a year-round glacier. It is halfway point to the trail's beginning, and it was there that I saw a small figure running. Yes, running—on the ice. It was still far below and distant, and I could not make it out. Our pace picked up; a minute passed. The figure loomed slightly larger below, and it was Alfons, with his extraordinary eyesight, who exclaimed behind me, "Jack. It's your sister Judy!" He was right, and I shouted, "Alfons, she's started up the trail . . . the ice." We were walking down faster and faster. Alfons said something about reaching her before she climbed too high. We did, and surely the Matterhorn had never seen such a sight in her long and glorious life as a brother, taking his sister by the hand and with a Bergfeuhrer who had now at last seen it all, went down the last of a long trail to a waiting family. Judy, age ten, had broken from my parents and Karl Franzen and some very good people of Zermatt and ignored the shouted pleas of her mother and father to race far up to meet me. The smile upon her lovely face as we walked down the end of the trail was the most splendid reward that a climber of the Matterhorn had ever received.

Matterhorn Briefing

You have taken that first step. Excellent. Now *my* job begins. And I need your help.

First off, we've got to clear our decks. First, dismiss from your mind any notion that this Guide is a travel book. Second, *The Adventurer's Guide* is not a technical manual of instruction. For a very simple reason: No *highly technical* expertise is required for the successful doing of any of our adventures. (That factor figured heavily in their selection.) The basic rules, yes; the physical and mental conditions required for each undertaking, absolutely. These we will explore forty fathoms down, in order that you yourself can evaluate your own qualifications and capacities for each adventure. Third, our relationship throughout these pages simply cannot be as reader and author. That is out. This book in its entirety is the first of its kind, and its objective is clear: to make your life a splendid thing high above the crowd, and to have you see things and do things that all the Walter Mittys in this world combined never dreamed of doing. But here is what I need from you: I must have your confidence; you must believe in me and in what I say. I have a loathing for generalities, and a great fondness for specifics. Examples with the human element involved will be the order of the day and night. I will at times recall with you some weird happenings that arose to hound and harass and to test me around the world when they are needed to prove a point by a living example.

Now all of this will help us, but it is not enough. It is one thing to prepare you for an expedition through the Third Street tunnel with gun and camera, but it's quite another matter to pack you off to break bread with a headhunter. There cannot be a credibility gap between us *at any time*. It will not help us one bit to maintain this author-reader nonsense. It must be as friend to friend, a conversation between us. The Pulitzer Prize I do not seek, but your embarking upon a great and unique adventure I do. In good talk with interesting friends, you don't stop constantly to work out a well-rounded phrase, or stop to consider if your grammar is perfect, or change in your mind an expression a dozen times before rolling it out to sicken your buddy. Of course not. You and I, we've got an entirely new project on our hands; let's make it work by sitting down together, with Cokes, smiles, and no barriers. Affectation I abhor, naturalness I like immensely. Forget the author bit. A conversation between new friends—that someday should make us old friends.

Now that I've gotten over that hurdle, I've got another one: you. When I tell you, "this can be done," I want you to believe me, and I will eventually prove it to you. But, on the other hand, I too must believe in *you*. How so? Simple. You're going to get specifics by the gross that will enable you to test yourself to satisfy every condition that I will impose for the successful completion of each adventure. Physical requirements we have mentioned, but psychological factors that enter into the world of High Adventure with a bang, believe me, must also be considered. In a few minutes we'll have graphic human examples wherein three perfect physical specimens, each of whom has just passed the most exhausting medical examinations, are absolutely unfit to climb the Matterhorn. Each of them is a superb athlete, a Mr. America, and yet he'd blow the first 500 feet of the lower level. Not that they cannot overcome their difficulties—in most cases, they can. But vital factors enter the High Adventure picture that you must judge yourself by, and therein lies your part in playing square with me.

Now for me—or anyone else, for that matter—to believe in you, you must believe in yourself. Why not start thinking, right now, of your climbing the Matterhorn as an actual, *real* possibility? Start saying to yourself—right now—"I *can* climb the Matterhorn! If this skinny kid could do it, well, so can I!" And above all, *never* say, "I am too young" or "I am too old."

Now, my friend, you understand why I had that young fellow climb the great Matterhorn. There are other reasons, of course; I wanted the spirit and enthusiasm of that boy to reach *you* and take hold. If we only took the time more often to look at things and happenings and people through the eyes of the young, I tell you the world that we had thought dead a very long time ago would come to life before us. And the colors? Ah, the reds would be so much redder, and the blues so much bluer. And our hopes, and dreams, and struggles, like theirs, would be new-born and kicking. Give me the eyes of that boy of fourteen, seeing what *he* saw, feeling as *he* did, meeting the challenges that *he* met, and I would receive a transfusion of spirit that no doctor on earth could supply.

That is why that boy climbed for you. And that is why, when he is sixteen, you'll join him as he lives with a clan of headhunting, headshrinking Indians—the famed Jivaros, in the jungles of the Oriente in Ecuador; you will swim with him the legendary Hellespont, naked like Leander, at midnight in the dead of winter; at seventeen you will track a man-killing tiger with him in the densest jungle on earth; at nineteen. . . .

You will learn of his mistakes, and profit by his doing, for the lessons will not be in a classroom or from an arm-chair researcher, but in the field as they actually happened.

34

It would be so easy, my new friend, to up-date these Adventures, instead of painstakingly, mentally researching in order to be accurate in every action and *thought*, but that would defeat our purpose in so many directions.

And in between the living of the deeds, we will have up-to-the-second briefings that should, and will, prepare you *in every way* for *your* Great Adventure.

And now to business.

We learned from our ascent and descent the rules of rock climbing with rope as they apply to the climbing of the Zermatt Ridge Route to the summit of the Matterhorn. This is the *only* route to be followed by the novice or moderately experienced climber. If you are an advanced, highly skilled mountaineer, and wish to tackle any of the other seven routes of climb, contact Alfons and you both take it up from there. Each of the all-important climbing rules that we are concerned with developed before your eyes as they were happening in action, not from statements on paper. So, they should stick to your climbing ribs from now on—especially as they came about the hard way and we all suffered with the learner. Because they are most important to you, we sum them up. Take them to heart:

1) *CLIMBING*. a. Take short steps. b. Move as upright as possible. c. Your *legs* are your climb. They *push* you up. Your arms are their helpers and balancers. d. Do not *pull* yourself up by your arms; they will quit you sooner or later. e. A rule to print: *body over feet*; the application keeps you *away* from the wall, a must for balance and safety. f. Make as few stops as possible. The longer your muscles are idle, the worse the tension effect upon them, i.e., quivering, trembling, pulsating, all resulting in loss of strength with tiredness taking charge. g. *Never reach above to the full extension of your arms*, unless you cannot find a handhold elsewhere. Two evils result: you will be *pulling* yourself up; and the stretching far upwards impairs balance and keeps you close to the wall, which you *must avoid*; the odds on your falling jump dramatically. Make it a ritual to find handholds that are *no* higher than your chest, certainly never past your neck unless absolutely necessary. h. Employ the *Three Point Hold* as much as possible: both feet and one hand in hold, free arm to search. Only move one arm or leg at a time. i. *Don't hug the wall*.

2) *GOING DOWN*. a. Three Point Hold again. b. *Reverse* procedure with stretching. *Reach*, feel, and find the *lowest* possible handhold. c. *Holding* power in hands and fingers. Legs are now for support and balance. d. Face *outward* as much as possible. Your center of gravity will be closest to the wall. e. When facing outward, arch your back slightly to put weight of body over feet. f. Face *in* when the wall is vertical or extremely steep. g. On small footholds or cracks (either up or down) use the edge of the

sole of the shoe rather than the toe. h. A good trick in either climbing or going down: for extra holding power, force hand or elbow sideways into large crack or hole—then *twist* them (this is called "jamming"). i. Extensions, outs-and-overs, bulges: *face in*. j. When feeling for your foot or hand hold, test it to be certain it is large enough; if not, keep feeling.

These are the basics for climbing the East, or Zermatt, Ridge of the Matterhorn. It will not be necessary for you to know the more technical procedures, such as belaying, rappelling, and aid climbing with the use of hardware such as pitons, chocks, carabiners, and the like. The same applies for snow and ice techniques, for the *AG* will recommend your climbing the Matterhorn only in climbing season (normally from late May through September or early October—but this is quite variable. When I visited Alfons in July 1973 bad weather still prevailed, and the guides were despairing over the strong possibility that the Matterhorn would remain unclimbable until August.)

To climb the Matterhorn you must:
1) Climb with an *expert* guide. Do *exactly* what he tells you to do every second.
2) Be in excellent physical condition.
3) Spend a minimum of five days in Zermatt becoming acclimated and practicing on small climbs the art of rock climbing with rope.
4) Possess the mental and psychological qualities demanded by the ascent and descent.

Number one you are supplied. Alfons Franzen has taken *400* parties to the summit and down—each a success. Number two we'll soon get to work on. Number three is up to you. The difficulty is with number four.

Specifics:
Take Sam.
A Charles Atlas product. Barbells sleep beside him in his swishing water bed. The distaff side melts when he trots down the beach. Twenty-nine years old, and muscles you wouldn't believe. Old Sammy is a sight to behold when he lifts Mary Lou high over his head, but ask him to climb very slowly a twenty-foot ladder and he'll tie up at the fifteenth rung. Muscle-bound, in capital letters. I break up when I think of a famed Western star who made it big with one of the first highly rated television series. Six feet seven, two hundred and fifty pounds, he is *all* muscle—no bone, no fat, no skin, just muscle. All was well and heroic until the script called for our boy to shoot a bow and arrow. The nineteen-inch biceps bulged magnificently as back went the arrow a fat foot and a half, and that was that. Another Sammy.

Take Ralph.

Nineteen years old, he's very large in the cross-country set. Twenty-six miles at a crack, and never a deep breath. Take him by the hand and lead him soothingly to a six-story building. Then up to the roof and have old Ralph look straight down and you've got a hospital case on your hands. Acrophobia.

Take Gordon.

Tall, tanned, and terrific. Give him a leopard skin and a spear and he's got it made. Now, put Gordon on the Matterhorn. About a hundred feet up. That's high enough. Now start him slowly upwards, instructing him to place each foot exactly where you have placed yours in front of him. Up ten feet more, and there's a narrow ledge one foot wide that our boy has to cross. Two steps, and old Gordie takes off like a bird. Certainly you arrest his flight with your nylon rope and ground him, but this kind of action for 14,782 feet is not only ridiculous, it's impossible. Gordon's problem? Imbalance. Back in the jungle he'll do just fine.

By the same token, mental quirks must also be considered when assessing one's capabilities for a specific Adventure. We'll consider these at the proper time

What does not show up on the surface—that's what concerns me, for I cannot see into your mind. This is where, as we discussed, your playing fair with me is vital. You will discover, my friend, as we move from each new Adventure and briefing, that I will be far more concerned with the *mental* qualities, and the psychological factors, for each climb, swim, trek, or expedition than I will be for your coming up to snuff with the physical requirements. For laid before you is every facet and degree of body exertion that each Adventure calls for, and you judge you and yours accordingly. Now, no friend of mine is dumb, I'll tell you that! So I *know* you won't double-cross yourself by cheating on the exam. Just remember: If one Adventure is not right on target for you—*another one will be*.

Now, for Sam, Ralph, and Gordon.

Old Sammy? He's got no problems at all; he'll skip the Matterhorn and the Hellespont, but he'll go to live with the Congolese Pygmies in the Ituri Forest, and when he strips down to his swimming trunks, they'll make him King.

Gordon? He has a problem. There is little I can do for him, although Cheendon knows I want to, but his lack of balance is due to faulty muscular or glandular coordination. The degree of imbalance varies considerably, but we have two simple tests to determine your sense of balance. Stretch a line along a level piece of land at least thirty feet long. Secure each end. Beginning at one end, walk to the other, placing each foot on the line. In other words, walk the length of it, using your arms to balance yourself. Secondly, have a member of your family, or a friend, with the same foot size as yours, walk barefoot with wet feet down a stretch of sidewalk or pavement, or whatever surface will retain his footprints, for a distance of thirty feet. If his feet dry out, soak them again. You follow his trail, placing your feet exactly in his footprints. Have the line of prints as much in a straight line as possible. If you do not leave the line once, or miss placing your feet in his prints once, as you progress to the finish line, I'll climb the Matterhorn with you anytime. To graduate with honors, locate a wall as high as possible, and as narrow as you can find. Repeat procedure one. If again you miss not once the line or prints, I'll meet you at the cable car in one hour. Now, if you slip off the line or the footsteps more than five times, all is not lost. Practice. That's all you need. Develop your sense of balance. However, if you fall off more than ten times, check into your problem.

Last, but certainly not the least in our feelings of concern, is Ralph. The line of demarcation separating the normal distrust of heights accompanied by that familiar queasy feeling in the pit of your stomach, and the sheer panic that often results in fainting and/or swaying with disastrous results, is wide indeed. There are many who revel in heights. There are those who panic at an altitude of less than ten feet. I mean this, and I will prove it by our good friend, Specific. I am going to spend a bit of time on this matter, for it concerns your climbing the Matterhorn. Kilimanjaro, for example, I am not concerned with, for it is not a precipitous mountain, although its height is staggering. To proceed in an orderly fashion, let's consider first the normal reaction to heights, not extreme, but moderate. In ninety-nine out of a hundred cases, this uneasiness is induced by 1) a new, unusual environment to which you are not accustomed, and 2) a complete lack of a sense of security. Result: Your body, like a flash, sends a panic message to your brain, and acute dizziness is the instant result.

Let us combine all three of the above into one example.

A group of Air Force officers is being instructed in mountain climbing. One of them—we'll call him Andy—is a captain with many wartime missions and decorations to his credit. Now remember, he is a *flying* officer. On his first instruction climb, he reached a height of *three feet*, and froze. More than that, his body was racked with shaking and trembling; there were footholds and handholds in abundance, but in panic he would not reach up for them. In a word, Andy was scared to death. He spread-eagled himself against the small cliff and refused to let go. Incredible? What I am describing is true, no dramatic license here; it happened exactly as I report the incident. In thirty days, Captain Andy was a credible climber, rappeling and using artificial aids in climbing rock at high altitudes that were otherwise unclimbable. Explanation: It was not a question of bravery or courage, far from it. It was simply a combination of all three conditions we have just outlined. He was at home in the air because he had a plane that he had confidence in; it would keep him safe. Secondly, *he* was flying the plane, knew what he was doing; he was trained for the job. Thirdly, he had absolutely no confidence in the rope or the knot that held him, he had no faith in the instructor, he had no idea whether that rock above him would support him—it might crumble. In his entire life, he had never climbed upwards on a steep wall. Other children had, he knew that, but he had not.

A patient teacher, a very gradual increase in height, a growing belief in his equipment, the discovery that rock would *not* crumble if he tested it first, a dawning knowledge that he *could* climb: You put all these together and you add the clincher—the continual exposure to height, the getting accustomed to this new environment so that his body did not telegraph his brain that he was in terrible danger—and you have yourself a climber. Want to sum it all up in one word? You're right: confidence.

(To gain this state of mind, accompanied by trained skills, you may wish to attend a climbing school, not only to assist you with the Matterhorn, but to prepare you for the climbing of *any* crag and give you a solid introduction to a magnificent sport. On page 50 is a list of selected climbing schools in the United States, as well as recommended magazines and books on climbing. The list is not complete, but the schools are the best. A session at one of them should prove to be very helpful. But be aware that, even if you are a novice climber, they are not necessary. Once again, climbing the Matterhorn does not require a great deal of technical, sophisticated knowledge of rock-climbing and mountaineering. While I urge you strongly to read one or more of the books listed, you can train at Zermatt during the week you are there prior to your climb (rarely are the climbing school sessions longer than this); Alfons will assign you a climbing instructor, at less cost than the schools'. For many, however, especially those with a fear of heights, the confidence and skills gained at a good school will be invaluable when they attack the Tiger of the Alps. I leave the choice to you.)

In conclusion, regarding this most important matter in mountain climbing, there are cases of acrophobia that appear to be incurable. Constant exposure to heights, beginning at low levels and gradually rising, does not seem to help. But there are so many splendid adventures that can be undertaken where the fear of the lofty has no bearing whatsoever. Flying to reach them has little effect on those who suffer from acrophobia.

So, if you have an extreme aversion to heights, and find the appeal of climbing small hills and taking the elevator to the 14th floor each luncheon break a frightening and depressing picture, turn to adventures-without-altitude and you'll stock up a store of memories that will never run out.

But, if you want to experience ecstasy and a joy of accomplishment such as you have never known in your life, be a Captain Andy and you *can* stand atop the Matterhorn.

Well, there you have them, the four conditions that must be met to climb the Matterhorn. And we picked up some pointers along the way that will help in your assessment of your own capabilities for other Adventures; they were of the "under the surface" variety that should be exposed early in the game anyway. Now, I'm ready for *your* questions. Fire away.

How about age? How old, how young? Well, for starters, hear the saga of the Reverend William Butler. The good man of the cloth climbed Longs Peak in Colorado on his birthday every single year until he was 84. He would have climbed it on his 85th, if he hadn't been killed riding his bicycle.

How high is Longs Peak? 14,256 feet!

How young should a child be before he starts climbing? His or her lungs and heart are not developed enough for higher climbs until at least fourteen. Of course, here again we run into variables. It is extremely difficult to set standards when it comes to either great mountains or any High Adventure; we have already seen proof of that. We will find a great deal more, but we'll stick to the mountains for now. In many of the more qualified climbing schools, children are started at five years of age. It sounds absurd, I know, but it is a very gradual, intelligent process. Again, it depends upon the individual child and the type of training he receives. When you stop to think about it, climbing is natural for a child: first the crib, then the playpen, the fence, the roof, the front-yard tree, then the Matterhorn. Well, not quite. What's important here is to strike a balance between providing your child (if you have one) with instruction and encouragement, and guarding against letting him have his head, for caution is not in a child's youthful vocabulary unless the parents print it there in indelible ink.

Do women make good mountaineers? This question was dramatically answered in the affirmative at 12:30 in the afternoon on May 16, 1975, when a 35-year-old Japanese housewife placed her small foot on the crest of Mount Everest. Her name is Junko Tabei, and she stands five feet even and weighs 92 pounds. Further confirmation is the fact that fully *half* of the rosters of mountain climbing clubs in the U.S. are women.

How small? How big? Men and Women? It doesn't make all that much difference. If you're laboring under the illusion that you have to be a Hercules or an Amazon to get by in this wonderful world of High Adventure, forget it. Look at Junko Tabei—or take me, for example. I'm five feet eleven and come in at 170: certainly nothing special.

Is strength the most important factor in becoming a good climber? In conquering the Matterhorn? No, definitely not. That is why so many young girls and women become excellent climbers. Coordination and agility take up the slack. Plus the all-important asset that Gordon lacks: balance. The strength required is mostly in the legs and hands.

GETTING IN SHAPE*

You do not need great strength to climb the Matterhorn: You need *stamina.* This means your cardiovascular system must be in top working order. The best way to achieve this is to run. Not jog. Run. Run every day for a mile or two. By this I mean don't shuffle along the way so many joggers do, bemoaning every step. Look down at your feet and say to yourself: "Someday soon these feet will be standing on top of the Matterhorn!" Then lift those knees, put a kick in your step, and move out! When you can consistently run two miles in about fifteen minutes you are in good condition.

Bicycling is another way. Ride your bike instead of driving your car whenever possible; take long weekend bike rides. I have a friend who gets in shape for skiing the easy way: He pedals a stationary bike in his living room while watching TV or talking to friends. Playing fast, active sports like tennis or handball, taking ten-mile hikes on a Saturday or Sunday—these are other ways as well. Do toe-lifts to develop your calves. Holding on to something for balance, stand up on the tip of your toes 200-300 times a day. Deep knee bends are excellent for your upper legs. When you are doing 100 a day with light weights you're doing fine. Do not use barbells on your shoulders as that's bad for your back; hold five-, ten-, or twenty-pound dumbbells in each hand at your side. (Girls should use no more than five pounds on the average.) It's not the weight here, but the quantity, the number of knee bends. That is what builds stamina, staying power—and that goes for all the above. The more you do the better. Especially running. All the others are supplements. Run every day.

What about the altitude? Can I get altitude sickness? Altitude affects people differently, so there's no way of telling in advance how it will affect you. Once I danced a little jig on top of Kilimanjaro and got slightly dizzy, which reminded me that I was 19,000 feet up in the sky and I should restrain my enthusiasm. But actual altitude sickness—heart pounding wildly, severe dizziness, and nausea—I have never experienced. The best way to avoid it—in addition of course to your being in good condition—is to acclimatize yourself in Zermatt. The village itself is over 5,000 feet high and you should stay there at least five to seven days before your climb. Do a little light hiking the first couple of days, getting used to the air (and your boots if they are new or rented). Then take a longer hike or two, on trails where tourists are seldom seen. There are over 200 miles of hiking trails around Zermatt. You can take any of several trams or cable cars to higher elevations, then hike awhile, getting used to the altitude. Alfons will arrange for a guide to accompany you if you wish. The atmosphere around the Christiania Hotel is very friendly,

Important note: Please consult your physician and get a thorough check-up before beginning a program of strenuous physical conditioning.

however, and you should have no trouble finding hiking companions. And if you want to put the alpine frosting on your climbing cake, take the cable from Zermatt to Trockner Steg, where there is skiing all summer long.

Once acclimated, you may still want to use a couple of tricks of mine to cover your altitude bets. The Matterhorn is not quite 15,000 feet high, so you will have no need of oxygen equipment, which is normally used only above 20,000 feet. Should you wish (although I don't think you will need it), you may purchase a light, small oxygen bottle from a number of mountaineering stores, or through your local sporting goods dealer. Alfons will carry it, and it can revitalize you if the altitude is affecting you. Using drugs on a mountain is very dangerous, especially amphetamines. Please avoid use of dexedrine, benzedrine, and other "uppers." Vitamin B12 and iron will help, as they strengthen the hemoglobin in your blood, allowing your blood to carry more oxygen. Take about 500 micrograms and 150 milligrams of each per day. Now I'd like to let you in on a secret of mine. It is a drug that is not widely known even among climbers, yet was given to U.S. Air Force pilots during World War II before the development of oxygen equipment in their planes. Its name is Persantin, and it has helped me on several climbs. I learned of it through a friend who lived in La Paz, Bolivia, for a number of years. La Paz is 12,000 feet high, and he claimed Persantin enabled him to easily adjust to living at that altitude. You need a prescription for Persantin so talk to your doctor about it.

You may have trouble sleeping at Hornli Hut since it's 10,000 feet up. Some climbers use sleeping pills to help them sleep at high altitudes, but this can be very dicey, as the British say. You're going to be getting up at 3 a.m., and if you start climbing groggy, before the effects of the pill have worn off completely, you can be in heavy trouble. So I'd recommend Persantin here rather than a sleeping pill. But don't overdo this Persantin bit—take very limited dosages. Remember, none of these tricks is a crutch, just minor insurance. *There is no substitute whatever for being in good condition.* I don't mean you shouldn't take advantage of this insurance, because if you develop a severe headache, nausea, dizziness, and general weakness Alfons is going to get you off that mountain right now. Just use these things as supplements to, not substitutes for, being in good shape.

A few final tips: Glucose tablets are excellent for a little extra energy; get them through your sporting goods store. Sucking on a lime or two will satisfy your thirst better than a lot of water.* Take three or four deep breaths every time you stop, such as waiting at the bottom of a cliff while Alfons climbs it first.

*Be sure, however, you drink at least eight cups, or two full quarts, of water per day when climbing.

BEING MENTALLY READY

What are the most important mental traits to possess to climb the Matterhorn and go on to other great mountains?

Ah, that's the question. Standing as high as Everest over all others is *will power.* Your body can be on the verge of surrendering a hundred times but if you *will it* to continue it *can.* And right behind it in quick step are three backups without which you cannot hope to be a climber who makes the top every time and commands the respect of those who climb with you. *Self-control:* It is absolutely necessary. If you *allow* yourself to lose control of your emotions, you are in a very tight situation then and there, and you have put a load on your guide's shoulders that is unforgivable. *Patience:* Its virtues are self-apparent in the rules of climb that we have established together, right? *Good humor:* You must be optimistic and not defeatist. The quarrelsome, the bitter, the nagging, the bad-tempered, the complaining have no place on a mountain. Say, come to think of it, the rules for climbing are pretty much the same for life in general, aren't they?

What about physical handicaps? Can people with serious ones climb the Matterhorn?

You bet they can. A girl climbed the highest peak in the Grand Tetons and she was one-armed. Bruno Wintersteller, an outstanding alpinist who has successfully negotiated the most difficult routes of climb in Europe, is one-legged. And you and I will never forget that gallant, blind man who climbed to the top of a great mountain because he wanted to "see" the Matterhorn. If you train yourself, and you have the desire, the examples of these splendid adventurers should not only inspire but *convince* you that the human spirit—especially yours—*can prevail.*

WHY PEOPLE CLIMB MOUNTAINS

One last question: Why, really, do people climb mountains? They don't climb a mountain just "because it's there," do they? There must be a better answer than that!

Why do men climb? A famous mountaineer, Lionel Terray, once wrote a book on climbing and climbers entitled *Conquistadors of the Useless.* And, indeed, *useless* is just what mountain climbing seems to many. Why risk your life, spend a great deal of money, subject yourself to incredible cold, discomfort, and struggle, generate an almost unimaginable effort of will, to climb to the top of a mountain—when all you do, once you get there, is turn around and come right back down? How ridiculous can you get??

Let's suppose, though, you overheard the following conversation:

Sam: "Jim, what do you really want most out of life?"
Jim: "Why, to be happy, I guess."
Sam: "Why?"
Jim: "Huh?"
Sam: "Why do you want to be happy? What for?"
Jim: "Well, I . . . er . . . uh . . . I don't understand."
Sam: "*Why do you want to be happy?* You don't know because there's no *reason* or *purpose* for being happy. That's the trouble with happiness: It's so pointless, so *useless* to be happy."

Now, would you agree with Sam that it's useless to be happy? Or would you tell him that he is seriously confused, because happiness is not a means for anything beyond itself? It is the end of the line, the final and ultimate *reason why*, the *that for which* we do things, and, as such, cannot be a *reason for* doing anything else.

The one problem with happiness is that we can't try and get it directly. Happiness can only come indirectly, as the accompaniment of and reward for doing particular, concrete things. We can't just "be happy." We must be *doing something* that makes us, thereby, happy. Like climbing a mountain.

The happiness, exultation, and satisfaction one experiences upon reaching the top of a mountain has a completeness, a totality, a finality to it that comes with nothing else I know of. The only thing that comes even close is being immersed in music of soaring celebration, such as the fourth movement of Beethoven's Seventh Symphony.

This finality and wholeness has two sources. Every one of us has goals in his life, and we all try, with varying degrees of effort and success, to achieve them. Most of these goals are, however, fuzzy. We may want to learn a skill or improve our relationship with a loved one—and these goals are achieved slowly, over a period of time, and may even be open-ended.

With a mountain it is different. You reach the top, place your foot on the summit, and that's it. In that very *second* your goal has been achieved. You are on *top*, there is nowhere else to go, all else is beneath you. You are surrounded by the magnificence of nature, by the stupendous beauty of sharp crags, shimmering ice, and sparkling snow, the world is at your feet and only the heavens are above you. Your exultation and soaring pride have that great depth that only victory through struggle and a gigantic effort of will can bring, and when you reach that holy spot—made holy by your achievement—all this comes upon you in a single moment, sharply, clearly, instantaneously, finally. There is no fuzziness. There is no doubt. There is no time and no future, only *now*. Your goal has been reached. You are *there*.

The second source lies in the fact that when on the summit of a great mountain, just as there is nowhere else to go physically, there is nowhere else to go mentally, spiritually.

Most of the goals in our daily lives are themselves means to further goals. We learn that skill so we can put it to use, improve that relationship so we can understand the other person better, have less friction, et cetera. Such a goal is an instrumental goal, serving as an instrument towards achieving another. But there is no instrumentality in climbing a mountain.

To reach the summit of a mountain that, with its beauty and awesomeness, has taken our breath away, is to achieve a goal that serves no other, a goal that is wholly and entirely intrinsic, within itself. It is precisely because it is so "useless" that we climb mountains. There is no further goal to reach once we stand proudly upon the summit. We stand there for *no other reason* than simply to *be* there, to have *gotten* there the way we did.

To climb a great mountain and place your feet upon its crest is to know that complete freedom of soul, that wholeness, that utter and final totality of happiness that can only be described as sacred— sacred for what you did to achieve it, to know it, and to experience it.

Any final suggestions?

As Alfons would say, "please attend me." Climbing a mountain takes psychological strategy. The one thing to avoid is *looking ahead*. "When will I get there?". . . ."I wonder when I'll reach the top?". . . ."How much *farther* is the top, Alfons?" With thoughts like these constantly running through your mind, you'll be amazed at how endless and exhausting is your climb.

Never think any farther than the next few steps. Forget about the top. Forget about the next ridge, the next traverse, about everything except the next few steps, where your feet and hands are going to go in the next minute. Remember: You are climbing the Matterhorn, the Queen, the Tiger of the Alps, the most famous mountain in the world. Feel every rock you touch. Feel the sun in your face, and the thin clean air in your lungs, the energy in your body and the strength in your legs. (Don't feel the weakness, feel the *strength*, however much there is left.) During those rare seconds you can afford to look at the spectacle of ice and snow and rock and sky surrounding you. Shout out loud—or say quietly to yourself, whatever is your style— "It's so *fantastic* to be alive!"

So my final word to you here, my friend of *The Adventurer's Guide*, is to enjoy the climb itself. Forget about the top. You'll be there soon enough, then be down off it and on to another adventure.

Matterhorn Particulars

Preliminary Note: Travel information that you can easily get from any travel agent or major airline is normally not included in the

AG. This particularly includes airfares from the U.S. to overseas, as there are so many different kinds and they are constantly changing. You should, by the way, have a competent travel agent make your travel arrangements (airline reservations, visas, advice on shots, etc.) when embarking on an adventure. His services are free, as he gets his commissions from the airlines.

At present, the most inexpensive way for the regular traveler to fly to Europe is on a "TGC," a Travel Group Charter. You need not belong to an "affinity group," but on a TGC flight, see your travel agent. Your local college may have some quite inexpensive student charter flights to Europe and possibly other destinations as well. Often, all you need do is sign up for a night course to be eligible. To obtain a free copy of the Charter Travel & Vacation Guide, listing over 3000 charter flights to Europe, Hawaii and the Orient, write to: Altatravel, 1108 Gayley Ave., Los Angeles, California 90024.

Most costs quoted in the *AG* will be in the local currency—with no exchange rates given, as they are as changeable as a chameleon in heat. The Worldwide Edition of the *Official Airline Guide* (issued monthly), which any travel agent has, will provide all current exchange rates.

Transportation
(from Geneva
to Zermatt)

You have your choice of three: train, car, or thumb.
Train: On the hour, trains leave Geneva for Brig. Transfer to the Brig-Visp-Zermatt Railway (all electric). Total time: three hours. Round-trip fare: Fifty SFR (Swiss Francs).
Car: direct to three and a half miles from Zermatt. No motorized vehicles of any kind are allowed in Zermatt. You park your car and board the electric train for the last three and a half miles for two SFR. Zermatt is 152 miles southeast of Geneva; allow six hours.

Guide

Alfons Franzen. He is still going strong after all these years. If your schedules are such that he is unable to climb with you, he will recommend a guide he knows well from the Zermatt Bergfuehrer Organization. Cost: 450 SFR per climber for two days, which includes the cable car up to Schwarzee, plus food and lodging at the Hornli Hut. All your climbing clothes (shoes included) can be rented for seventy-five SFR per three days. Alfons can arrange for a professional photographer to accompany you and photograph your climb, in super 8mm or stills, for 300 SFR (plus film).

Hotel Accommodations

I, of course, prefer the Christiania. It is owned by Karl and Alfons Franzen, and if you stay there you will be treated superbly. Upon your arrival you will be taken in a gaily painted buggy fueled with genuine horsepower (no cars in Zermatt, remember?) far up the hill overlooking all, with the most noble of mountains before your eyes twenty-four hours a day. If the Christiania is booked, Alfons will make your reservations at the Mont Cervin, the Victoria, or the Monte Rosa. I also recommend the Beau-Site, which is comfortable and has a good menu, while its rates are much less than the famed Mont Cervin downtown. The phone number of the Christiania is Route 028 Zermatt 77779. You may contact Alfons at that number. Address all written communications to: Alfons Franzen, Hotel Christiania, Zermatt, Switzerland.

Equipment

Alfons will supply all equipment required for your climb, but if you wish to bring the most important articles, the AG suggests the following:

Climbing Boots

Without any question, this is Number One. If it is at all possible, I want you to have your own pair of boots. What you need is a moderately heavy mountaineering boot that weighs two to two and a half pounds (four to five pounds the pair), and is six to eight inches high. It should be made of full-grain leather, which is thicker, more waterproof, and more durable than suede. It should be lined with leather inside as well, have no spongy insole that will wear out (buy a good firm one if you want, replace as necessary), have padded foam ankle pads, tongue, and "skree guard" (foam padding around the top so it won't cut into your Achilles tendon). The lacing should go to the toe. There should be a "counter" or stiffener in the heel and the toe, plus a steel or fiberglass shank the length of the instep. When first inspecting the boot, grab the heel and toe and try to bend the boot. Then grab the toe with both hands and push in on the insole with both thumbs. If it bends and pushes much at all, forget it. You want a stiff boot. You want a Vibram (or similar material) lug sole. It will be either stitched on (a welt) or cemented on to the boot under heat and pressure (Littleway construction). The latter is better as the sole does not overhang (extend beyond the boot, forming a ledge), so you can use smaller footholds. But if you decide on a boot with a welt, be sure it is double-stitched and narrow.

There are four boot manufacturers I would like to recommend: *Vasque* (American), *Lowa* (German), *Raichle* (Swiss), and *Galibier* (French). There are other excellent boot makers, but these I feel are the best. You may secure a brochure from them by writing to the addresses at the end of this chapter. I won't suggest any particular models as the names are always changing. If asked to state a preference among these four, I would opt for Vasque. While all four make boots of the finest quality, all have idiosyncrasies in manufacture. For example, a Lowa may fit better on your foot than a Vasque, but be vice versa for your buddy. If possible, try several models on. Remember: You need a mountaineering boot, one good for extensive hiking as well as rock climbing. You don't want a lightweight hiking boot, nor do you need a technical climbing shoe (klettershue) on the Matterhorn.

If at all possible, go to a mountaineering store and get outfitted on the spot. If, however, you have to order by mail, be sure to state your usual shoe size and width. Put on the socks (we'll take this article up in a moment) you intend to wear. Place your weight evenly on both feet. Put a piece of cardboard under each foot. Have an outline drawn around each foot. Hold the pen or pencil vertically! I really don't like this mail-order business, though—boots are so important. You simply must try and get to a mountaineering store.

When trying them on: 1. Lace them on firmly, especially around the instep. Stand straight, weight evenly placed. 2. Have the toe of each boot pressed firmly down three-quarters of an inch back from the front; your big toe should be at that point. 3. Wiggle your toes up and down, curl them backwards; I want you to have freedom of toe movement. 4. The ball of your foot should not be pinched. 5. Now have a friend hold the toe and heel of the boot rigid while you twist with all you've got from side to side. It should fit firmly. The heel of your foot should not move from side to side.

One final word on your boots: Break them in well. Wear them every chance you get, around the house, to the store, for at least thirty to forty hours wearing (and walking) time. Then go on a few easy hikes with them. Never, never do any extensive or difficult climbing until your boots are broken in thoroughly.

Socks

At all times, regardless of conditions, climate or otherwise, wear 100 percent wool socks. Blisters will be held off, and they absorb moisture much better than any other material. Be sure they fit properly! You should wear knickers, not long pants, that are worn with long knicker wool socks. Be sure to use a thin cotton liner sock as well.

I have spent considerable time on your footgear because it is the most important item you will be concerned with, save for one thing—the rope that binds you to your guide. You will find that when Alfons places it around you it will now be made of nylon. It will be at least a hundred feet long (the average used to be eighty), and very possibly a hundred and twenty. No more hemp. Nylon is elastic, thereby stretching; hemp allowed for little taking up of slack in case of a tumble. But this is Alfons' territory—relax.

Other

Have an excellent pair of sunglasses. The best are cadmium-coated to filter out all ultra-violet and infrared rays (e.g., Swiss Everest Glasses, sold by Recreational Equipment, with side-protectors). American Optical *Calobar* and Bausch & Lomb *Ray-Ban* are also very good.

Select a good wool cap. Bring a second pair of bootlaces, both nylon. Have a good wool sweater. Wear knickers—cord, tweed, or wool. As for gloves or mittens? Let Alfons supply you with the proper pair. He will also have a climbing helmet for you, but should you want your own, Recreational Equipment offers several models.

Below is a list of recommended books, climbing schools, magazines, boot manufacturers, and mountaineering stores. I really do hope you will become involved in rock climbing and mountaineering, for it is such a magnificent sport. In the succeeding editions of *The Adventurer's Guide* that I hope to be writing, I'd like you to join me in climbing Kilimanjaro; glacier-strewn peaks in New Guinea; the giant of the Andes, Aconcagua; that majestic abode of the gods in Greece, Mount Olympus; Fujiyama; sacred mountains high above the jungles of Ceylon; snow-covered peaks in the remotest center of the Sahara; and maybe, even Mt. Everest. But above them all is the Matterhorn. Before all the others, you must first place your feet upon her knife-blade crest, look at all that is beneath you, and say: "Nothing in life matters except experiencing what I am feeling right now."

Books

1. *Basic Rockcraft* by Royal Robbins. Simply and quickly explains all the basic techniques of rock climbing. $1.95
2. *Basic Mountaineering*, a pamphlet put out by the San Diego chapter of the Sierra Club. Very good. $2.50
3. *Mountaineering: Freedom of the Hills* by the Seattle Mountaineers. The best text extant. $6.75

4. *The Matterhorn* by Guido Rey. The classic book on the Classic Mountain. (Now out of print; secure through library.)

Magazines
(Note: Some of these magazines have a tendency towards elitism, and occasionally prate about the "immorality of bolting," or such. As a fan of Cesari Maestri, I agree with him that all that really matters is what you and only you gain from the experience on a mountain.)

1. *Climbing*, American Mountaineering and Rockclimbing Magazine. Box E, Aspen, Colorado 81611
2. *Off Belay*, 12416 169th St. S.E., Renton, Washington 98055
3. *Mountain*, 30 Collingwood Ave., London N.10, England.
4. *Ascent*, the Sierra Club Mountaineering Journal, 1398 Solano Ave., Albany, California 94706.
5. American Alpine Journal, the annual publication of the American Alpine Club (and undoubtedly the most prestigious journal in the climbing world), 113 East 90th St., New York, New York 10028

Climbing
Schools

1. Mount Hood School of Mountaineering, 9920 S.W. Terwilliger Blvd., Portland, Oregon 97219. Phone (503) 246-9830.
2. Palisade School of Mountaineering, 1398 Solano Ave., Albany, California 94706. Phone (415) 527-8100.
3. Rainier Mountaineering, 201 St. Helens, Tacoma, Washington 94802. Phone (206) 569-2227.
4. Yosemite Mountaineering, Yosemite Valley, California. Phone (209) 372-4505.
5. Dick Pownall Climbing School, 267 W. Rockledge Road, Vail, Colorado. Phone (303) 476-5418.
6. Eastern Mountain Sports School of Mountaineering, 1041 Commonwealth Ave., Boston, Massachusetts. Phone (617) 254-4250.
7. Rockcraft, 906 Durant St. Modesto, California 95350. Phone (209) 521-7515.

Boot Manufacturers

1. Vasque. Red Wing Shoe Co., Red Wing, Minnesota 55066.
2. Lowa. (US Distributor) The North Face, 2804 Telegraph Ave., Berkeley, California 94702.
3. Raichle. (US Distributor) Raichle Molitor Inc., Natick, Massachusetts 01760.
4. Galibier. (US Distributor) Mountain Paraphernalia, 906 Durant St., Modesto, California 95350 (same as Rockcraft above; Royal Robbins runs both).

50

Mountaineering
Stores

1. Recreational Equipment, 1525 11th Ave., Seattle, Washington 98122. Phone (206) 323-8333.
2. Eddie Bauer, Seattle, Washington 98124. Phone (406) 622-2766.
3. The Ski Hut, 1615 University Ave., Berkeley, California 94703. Phone (415) 843-6505.
4. The North Face, 2804 Telegraph Ave., Berkeley, California 94702. Phone (415) 548-1371.
5. Eastern Mountain Sports, 1041 Commonwealth Ave., Boston, Massachusetts 02215. Phone (617) 254-4250.

Note: These lists are partial, the last especially so. If you write to any of the schools, manufacturers, or stores listed, they will send you excellent brochures. (I am particularly impressed, for instance, by Recreational Equipment's. REI is managed by Jim Whittaker, the first American to climb Mt. Everest). By scanning the ads in the magazines, or by writing to either your local Sierra Club chapter or The American Alpine Club (at 113 East 90th St., New York, New York 10028), you can easily find out where your nearest climbing school or mountaineering store is located.

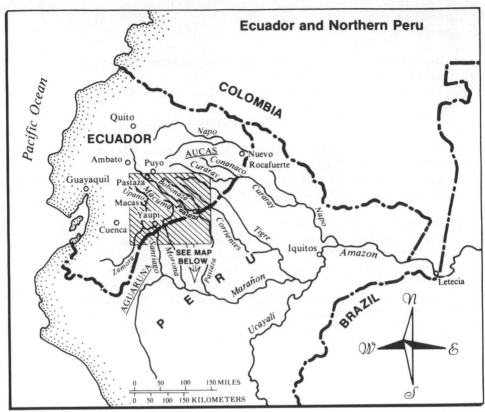

Ecuador and Northern Peru

Pacific Ocean

COLOMBIA

Quito

ECUADOR

AUCAS

Napo

Ambato   Puyo   Nuevo Rocafuerte

Cononaco

Curaray

Guayaquil

Pastaza   Bobonaza

Upano   Macuma   Pastaza

Macas

Yaupi   Corrientes   Tigre

Cuenca

Napo

Iquitos   Amazon

SEE MAP BELOW

Zamora   Santiago   Morona   Marañon   Letecia

BRAZIL

AGUARUNA   Pastaza

P   E   R   U

Ucayali

N

W   E

S

0   50   100   150 MILES

0   50   100   150 KILOMETERS

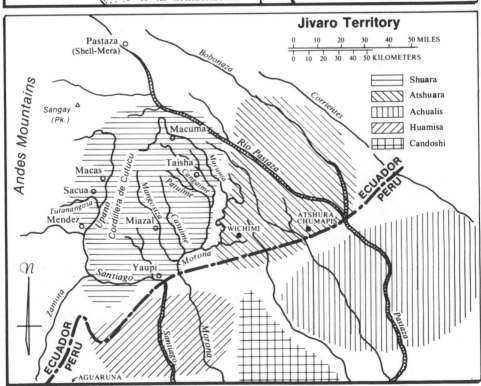

Jivaro Territory

Pastaza (Shell-Mera)

Bobonaza

Corrientes

0   10   20   30   40   50 MILES

0   10   20   30   40   50 KILOMETERS

	Shuara
	Atshuara
	Achualis
	Huamisa
	Candoshi

Andes Mountains

Sangay (Pk.)

Macuma

Rio Pastaza

Macas

Taisha

Sacua

Macuma

Cangaime

Patuime

ECUADOR
PERU

Tutanangosa

Miazal

Upano   Cordillera de Cutucú   Mangosiza   Cusuime

Mendez

WICHIMI

ATSHURA CHUMAPIS

Yaupi

Morona

Santiago   Morona

Pastaza

N

Zamora

ECUADOR
PERU

AGUARUNA

2

LIVING WITH
HEADHUNTERS

The going was rough, very rough indeed. The towering jungle trees, interlocked above us, permitted only an occasional shaft of light to pierce the dripping darkness; this constant wetness had made the trail a slippery, sucking thing of frustration. There was no hacking and cutting for the figure in front of me. The jungle base was rotted vegetation and fallen trunks of trees, giant roots and vines that you stumbled over in the dimness, but there was no classic scene of slash and penetrate. One hour, two hours—a sudden burst of chattering voices directly above me would lift my head and I would search for their owners; a screeching to my left, coming as quick as a cough, would swivel my eyes in that direction. I never even saw a movement, much less a body, but I would get a blow in the face by a vine as thick as a man's wrist that had been waiting for me as it hung straight down from forty feet, and I'd hit the glistening red-brown mud on all fours once again. Thirty minutes more, and then a turning and a raising of a left hand stopped me. "We will reach the Shuaria in about fifteen minutes. The *Curaka* knows, of course, of our coming. All has been arranged, but it is necessary to follow custom. Now, repeat after me this word: *Winyáhei* (I come!)." I did so, again and again. *Winyáhei! Winyáhei!* "Good. Now you are to shout it, right after I call it out first. Then we repeat it twice more. Alright. Then I will yell another word twice, but this you will not repeat. I want you learn it though, so repeat it: *Yachuta! Yachuta!* (My brother, my brother!)."

Five minutes passed, and the warm rain stopped. The dripping kept in step with us, but the darkness grew less intense about us and seemed to lift my companion's spirits, for he began to talk without turning or stopping; it was almost as if he were giving a lecture.

"There has been no cultural nation in the history of the earth like the Jivaro. Only he shrinks the heads of his enemies and how stupid the world is to believe that he does it solely to have a trophy, to hold it high and shout 'See? I have killed my enemy, here is the proof!' So much has been written, so little is true; sensationalism, writers making up things, seeing things as *they* want to see them, writing as if they *knew*, as if they understood the why and the how of their existence."

He stopped. No chattering of monkeys, no screeching of parrots now, no din of insects. There was just the dripping, the strong jungle smell, and the two of us standing alone in that deep-green, shining cathedral.

"The Jivaro's whole world is filled with spirits, and magic, and witchcraft. See that tall, skinny palm over there? It is the *chonta*. To the Jivaro it has great power; a spirit lives within it that brings fear to all evil spirits and demons, and therefore all his spears are made of its hard wood. The *tsantsa* [shrunken human head] must be tied to a *chonta* lance at the victory feast; any other spear with an iron point would not keep the bad spirits away. Even the three pins passing through the lips of the *tsantsa* when it is being shrunk are of *chonta*. It has great supernatural power. The spirit living within it is the *wakani*." He looked up, as if he could see through that stitched ceiling to the sky, and his voice rose. "The Rain God, who lives in the mountain peaks, the Anaconda God, who lives in rapids, the Moon, the Sun, the Earth Mother: All are living spirits. The witch doctor, when he dies, becomes a bear to be feared if his murder is not avenged. The warrior's soul after death is a jaguar if he was brave. A child is a sweet and beautiful bird. . . ." His voice trailed off. He started to turn, then, abruptly, "Did you know that a Jivaro *never* uses a blow gun and poisoned dart against a human being? Even against his deadliest enemy? And he does not acknowledge natural death, did you know that? He cannot even imagine such a conception; death comes from supernatural causes, brought into being by his enemies who force or hire a witch doctor to direct an arrow, a *magic dart*, the all-powerful *tunchi*, to enter his body to inflict disease, death, or a horrible accident. Death to a Jivaro is always *murder*, and murder must be avenged or the spirit

54

will. . . ." This time he did stop speaking, for he had looked at his watch and then instantly turned and started up the small hill above us, and for the first time I saw extremely thin, glittering rivulets coursing down its face above us. A few struggling, slipping steps upwards and he looked back over his shoulder at me and said, "Placer gold."

For the last minute or so we had for the first time been able to trek side by side. Looking ahead now I could see no change whatsoever in the character of the growth above and about us, when Ralph, of an instant, stopped me with his outflung right arm. "We are at the edge of the Shuaria," he said quietly, as he again looked quickly down at his wristwatch, "and we are early. Tangamashi expects us when the sun is directly over his *hea*; we wait." He stepped over to a large fallen tree trunk, first inspecting it closely, and sat down.

A Jivaro time out; okay, we won't waste it. It's high time anyway that I fill you in as to what put us here in the jungle of the Oriente waiting for a call from a headhunter.

Actually, it had all started a year before. I was laying out my next summer's dreams of doing some climbing in the Andes, and, as I had decided my major at UCLA would be anthropology, exploring a number of fascinating ancient Inca ruins (as well as trying to figure out how to talk my folks into letting me go, and how to pay for it!). It was then that I discovered a strange, storybook kind of rumor. It told of an American doctor who had spent his life in the headhunter country of Ecuador in a quest for a cure to cancer and other maladies. Year after year, he had been collecting herbs and roots and plants used by the headshrinking Jivaros, preparing them in hundreds of liquid formulas in a laboratory in the jungle outpost of Sacua. In order to do this, he had painstakingly gained the friendship and the confidence of the Indians, and had raised a family in Sacua. One of his children, a son named Ralph, had been brought up both as an American, going to school for certain periods in the states, and as a Jivaro, becoming a blood brother, so to speak, of certain clans. I checked the story out with the Ecuadorian Consul General in Los Angeles and found that it was true. Somehow I managed to both save up enough and get the parental ok—so, when summer came, I was off.

Four days ago I finished my expedition to Peru and am happy to report to you that all went well, except for two near things: One occurred in the Temple of the Moon at Machu Picchu, where I had an impromptu encounter with a coral snake; the other a hundred miles or so away above a Quechua Indian village, with several hundred Quechuas squatting in a great half-circle on many rock tiers and Inca terraces, watching me trying to negotiate a crumbling sheer cliff I had very unwisely attempted.

Two days ago I arrived in Quito and found Dr. Wilburn Ferguson—he did indeed exist. He was on his way to the States, and in four hours I would have missed him. I concluded with ". . . .and so, doctor, my interest is threefold. Number One, I wish to present a qualified paper to my Department of Anthropology. Number Two, I want to discover personally as much of the truth as possible about the Jivaro—by living with him, by taking part in his daily activities, by living his way of life. The Jivaro have come to fascinate me, doctor, not only because they are the only tribe in the world that shrinks human heads, but because of their legendary independence—for they are also the only tribe to have ever successfully rebelled against the Spanish.*

"What I really want, then, is to get inside the Jivaro's mind. I realize that this will require an interpreter that is not a guide of other blood or tribe, but one who is, in effect, a Jivaro himself. I have spent considerable time, during the past year, reading about and researching the Jivaro, and there is so much obvious padding, imagination employed, dramatic license used, much of which I suspect is the result of incorrect or inadequate questioning and answering through interpreter. So many interpreters fake so much to impress you or to keep their job—you must know that, doctor, far better than I. And then, of course, personal feelings and impressions influence so much, and discolor so greatly, the end results, making a great deal of what I've read highly subjective.

"By the same token, the Jivaro *Curaka* that I may fortunately meet must have integrity and honesty as well—or I'm finished before I start. Number Three, doctor, six words: It will be a great adventure."

"You know of my son, Ralph?" the doctor asked.

"Yes, doctor, I do," I replied, and quickly added, "His help is really the key to my goal, that and a clan you know, that has accepted you and Ralph. I am hopeful, too, that the *Curaka* will be an old and trusted friend of yours. My dream is simply that when I enter the Shuaria that I will live the life of every Jivaro there exactly as he does, that Ralph will have told them beforehand that I

*The famous Jivaro uprising in 1599 is discussed on page 108.

am a student of their culture, that I respect their customs and beliefs, that both my mind and heart are open, that I come to them to study and understand, in all things, the Shuara. And that's it."

The doctor smiled for the first time, and said, "Son, you have done your homework well. You also correctly identified my Jivaros as they call themselves: *Shuara*." The grey-haired, smooth-faced, stocky legendary man of medicine of the headhunters sat there without saying a word; his eyes behind the slightly tinted bifocal lenses were unblinking as they studied me. How many twisted, broken bones of exotic primitives had this man set deep in the jungle? What had triggered this quest that had consumed his life in a dark green world of his own? Thirty years. Did he have within his reach now the. . . .

"Young man, you shall have your clan, and your *Curaka*, and my son will take you to them. Many years ago I saved the life of a Shuara witch doctor's wife. This shaman was also the clan's *Curaka*, and when his magic roots and herbs failed for once he had to come to Sacua for me. Days later, in his Shuaria, when we both knew that Atsáyü would live, there began a friendship that has grown stronger and more trusting each year for a quarter of a century. This Shuar,* young man, is a chief of great intelligence and wisdom, and a man of honor. He has taken many, many heads, he has never broken his word, he is a warrior beyond compare, and he has virtues that. . .but I will not say anything more. It is now for you to find out because he is the *Curaka* that you will meet. His name is Tangamashi."

"*Winydhei*!" I called it out for the first time in my life—"I come!"—to a renowned taker of heads, a famous warrior, the *Curaka* of a headhunter clan in the Oriente of Ecuador. It was 12:01 p.m. on the afternoon of August 17, 1960.

"*Winiti*!" rang out clear and strong, penetrating easily to where we stood in the gloom of the forest. "May you come!" We moved forward, and in ten yards stepped into bright and, to us, almost blinding sunlight. Hour after hour we had not seen much of the sky, nor had our eyes been exposed to strong light, and suddenly, like a giant black window shade being ripped off, the scene before us blurred and burned for long seconds, then slowly cleared into focus as we walked forward in step, side by side. My sights were

*Singular for Shuara is Shuar.

57

zeroed-in on a figure standing alone some one hundred and fifty feet directly in front of us, but the periphery of my vision took in the drastic environmental change. We had moved out of a tree-enshrouded, vine-encrusted, bamboo-casketed world into a burned-out, chopped-out clearing, with figures moving here and there in the far background. But that figure alone, motionless, waiting. Tangamashi.

At one hundred and fifty feet, three instant impressions: color, height, muscles. A shock; his color is light, very light—make it half copper, half tin. Short, how about five feet seven. Smooth muscles, skin looks oiled. Hair? Can't see it, but there are reds and yellow around his forehead—a band, a *tawasamba*, certainly: toucan feathers. Skirt—right, it's an *itipi*. Ah, no lance, no blow gun. Look at that collar around his neck, it's pure white and—wait till I get closer—but look, Jack, at those necklaces. Four, five, hanging to his chest—then his stomach, his waist, birds on the bottom loop, that coal-black one with the blue beak, that orange one next to it . . . what are those narrow, long, round rods between the snail shells and seed pods? I've got it: bones, monkey bones—dozens of them. Where are his ears? Can't see them, but look, there are red and yellow bunches of feathers hanging from where they should be, toucan feathers matching his *tawasamba*.

We stood silently facing—Tangamashi. A flash of an impression, all of three seconds. Eyes—the most important of all things in a human face: the black, ebony ones thirty-six inches away were serene, composed, tranquil. Mouth—the second most important for a clue to emotion or character: even, not turned down, at rest, no uplifting for the beginnings of a smile, no pressing in of bitterness or displeasure, no pressure from lip above nor lip below to control suppressed anger or fury. A capsule diagnosis, born of suspense and undiluted anticipation: a man at peace with himself and all about him. The *Curaka*. A thought flashed through my mind: Seventeen hours ago, that's right, seventeen hours ago, I had been told in whispered Spanish: *Este cacique ha llevado treinta cabezas.* (This chief has taken thirty heads.)

I stood there listening to my first two-way exposure to the Jivaro language. The sound of "Jack" I caught, it came out as "zhuck" and hard on its heels came "Whee-lehr" with a "whee" rising in tone, and the "lehr" falling. It commanded a turning of the befeathered head and an abrupt, unexpected outthrusting of a bronzed hand that was met as quickly by my own. There were two severe pumpings up and down, then an instant release.

58

And now I had an opportunity for a BCU, as the film makers so fondly designate an extremely tight close-up, of a champion head-taker. Face to face with Tangamashi was a soul-searching experience of inflated proportion at the very least, and the use of words like avid and intense are properly employed to describe my nose to nose inspection. I took care not to look directly into his eyes, for the Jivaro view this as a hostile act, but I could see that, as I have already noted, his eyes were clear, there was no gleam of fanaticism, no wildness lurking in their depths. The strong face was unlined, except for squint tracings, no deep grooves furrowed their way down his cheeks on either side of his normal nose. No muscles throbbed in neck or jowl. So having taken facial inventory and found not a monster but a man I liked at first sight, I was now free to gaze with wonder and admiration at a truly unique and masterful paint job.

On each cheekbone, a pure red butterfly; across the bridge of his nose, a squared, geometric-appearing figure with a box in the center and two boxes on either side of the straight nose, all painted in the same flaming red, which came from crushed *achiote* seeds. An inch or so below each fiery butterfly, an X. At the very tip of his nose, a crimson spot, matching the X's and all above. There were no horizontal bars, no black, heavy lines. There were no ear cones. It hit me like a slap —no ear cones. It came over me in one gratifying moment: This was a Jivaro, a Shuar. This man before me was not a posed picture, with all the regalia for different times and specific events and special occasions, piled on at one time for a spectacular, staged commercial still. The doctor had kept his promise; Ralph had passed the word by forest runner of the young man and his mission, and Tangamashi had accepted it. I was to live with the Shuaras as one of them, not as a writer with a publisher waiting, not as a film maker for television or theatres, not as a lecturer with pith helmet and ladies clubs already clapping, but as an anthropologist/adventurer with only one goal: to know the Shuara.

"Jack, Tangamashi has invited us to enter his *hea.*" As a trained, scientific observer I had, quite frankly, seen hardly anything from the moment that we had emerged from the jungle, except that solitary, lone figure. I mentally resolved not to let that happen again, as I saw for the first time that the Shuaria (or *hea* in Jivaroan) actually was located on a hill, not precipitous, but a steady incline to high ground. Of course, self-defense—a characteristic of all Shuarias. And furthermore, I knew, or at least assumed, that a swift-moving river, laden with fish, would be close by: a market-place 'round the corner for the busy headhunter housewife.

There was no conversation as we three, side by side, walked up the slope; a break for me as I was able to quickly look about for the first time. A pastoral scene, bucolic, was the setting. Over there to my left, a Shuar warrior was—now wait a second, Jack—weaving? Surely that was a vertical loom encased in a sort of frame? Certainly, why was I surprised? Men do all the spinning, and weaving, and make all the clothes, even the women's (from cotton grown in their gardens), simply because in the Jivaros' animalistic world every natural object about them has a soul that exists apart from its material body: A spirit that lives in every plant, rock, tree, bush, whatever, that is either female or male. Fire is female, therefore the woman does all the cooking. Cotton and basket material and certain plants or vegetables like corn have male souls, therefore the man does everything connected with them. The Jivaro woman does all the pottery work, the bowls, the utensils, because clay is of the earth, and it has a woman's soul—and on and on.

Beyond my weaver were three women sitting before large bowls. They were in constant motion but the distance was too great to determine what they were doing, and looking past them I could see figures bending over in a fairly large field cleared of jungle. Voices brought my head swinging to my right, and there came two Shuara carrying some kind of animal with long arms, and back of them . . .a slowing of the pace beside me brought my eyes quickly back to stage center.

The *hea*: at long last, not a picture, but the real thing. Make it forty-five feet long, and judging by its elliptical, thatched roof, at least twenty, no, check that, twenty-five feet deep. Cone shaped, its walls were obviously made of *chonta* poles, and there appeared to be two doors, each quite small and located at either end. We veered towards the one on our left, and since we were now about ten feet away I could plainly see that the *chonta* poles had been driven into the ground and then lashed tightly with lianas. The thatched roof, apparently very thick, extended over the tight walls some two or so feet, affording a practical overhang, and it stopped about six feet above the ground.

It was fairly light inside, with beams of sunlight filtering through the spaces between the *chonta* poles. I had been sitting on a footstool for the past ten minutes, sorting out in my mind all that I had been told and had observed in that single house of a Shuara clan. First of all, take a look at it: Three rows of heavy *chonta* posts

60

are supporting the roof, spaced about ten or twelve feet apart. As you look down the long room there are no partitions, only groupings here and there of platforms, some six feet long (some shorter) and four to five feet wide held up by *chonta* legs at each corner and none more than one to two feet above the hard-packed dirt floor. There are three much higher platforms at the far end, and wooden stakes driven in at an upward angle are placed irregularly along the walls; a few are only four feet off the ground, others are six feet high. The low platforms are for sleeping, the others for storage, while the stakes are for clothes and ornaments to hang from the walls. The far end is strictly for the women and girls, my end for the males of the clan. All sleep in this one, great room, and I can see small mounds of round rocks, smoke-blackened and lying in ashes with charred embers, at the foot of several of the sleeping platforms, obviously the Shuara solution for a cold, rainy night (yes, it gets *cold* in the jungle at night).

I was holding a pottery bowl the size of a large cantaloupe; it had been handed to me by Atsáyü, Tangamashi's wife, within a minute of my sitting down. Ralph and the *Curaka* were holding and drinking from theirs some fifteen feet away. I had met Pidro, Tangamashi's brother; Sakimbyo, the *Curaka*'s brother-in-law, and, of course, Atsáyü, all of whom, including the wives and children of Pidro and Sakimbyo, lived in the house—and I was to meet more. As we are having a Shuara "siesta," with the quiet conversation in their language between the two men in the background, with an occasional sentence or question from Pidro and Sakimbyo who are sitting on stools around them in this darkened strange house, I'll ask you to join me while together we review a little basic anthropological data on the Jivaro.

Certain facts are indisputable. They have held true for centuries and, where the Jivaro has managed to hold his own against the encroachments of the *civilizados* and the influence of the missionaries to destroy his rare culture, stand today. Regrettably, the Jivaro is now making his last-ditch effort in isolated spots in the vast interior of his country where he still lives his most unique existence. They can be found, and *you*, in a Great Adventure, *will find them*.

The anthropologists divide the Jivaros into five main groups:* the Shuara and the Atshuara, both in Ecuador, and the Huambisa,

*See map, page 52.

Aguaruna, and Achuali in Peru. Each speak a slightly different dialect of Jivaroan. All believe death is murder and practice blood-revenge on their enemies, but only the Shuara, Huambisa, and Aguaruna commonly take and shrink their enemies' heads. The Atshuara, Achuali, and the Candoshi (a non-Jivaro tribe who picked up the practice from their neighboring Achualis) do so occasionally. (None like to be called Jivaro, which means "heathen" or "savage" in Spanish. I use the term Jivaro, then, only when referring to all five groups as a cultural whole.)

The Jivaros are primarily "slash and burn" horticulturalists, practicing the rain forest type of seminomadic gardening, hunting, and fishing in the Amazonic jungle of Ecuador and northern Peru. They have no villages, no large tribes; they live in small clans scattered throughout the jungle. Each clan lives in what we are now sitting—a single, cone-shaped hut called a *hea* or Shuaria. Each clan is completely independent from the others, with its own household, small cleared fields, and *Curaka*. The oldest family father is the headman of each community, and is the absolute ruler of his house people. He is called *unta*, the "old one," and also bears the title of *Curaka*, if he has led successful headtaking raids.

Since each clan is a separate entity from its neighbor, we have the strange, unique situation of a cultural nation in which all clans speak the same language, have the same superstitions, customs, ceremonies, legends, magic, and myths as all live in an animistic world—and couldn't care less for their neighbors five miles away as the *chingi* flies. As a cold matter of fact, that clan on the other side of that far ridge over there could be—and often is—a deadly enemy, and has the heads to prove it.

I rose from my hand-hewn seat, stretched, and looked inquiringly at the huddle in the *hea*. I wanted to exit and investigate, but I wished not to be caught *in flagrante delicto* if headhunter protocol looked askance at a split without permission. But they paid me not the slightest attention, so out I went, stooping down to exit through the low door. Blinking at the instant glare (*you* take sunglasses), I looked about. My weaver had gone, but just beyond where he had been plying his trade was a Shuara girl doing something to a baby.

I stopped ten feet away and looked upon a scene of such rare quality that I knew instantly that if I were not permitted to photograph it, not a living soul who was not a Jivaro would believe me. For I had spent a year reading every book I could find about them, and here was another beauty they had missed completely.

I was rooted to the spot, mud-covered, gold-flecked, astonished. The mother, a young girl really, was wearing a full robe, seemingly of cotton, dyed blue, secured somehow over her right shoulder, leaving the left one bared. Her long, dead-of-night hair, parted in the middle, dropped in a thick flow over her shoulders almost to the small of her arched back. Her face was a bit broader than Tangamashi's and a delicate shade darker; the skin was unblemished, no pockmarks, no eruptions (I thought, do they use some cream or liquid from a plant or bush? I can make a fortune!); her eyes were round and deep brown.

She was giving her baby boy a bath. Now remember what Alfons was eager to say when we climbed the Matterhorn two years ago? "Attend me." Well, my friend, attend me. Beside her was a large, thick bowl filled with water. As I watched her in out-and-out fascination, she lifted the bowl to her mouth, took a copious mouthful, held it in for a second, took aim after laying the pottery down, pursed her full, well-shaped lips, and let fly a stream full-fair upon her son's chest. A quick reaching of her left hand and a vigorous scrubbing ensued, reinforced by several more shots from mother's oral jet spray. This routine was repeated, time after time, until, I must admit, baby was 99.99 percent pure.

"Jack, let's go down to the river. Tangamashi's youngest daughter will wash your clothes while you're taking a swim to remove all that mud. While you're drying out, we will eat. Okay?"

The river was boiling, fast-moving. Huge boulders thrusting up, here and there, in the path of the rushing water, creating multiple rapids, with here and there eddying pools of quiet, gently moving, white-flecked, blue-green waters. Downstream, about thirty yards from where I stood, two women were dipping clothes into the swift-moving water, lifting them out and then slapping them upon big, smooth rocks beside them. There was a large pottery bowl among the laundry crew, and they would take turns reaching into it with cupped hands and bringing up small amounts of what appeared to be a fine, white powder, which would then be rubbed into the clothes. "Commercial soap?" I asked. "Sometimes, from Sacua. But apparently they like best the soap they make themselves. Tangamashi is strong for the old ways; he's hard to change." This from Ralph, who was standing beside me.

I had been cavorting in the cold, clear water—fighting my way upstream against the rapids, being dragged backwards, fending off giant, spray-enveloped rocks—after turning over my white shirt with the long sleeves, blue jeans, white woolen socks, and heavy boots (in our briefing, we'll have much to say regarding your outfit in the jungle) to a smiling girl much younger than myself. Then it was up to the top of a huge, glass-smooth boulder to let the Shuara sun dry and warm me. But not for long, for here they came, Atsáyü and another older woman, bearing two bowls apiece, which they gently placed on the hot rock beside me. I nodded, smiled, thanked them in Spanish, and turned to a close inspection of my first headhunter's meal.

I studied the four bowls. Number 1: A thick, almost solid, white porridge. Number 2: A stew, with small pieces of dark meat bobbing about in a thin gravy studded with cut-up, yes—it must be yucca; short, green tubers—beans?; reddish chunks of—yams?; and swimming about from rim to rim, specks of red powder— paprika? Number 3: Easy. Bananas. Number 4: Liquid, light brown in color, with a foaming head that was holding its own. (Obviously the same drink I had been given in the *hea*.)

It must be established now that I have still another physical failing. Apart from my ridiculous eyesight—and thank the gods for my contacts—I have very little sense of smell. But I have found that through the years it is more of a blessing than a handicap. Girls, for example, all smell alike, and where I've been in this world, that *is* a blessing. Foods? Ah, the proof of the goodness is in the tasting. I never receive olfactory messages that turn me off at anybody's table, be it in a Tartar chieftain's tent or a Montagnard's abode on stilts in the Central Highlands of Indochina. Let there be no mistake about it, in the wild regions of the earth it is quite true that a keen sense of smell can be a lifesaver. To compensate I have concentrated on developing an extra consciousness of what is happening about me, the constant observance of conditions and clues, that will tip me off to what's afoot, as Mr. Holmes was fond of saying.

I lifted my bowl, I sipped it, I downed the whole bowl. I had drained the first offering in the domicile of mine host, but that had been a gesture of good form only; I had not dwelt upon the matter. It was beer, with a slight overdose of malt, I concluded. If its production was along the lines that I figured—well, forget *that*, Jack. Therein lies the old upchuck—mind over matter, son, and don't you forget it. Next, my newly cleansed fingers probed the stew, emerging with the largest chunk—always go for broke—and thrusting it into my waiting mouth, I took to chewing. To be charitable to the chef, it was just a bit on the firm side, with a touch of the gamey to it, but its impact was somewhat softened by what I now knew to be paprika and the longer I chewed the better I liked it; it just took some getting used to, I decided, and, after all, it had been a long time between meals. So, it was up with the bowl, and I made the pleasurable discovery that salt had been added, for the vegetables were seasoned and delicious. I finished off the bowls in good time, leaned down to do the washing of the service on the spot, and then, staring down into the leaping waters, meditated upon the menu. If I were correct, the drink had been *chicha* (manioc beer); the thick porridge, boiled yucca, (a starchy, potato-like tuber, also known as manioc); the meat, monkey; and the bananas, bananas. I knew that the larder could possibly have offered a different dish due to the relative proximity of the trading outpost, Sacua, but these people were sharing with me the old life that they were still clinging to—and it got to me. But at the same time, I remember cautioning myself: These people are extremely volatile by nature; they are impulsive and choleric, with the instant flaring of the savage primitive. They are professional warriors, and still live in their world of spirits and demons. If a death, or illness, or accident should occur when I am with them, I may be blamed. True, I continued to myself, they *never* attack or kill a white man *if* the white man does not attempt to harm them, or take advantage of a member of their clan.

My *compadre* slithered up to join me on my heated boulder. "Ralph, level with me right now. I've been considering my status amongst your Shuara brothers and sisters. I honestly would not feel right or at ease with the game if this was all cut and dried. I am not waving the flag for reckless adventure, you know that, but there is little room here for the foolish and the feisty, right?"

He studied me for a few seconds, then, "Did my father say anything to you about a German?" I shook my head. "Okay, I think you should be told about him right at the start of your stay here, not," and he paused here for a second, smiled, and with increased feeling to his words, continued with, "that you would ever do such a damn fool thing. But if you're worried that life here will be 'cut and dried' as you put it, nothing, absolutely nothing, could be further from the truth." He stopped to wave and call out something in Jivaro to the *Curaka*'s daughter who had just held up my pants for a distant inspection, and she answered with a quick laugh, obviously pleased that Ralph and I were proud of her work. "See, Ralph, these people of yours are just great, I can't believe that . . ." He interrupted me with a wave of his hand, and turning to look down at the rushing water just below us, quietly continued.

"Now listen carefully, Jack. This German, he was an engineer I think Dad said, was escorted to another clan's Shuaria some distance from here a couple of weeks ago by my father himself. The second or third day, this man came in from the fields where he had gone without Dad and was acting like he had just discovered pure, black oil bubbling up from the jungle floor somewheres. He was talking loud, and running around like a *unta pakki*—that's a big, wild hog, Jack. Dad suddenly had a terrible premonition . . . and he was right. Thirty minutes later, my father had the revolting facts: This stupid, unthinking son of a bitch had raped one of the *Curaka*'s daughters. What had taken him twenty years, at least, to be accepted himself and to be allowed to bring a stranger into their Shuaria as his friend was gone." Ralph stopped. This was a tough job for him, just talking about it. After a long minute, with the sounds of laughter coming from downstream to stab me with the realization that they were just like the. . . ."I'm sorry, Jack. Well, my father's feelings and reaction can well be imagined; he wanted to kill him on the spot. He knew that it would be completely useless to try and explain to his old friend anything at the moment, somehow he would try later, and as much as he hated doing it, he would have to help the German escape before the girl was able to tell her father upon his return what had happened. He grabbed the German by the arm, and started running across the clearing of the Shuaria. They made it and entered the jungle, going as fast as they could down the trail for at least a quarter of a mile. The German was panting heavily—a fairly young man, while you know how old my Dad is. It was a great strain on him, but he kept on and on and on till it became night. As you know, Jack, you cannot travel in the dark in the Oriente, but at daybreak they were off and running again. They finally came out of a very thick area, trotted around a curve—and stopped dead. In the very center of the trail stood Shuara warriors. Without a sound, one of them took his war lance and drove it straight into the ground, while the other quickly placed a tightly wound bunch of leaves upon the top of the lance: the Shuara declaration of war. My father stood absolutely motionless until the Shuara vanished into the jungle, and turning to that miserable German he told him that the Shuara had just signed their death warrants. The man laughed, that's right, he laughed, and said something like this to Dad, 'I can handle these people; I shouldn't have run away in the first place. You go on, Ferguson, if you're frightened. I'll take care of them.' Without another word, my father started walking down the trail, passed the lance, and hit it for Sacua as fast as he could. He had done his best, and to hell with the rapist.

"Dad made it safely home, and then flew to Quito where you saw him a couple of days ago. We have not heard a thing about the German since. One day, Dad will go back and attempt to be friends again, and apologize for what had happened."

(Ten months later, when Ralph Ferguson came to Los Angeles to appear on "This Is Your Life," I asked him about the German. This was his answer to me: "My father returned to that clan just a few months ago. The *Curaka* presented him with the German's head." (See pages of photo insert.) At the time I sat upon that rock overlooking the river on the first day of my arrival at the Shuaria of Tangamashi, neither Ralph nor I had any inkling of the fate of the German. But I tell you this: As I sit here now, talking to you years later and thousands of miles away, with the fog rolling in about me from the ocean, and so late at night, I am getting a little queasy as I think about myself sitting there on that rock, beside that river, when all unknowing to me, perhaps at that very minute, a vicious downstroke of a razor-sharp machete was severing the head from the body of that German. And that later that afternoon, as I was learning the ways of the Shuara, his head was being shrunk only miles away.)

Fifteen minutes later, I was squatting in my shorts beside a headhunter of wide renown, watching him dip a foot-long dart into a pot of *curare*. Now if that isn't a picture that would have Ripley himself spinning in his crypt, I pass. Tangamashi was talking, Ralph was translating, for we were preparing for my first hunt in the Oriente.

"Jack, Tangamashi will not use poisoned darts upon the birds, although he will upon the monkeys that we will find in the forest this afternoon. He says to you, 'I do this to make the death dart plain to see.'" Tangamashi took the foot-long sliver of wood that he had just dipped into the brown, gummy substance, and raised it to his mouth—and licked it! He lowered it to stick its base into the ground, where it vibrated back and forth, and smiled—slightly. It was the first cracking of the facial armor that day. "He did that, Jack, to show you that the poison *curare*, which only he and Pidro can prepare, as *uvisheens*, is harmless unless it enters, as he has just put it, 'the blood where it runs.' In other words, the bloodstream; you can swallow it by the spoonful, and it won't hurt you a bit."

We were in single file, with Tangamashi leading, I second, and Ralph just behind me. The *Curaka* held the eight-foot *oom* (blowgun) in front of him, tilted upwards, with his left hand about three feet from its base, where his right hand grasped it firmly. Not more than a minute ago he had taken a foot-long dart from his *tunta* (quiver), and taking a little ball of kapoc from a gourd attached to the quiver had pierced it with the blunt base of the sliver, letting it ride like a small collar about the dart. A whisper from Ralph, "He does that to keep the arrow straight as it passes through the barrel, Jack, and it also fills the space there so the full blast of his breath will project the dart instead of some escaping around it." Suddenly Tangamashi froze; he inserted the *tsentsek* (dart) in the barrel, placed the gun to his mouth and aimed it high; his cheeks puffed out and went flat. He walked forward ten feet, reached down, and picked up a hummingbird—still alive! "He will shoot them through the neck to paralyze them; he wants to keep them alive so that Atsáyü can have them fresh for the pot." It was Ralph of course, whispering once again behind me. This is absolutely impossible, I said to myself. Paralyze them? Let's see him do it again. And he did, again and again. I report to you that he bagged thirty birds, and killed but one. His skill was uncanny, and the classic topper of the day was Ralph saying to me, as we trekked back to the *hea*, "Do not look at Tangamashi, or say anything to him; he is very mad, Jack, at himself. He cannot see how he killed that one bird!" Have you ever eaten a hummingbird, prepared by a headhunter wife deep in the Amazon jungle? Is that a tale to tell to your grandchildren? "How did it taste, Grandpa?" Well, you will: And you will find it delicious! This is only one of the exclamation points that you and I will place after *your* life.

That first night, I sat surrounded by headhunters in front of a blazing fire that had been sprinkled with a black powder that kept us free of mosquitoes and all night-flying jungle insects, and heard the story of the first shrunken head from the lips of Tangamashi. He would speak for thirty seconds or so, and then Ralph would quietly tell me of his words.

"One day a great *pangi* (anaconda snake) came from Sanguay and slithered down the mountainside into the waters of a large lake at the bottom of the mountain and disappeared. From that day on, any Shuar who ventured near the waters of the lake was seized and eaten by *pangi*. Many Shuara were eaten by the huge *pangi*—what could they do? In deep and final despair, they went to the most powerful of all *uvisheens* and asked for his help. The *uvisheen* came to the lake, and with great courage and the loss of many brave Shuara, the people followed his plan and captured the *pangi*. The *uvisheen* then severed *Pangi*'s head from his body, took out the skull, soaked the head with many herbs in boiling water, and made it very small. 'See,' he cried to his people, 'it is now very little and cannot hurt you. It is too small to swallow you, and the spirit of *Pangi* is inside; it has returned because it recognized itself and now lives within what I hold in my hand. I will teach you how to keep it there, and it will never escape to harm you again.'

"And this he did. Then the Shuara said, 'If we can do such a thing to the body and spirit of *Pangi*, why cannot we do the same thing to our enemies who have killed one of us?' And it was done."

Now there is a mountain called Sanguay; I have seen it many times. Sanguay is an active volcano; to this fact I can personally attest. It does not require a great deal of imagination to see Sanguay erupting in ancient times, and resulting rivers of molten lava flowing down the sides of the mountain to hissingly enter the waters of a large lake. It follows that this would have a highly upsetting effect on the local aboriginal Anacondas inhabiting the lake, and their food supply. (The South American Boa, *Eunectus murinus*, grows to a length of over twenty feet and as big around as a man's thigh.) It would be fair to assume that, due to their depleted natural larder, they would turn, in desperation, to the Shuara bathing in the waters of the lake. Nor do I then, in turn, find it difficult to picture a famous witch doctor capturing a really huge boa living by the lake. With the first head severed and shrunk, you have a story that grows with the centuries—and becomes a great legend.

Today, the anaconda snake, the enormous serpent *Pangi*, is the most powerful and revered of all the thousand and one spirits that inhabit the Jivaro's world. *Pangi*, the father of witchcraft—and the original shrunken head.

"Now raise your arm so that it extends straight out from your body. Right. Turn your fist over so the knuckles are pointing up; close your fist over the shaft. Bring your forearm up till it forms a right angle. Good. Now bring the lance back as far as you can—without drawing your chest sideways to the right—keep your chest facing your target every second." Ralph was repeating the English words that fit as closely as possible the commands that Tangamashi was giving me—I was having my first lesson in the use of the Shuara lance; it was less than an hour after sunrise. Last night, Ralph had given me a briefing on the basic weapon of the Jivaro in war and in hunting.

"To a Shuar, Jack, it is a *thrusting* weapon, almost always in a motion *downwards*, at an angle. It is rarely thrown. He lunges, parries, thrusts, at close quarters. He rushes the enemy; he *drives* the lance into the body. There is rarely the thrown spear that is the trademark of the Auca. And never, never go into *his* country. Don't even try!" It was the second reference to these Indians in as many days by Ralph. I knew, of course, that they had killed a group of missionaries just a couple of years ago. The whole world knew that. And only the Cheendon knew how many hundreds of oil workers, both white and brown, had been done in by the Aucas. No accurate count had ever been kept of Indians of other tribes that had been speared for encroaching upon the jungles of the Aucas. Why, I thought, just a few days ago I had been told in Macas that if I were to go down the Napo River and drift too close to the south bank, a swarm of spears would come flying out of the forest to transfix me and my dugout. The Naked Aucas. Someday, somehow, I'm coming back here and I'll. . . ."Jack!" Ralph's raised voice brought me to attention in a hurry. "Please concentrate. The *Curaka* says that he will have a *wambishku* ride upon your lance to keep it straight." Well, I said to myself, welcome aboard, *wambishku*, whoever you are, welcome aboard.

Tangamashi walked over to a young tree, peeling a banana as he did so. Standing in front of it, he took the fruit and, with a mighty splat, squashed it against the trunk at about chest level. Turning around, he marched back to his judge's stand, nodded to Ralph, who, in turn, stated, "Jack, there stands your *enemigo*. You see that banana stain? That is the heart of your enemy. He is going to kill you! You must attack him *first*. Do exactly as you have practiced—the body behind the thrust, right? But this time you will never take your eyes off his heart. Understand? You suddenly see your enemy—and you will rush him. Now, Tangamashi wants you to be walking along in the jungle, and all at once, there he is—your deadly enemy. You will follow my orders. That is how the *Curaka* wants it done. All set?

"Now turn around, walk back aways into the jungle. When I call out, you re-enter the clearing and walk towards us. Imagine, you will be on a trail, the growth is terribly thick, you are looking out for an ambush. When I yell, you see the splash. It is the enemy. Run forward, judge your timing, left foot forward, remember everything. You thrust—you kill. And never take your eyes off his heart, never. All right, go."

I turned, walked to the end of the clearing and into the thick growth. When I heard the shouted "Now!," I spun around and started creeping back. I entered the clearing, bent over, and suddenly, "Jack, Tangamashi says, 'stand up straighter.' You cannot get—what he means is, you know, no real power from the ground up if you're bent over too much." I stood more erect, walking slowly, head swiveling. "There he is!" My eyes whipped to the splash, my arm shot up at a right angle, the lance held high and pointing at the blob. I took six running steps, the lance shot down and pierced the yellow, pulpy stain.

Thirty minutes later, Tangamashi was half-satisfied, and make no mistake about it, I was tired. I had gone that route at least twenty times, until at last there was no more banana. I was saved from another peeling by the welcome arrival of Atsáyü and Sakimbyo's wife, Tangamashi's daughter, bearing food—a Shuara picnic.

We sat in the shade and ate boiled yams and fried bananas. Ralph, Tangamashi, and the girls talked softly. The jungle was quiet, except for the hum of insects. I leaned back on my log and looked up. There is a great beauty to the jungle, I thought. A surging, chaotic beauty. At first it seems that life has gone berserk, a place of wild abandon, fearful and dangerous. Yet it is a place of enormous peace.

There is so much *life* in the jungle. Living, moving, pulsating, wild and free. There is more that *lives* in the jungle than in any desert, mountain, or even ocean. Yes, it is full of headhunters, insects, poisonous snakes, and spiders. But it is so much safer to walk through than the streets of New York City.

The Shuar uses the lance, and the shotgun, in time of war. No blow guns and poisoned darts are ever used on human beings. He believes that if they were used on humans, they would lose their power when employed in hunting. Further, contrary to the mystery novels that present *curare* as the fastest-acting deadly poison that summons death by laser beam, this alleged wiper-outer of countless humans is slow in acting, and takes a considerable amount to score a kill (much more than can be put on the end of a dart; this amount is enough only to stun or paralyze a monkey temporarily). There is also a simple antidote which I now advise every good detective and private eye to carry with him at all times: sugar.

The Shuar kills his enemy with the lance. He kills not for money, not for politics, not as a mercenary hired to murder, not to wipe out a religion in favor of his own, not to conquer an alien nation, not to put a new ruler-thug in power, not to supplant one ideology over another, not to loot the resources of the tribe over the hill, not to. . . .why go on? The Shuar kills, as do all Jivaros, to avenge the murder of one of his clan. It is as simple as that. Blood revenge is a religious ritual of justice, for which he must summon the spirit of the *chonta*. An eye for an eye, a tooth for a tooth.

Now, remember what we discussed in the Introduction about the valuable perspective that living in a culture so removed from our own provides? Well, here is an excellent case in point.

To the Shuar, all death is murder.* This is a view that he holds in common with primitive tribes throughout the world—with the Azande and Lovedu in Africa, the Dobuans in the western Pacific, the Navaho of North America, the Aritama in Colombia, and a great many others. One such is the Tiv, who occupy the Benue valley of Nigeria. A sociologist who studied them makes the comment:

> The Tiv, like many other primitive people, do not recognize natural death. If someone dies it is always attributed to the envious black magic of another. (Schoeck, p. 57)

And on the Aritama, he notes:

> There is only one explanation for unforseen events: the envious black magic of another villager. The Aritama do not believe in the possibility of natural death. Every illness is caused by a personal enemy. (p. 52)

The institution of witchcraft and the practice of black magic in primitive and peasant societies is seen here as being motivated primarily by envy, and has as its source the envious man's theory of causality in human affairs: that one can be prosperous and happy only at the expense of others, that one man's gain necessitates another man's loss.

Anyone who has much familiarity with primitive and peasant societies throughout the world can recognize the extent to which the people in them are dominated and haunted by envy, and the fear of envy, the "evil eye." But how different are we? A particularly acute insight is offered by the scholar quoted above:

---

*Except that caused by white man's contagious diseases, such as influenza and small-pox. Death-murder for the Jivaro is of three kinds: actual murder (by lance, shotgun, or poison), witchcraft murder (by unexplained illness), and demon murder (what we would call "accidental" death, such as by drowning, snakebite, or being crushed by a falling tree). Only the first two are avenged.

72

A self-pitying inclination to contemplate another's superiority or advantages, combined with a vague belief in his being the cause of one's own deprivation, is also to be found among educated members of our modern societies who really ought to know better. The primitive people's belief in black magic differs little from modern ideas. Whereas the socialist believes himself robbed by the employer, just as the politician in a developing country believes himself robbed by the industrial countries, so primitive man believes himself robbed by his neighbor, the latter having succeeded by black magic in spiriting away to his own fields part of the former's harvest. (p. 41)

That envy plays a major role, then, in the Shuar's culture is not exceptional. What is exceptional and, given the context, quite admirable, is how he deals with it: with a fierce pride in his independence, with the point of a lance, not allowing himself to be eaten away and tortured inside by the cancer of hypocrisy and the repression of fears and hates.

Yes, the Shuar cuts off his enemy's head and shrinks it. An act of barbaric, Dionysian savagery that both nauseates and intrigues us. The latter, perhaps, because there is a wild and primitive innocence about the headhunter. He lacks the sanctimonious pretense of, for example, certain of our Puritan forefathers who offered $134 in cash, not trade, for a male Indian's scalp, $50 on the Bible-thumping barrelhead for a female scalp, and $10 in trade for an Indian *child's* or *baby's* scalp. He is not imbued with the infinite obscenity of a leering, drooling beast such as Lenin, Hitler, or Stalin, turning entire nations into charnel houses. "Thou shalt kill thine enemy" we may feel is tragically misguided as a moral commandment, but at least the Shuar has no use for monstrous bromides about the True Faith, the Public Interest, or the Common Good.

Tangamashi rose, adjusted his *itipi*, set straight his crown of glowing toucan feathers, and made an announcement. Whatever it was broke up the luncheon, and I followed the group as they headed back towards the *hea*. I did not forget to pick up my lance.

I was awakened two hours later from my siesta by, to my surprise, not Ralph but Sakimbyo; he motioned for me to follow him, and we walked out into the hot bright sunlight. There stood Ralph listening to the *Curaka*, who was speaking with surprising animation for him, and pointing with fully extended arm towards the jungle to my right. My man from Sacua nodded, turned to me, and started speaking before I had reached him. "Now," he announced, "you're up against it."

It wasn't a particularly pleasant greeting, I thought, as approaching him I looked around and saw being repeated one of the first sights to have registered with me on my arrival. Atsáyü and another woman to whom I had not yet been introduced were bending over two large bowls. Remember?

"Tangamashi has been favorably impressed by you," Ralph informed me, and then with one of his infrequent, quick grins, "for the life of me, I can't figure out why." That brought from me, "I'll drink to that," looking over at Atsáyü and finally getting the message concerning her activity, which consisted of chewing yucca and spitting frequently into the large pots. Fermented, the masticated yucca becomes *chicha*.

"You, my boy, are about to engage in what the Shuara lightly describe as *awuimaipa*, which I very roughly make out to be something like not letting an enemy escape—and in this case, the enemy is most certainly you. It's a kind of test, really, what we'd call a war game. Wait a minute."

Tangamashi, between drinks from a bowl that his daughter had just brought, nodded several times as Ralph adressed him. "Okay, Jack. Tangamashi himself will take you out north of here to a certain trail that ends up finally back in the Shuaria, or at least that yucca field over there. You will be the enemy who is sneaking up to attack the *hea*; of course it should still be dark, as you know, but you are to try to avoid the traps on the trail that are now being finished by Pidro. The *Curaka* thinks that you will detect them. As I have told you, these people attack just before dawn when it is still dark, so you realize that in blackness the traps would be twice as hard to avoid. The enemy knows this, of course, so he tries to make his way up to the *hea* by staying off the trails. My father has told me that when he first came here years before I was born, Tangamashi had placed at one time over *thirty* such traps all around his Shuaria, just for the few days when he knew an attack was coming. How he kept track of them all I'll never know."

Ralph stopped, for Tangamashi had called out to him with what obviously were more instructions for me—but thirty? "Jack, these people do not fool around. These traps are real, and I don't like it at all," and he turned to the *Curaka* and for the first time raised his voice and got a little excited. He strikes you at first as being introverted, quiet and very soft-spoken, almost shy. But there is *mucho hombre* under that deceiving exterior. Finally, "Well, I've managed one change, and he's agreed to. . . .but I don't know . . . .I'm not supposed to give you any help, but to hell with that.

74

Every step, and make them *slow*, look for fresh signs of leaves and dirt in front of you; it will be hard, believe me. Above all, look for a *liana*, you know, a vine, stretched across the trail. It'll be brown, I'll bet on it; they are usually black because of the night, but in daylight now, they'll think of that, too."

Tangamashi was beside us, Tamashyo panting slightly, eyes gleaming, along with him. I had the instant thought that this embryonic warrior was hoping for the worst. Three quick words from the *Curaka*, and we began following Tangamashi in single file across the Shuaria's clearing towards the yucca patch to the north.

"There is your trail; it comes out of the jungle into the field directly in front of the *hea*. Now listen to Tanga . . ." Ralph had not finished speaking his name when that Shuara gentleman suddenly, without warning, let out a yell that I swear they heard in Lima, Peru.

My nerves at the moment were not in the best of shape anyway, but with that horrible, drawn-out scream I damn near dropped dead on the spot. No traps were needed; I was through before I started. Ralph continued talking as if nothing had happened, but his words came from a great distance; I simply could not continue breathing again. Tangamashi was tremendously pleased with him-self—that much was obvious—and Ralph seemed more concerned with the traps than with my return from death. "What in *hell* was *that?*" I finally managed.

"That," replied Ralph, with a certain air of preoccupation, "was the great war cry of the Shuara. The *Curaka* thinks it is the surest way to warn you if you miss a trap and are about to. . . ." His voice faded away and I couldn't have agreed more; how right he was. With normal breathing slowly returning, I asked, "Is it a word," and I came up with a beauty that I am proud of to this day, "or a paroxysm?"

No smile, only, "They speak of it as 'Tuo!', but it gains something in the yelling." On that statement I would not com-ment. "All right, Jack. It is time." We three were alone, standing in a very deep pocket of intense growth. "Good luck," from Ralph, and I turned to start down the path.

It varied in width, this path, for that was its proper description, not really a trail. As I walked slowly and carefully, it was three feet wide here, only a foot there. The growth was not too thick, there were no bananas, nothing cultivated or planted along the way. Trees here, clumps there, heavily matted carpeting sinking under my carefully placed boots. No monkeys chattering, no parrots screeching, no bark of a toucan, no cawing of a hawk—it was all very still that late afternoon in the Shuara's jungle. My breathing was the only audible sound, my mouth was open, and the air was escaping from my flushed face in loud hisses and pants.

My muscles, I discovered, were taut. This is bad, very bad, I told myself. I must keep them relaxed—if I have to jump, they must be loose. Eyes, eyes. . . .keep them on the move, constantly, look for dark shadows, freshly moved earth or leaves, strings, vines, a heavy cluster of foliage, a slight depression, a higher growing clump in the ground ahead of you, keep those eyes searching.

Madre de dios, there he is. Don't move. He's big. Check those colors, and don't move. Bright green and shining yellow? Yeah. Eyes? Round and brown. That's a *boa*, half-grown, about ten feet. Step around him, he won't lunge at you. All right, go, but slowly. Why doesn't his head turn? Why—he's dead. Stop. It's a trap to make you go around him. Look at the ground behind him and to the right. That's it: a brown vine stretched across the only way to travel around *pangi*. I slid to my knees, reached for a long piece of half-rotted wood, squeezed myself as far to the right of the *liana* as I could, snaked the limb forward and, with my left hand extended almost to a straight out position, shoved the wood ahead to strike the line. Nothing happened. I tried again, harder. Nothing—and then it hit me. A dud. That's it—if I had cracked up here, I was 86'ed before I had made the first quarter pole. A test. Darned clever, these headhunters.

For the first time, I looked about me, and there was the *Curaka* himself, muscled body hugging the greensward. I smiled at Tangamashi, who lay there, resting. He showed not one bit of expression. I rose to my feet, took one step in order to turn around. "Ralph," I called out, for I could not see him, "we took the first trick, I. . . ." WHAM!........ a tremendous blow struck me on my right shoulder blade. I was hurled forward, straight towards Tangamashi, who was still lying on the ground. I saw him beneath me as if in a heavy fog, for my vision was going, and I was vaguely aware that I had fallen on him, with a crunching, sodden thunk of dead-weight impact. I remember a vicious, sharp, penetrating pain that was sweeping now over my entire back, and I recall, oh, how I recall, saying over and over to myself—nothing, nothing at all. It would be easy and colorful to tell you such accepted, dramatic formulae as "the bastards have done me in!" or "the swine have killed me!" or "my god, to be suckered by these damned headhunters!" But, my friend, if we are going to make *The Adventurer's Guide* a success, everything must be as it was, and as it is—so, I tell you, when I get in a *real* bind, I think of nothing except how to *get out of it* . . . grab that ledge . . . roll with the blow . . . massage that cramp, Jack, like squeezing an orange . . . freeze. . . .don't move an inch . . . wait . . . hold your breath . . . and on and on. You simply cannot afford the luxury of self-incrimination, pity, anger, and the like. You're wasting time and energy, and it's ten to one you end up very dead, or, at the very least, out of commission for one long time.

"To begin with, Jack, it was a *tambunchi*, and they have used it for centuries to kill their enemies who are making a surprise attack at night upon their Shuaria. Now I shall show you how they prepare it. But I'll tell you this: Pidro added a refinement, which was a real compliment to you; for it they have no Shuara words, so they use the Spanish *doble trampa*, which means double trap. Okay, now we'll take it step by step."

With Pidro and Tangamashi and Tamashyo watching, Ralph moved to a point past my liana to where a sapling about six feet high and some two inches round now stood upright. There was a cross pole attached to it some eighteen inches from the top with a projecting, thick stick heavily wrapped in an *itipi* at its point facing us, which in turn was stuffed with packed foliage of some sort. The best way to describe it is by having you imagine a wooden arm extending out towards you with a huge fist at the end. He bent the small trunk backwards until it disappeared in a rather thick bush behind it and then took a heavy vine and with a quick turn secured it to the ground. Then, a foot closer to me he picked up a second vine, pulled it across the path in front of the rear liana, and secured it. When he was finished, nothing could be seen— nothing, especially as in his closing seconds of preparation he had carefully strewn leaves and jungle matter in front and over both lines.

"Now, Jack, you spotted the first line—good. You carefully disturbed it with your stick, and it failed to operate. You assumed it was a test, nothing more. You stood up, you took a step forward to turn around, you started to call out to me, your right foot was moving, and it touched the *second* line—bang went the release and you were struck, fortunately, in the back as you were in the process of turning. I have told you before, Jack, these boys play rough. If you had been facing the trunk as it snapped forward at something better than a hundred miles an hour, and it had hit you in the face—well, for starters, no teeth, no nose. Shall I go on?" No comment from your humble adventurer. "Now to make you feel a lot better, watch very carefully what Pidro is going to do now."

Lowering himself to the jungle floor with the inherent grace of a courting cougar, the cursing *uvisheen* scuttled noiselessly forward to the right of the path, reached forward, touched the string, and a blur that hummed flashed upwards, to vibrate back and forth with eye-aching speed. When it finally stopped Pidro stood up, untied the lashings (vines) that held the extended fist, and then, receiving from Tangamashi the most diabolical device that I had ever seen, proceeded to lash it into place where before my substitute had waited for me. Affixing again the releasing device, but this time only employing a single line across the trail in front of it, he stepped back and admired his handicraft. I assure you, it would have been impossible for any of us to have spotted the severely bent-back tree trunk, much less the connecting liana. When the bare foot of the attacker touches the front stretched-out vine, the vicious bow is released and the *real* device strikes with horrible strength and force the face or chest of the advancing enemy.

What is hurled into his body with blinding speed? To the upper end of the sapling, lashed so tightly that it becomes a part of the trunk, is a comb, two feet or more wide, forming what could be called a cross. The teeth are four, five, six, seven, or eight in number; each is a chonta stake, a foot or more in length, and sharpened to a needle-like point. Side by side, when they are bent back with the pole to which they are attached, they point, in a horrible, gleaming row, up to the sky. When the release is tripped, they flash forward, level off—and strike with inhuman velocity the chest, face, or head of the victim. The speed is so great, so sharp and pointed the stakes, that the victim remains impaled upon the tree trunk, with the teeth of the giant comb piercing his face or chest, sticking out in a row in his rear, and supporting his body, holding it dangling in the humid, jungle dampness.

"Jack, Tangamashi asked Pidro to set up this real *tambunchi* for your training. I told you I had received a change in his plan. This was it. But is also true that the *Curaka* and Pidro would not have installed the *doble trampa*, the double trap, if they had set up the death stakes, and, after all, you did discover the first liana, so I guess all would have gone well anyway." Thanks, old buddy Ralph, I said to myself, thanks for the "guess" bit.

78

Considering his handiwork, after spending a good minute upon the concealing process, Pidro stepped back and spoke to Ralph, who looked at me and said, "Alright, Jack, they want you to go back down the trail, walk up here again, spot the vine, crouch down, make your approach, and release the death teeth." A few minutes later, from my prone position on the dank, thick floor, I looked up and over me to the oscillating, hissing passage of the death stakes, a blur in their arcs forty-eight inches above my uplifted face.

After that initiation, the rest was easy. I spotted a "hole of death" without managing to fall in and get impaled on the pointed stakes on the bottom, and another padded *tambunchi*. On the way back, Ralph explained to me that the padded version of the *tambunchi* was a "sex trap."

"A what?" I asked.

"A sex trap. A husband will set one out on a trail near his wife's garden if he suspects her of fooling around. When her boyfriend comes to pay her a visit in the garden. . . .wham!"

"Really! Is there much of that?"

"Quite a bit. You should see how much fun they have at the *tsantsa* feasts! Premarital rendezvous between boys and girls of friendly clans are very common too. The parents are pretty tolerant about it. Sex is the Great American Hang-Up—not the Jivaros'."

I began to lose track of minutes, hours, days, and nights. It seemed at times that this life should have been one immense dream or cut from the pages of a fictional fantasy. It was the saturated uniqueness of the life that all have heard of but know so little. Who has not caught their breath at the vision of a head being severed from a body and then being reduced in size to that of an orange, or at the sound of the words *curare, blowgun, poisoned dart?*

How many times, in how many detective novels, had I read of *curare* being used by the murderer, in how many scenes of jungle pictures had the poisoned dart and arrow been the focal point of attack? We know it is not used upon humans, that the small amount on the end of a *tsentsek* is enough only to temporarily stun or paralyze a small animal, such as a monkey. But did you ever read, or have described to you, how *curare* is produced in the Amazon jungle? What the witch doctor (who has the monopoly) does in the *curare* ceremony? Come into the forest with me, my friend, away from the clan and the *hea*, just you and me—and two *curare uvisheens*.

The chanting is low as the two figures move in a sideways swaying motion around a very large, cracked earthenware pot, blackened by a hundred fires. As in all things, the spirits are soothed, wooed, and won; there is superstition and religious rites even here in the brewing of a deadly poison, and the painted faces have added geometric figures that we have never seen before. The witch doctor stops and gestures to his partner, who in turn instantly places a brown, rounded cloth over the pot. There is a lowering of the shaman's voice; we cannot make out the words nor will we ever be told their meaning. A spinning by each warrior to a short row of small piles, a plucking out of a handful of one, then another, and the hands place the vines, and roots, and leaves upon the cloth. The shaman picks up another, smaller blackened pot that had been suspended over a small fire behind him, and pours a brown, boiling liquid over the materials on the cloth. A constant dripping commences into the pot beneath.

The chanting grows louder; more vines, more roots. The brown liquid is poured again, a very small amount this time, and the two sit down. Five minutes of silence—then one *uvisheen* rises and disappears into the jungle; he is back in thirty seconds, shielding a small, deep cup decorated with black markings. We know what is in that container, and we know that it is not what is used so often by the Indian chemist, i.e., the substance derived from the *Strychnos toxifera*. Oh, yes, that will do the job but our witch doctor has been very busy indeed, all by himself, in a far, dark corner, exuding a very dark, almost black mastic-appearing matter of a thick, gummy, resinous nature from the roots of a shiny, color-changing, clinging, twisting vine that grows wild in the jungle: Its name is *pareira*. There is this one last cup to be emptied; it was prepared a while ago when the shaman was in his own, deep-shadowed place alone. He removes the cloth serving as a strainer and pours the cup's contents directly into the steaming kettle. Its contents flow into the bubbling pot, but oh, so very, very slowly. It will make of the viscous substance a paste of gluey, black consistency. . . .and it is finished . . . it is *curare*.

Be prepared for an "authority" to inform you that the famed poison is not complete without the witch doctor adding in the final minutes such intriguing ingredients as spiders, ants, the hood of a Vampire bat (it has such a ghastly odor that even I smelled it!), plump red beetles, and much more. But all of these things are window dressing for the witch doctor. They affect not one whit the killing power of the poison. But peppers of the Capsicium family are an important addition, as are juices that are scraped from the lianas of *nacu sari, curupa, caspi* and *bucuna ucho*—all these make the *tseas* much stronger. Out of the twenty-five or thirty leaves used, not more than five or six really contribute to the end product.

If we watched another witch doctor, at another time, we would see the *tseas* (*curare*) end up as a rich, dark, thick pot of brown chocolate. By the way, the witch doctor preparing the basic ingredient (the alkaloids *Strychnos* and our own *Pareira*) spends many days, sometimes a week, alone in the jungle, preparing it. At no time can anyone in his clan seek him out, especially women. It is hardly necessary for us to be reminded that the Jivaros' *curare* has become one of the most widely used and valuable drugs in the world today.

Alright, we know how to make the poison; now we need the blowgun, the *oom*. Join me in that clearing over there—okay?—and we'll watch Naita finishing one for you. Days ago he had split a thin, young chonta palm trunk with his machete into two halves about eight feet long apiece, both of which he carefully scraped with a small wet stone and sand so that one side is flat and the other a half-circle. He has just cut a long pole that extended past the two halves; he places this rod inside the half-circle, fits the flat sides together around the rod, and binds the two pieces together with lianas. Now, see, he pours wet sand into the tube and starts working the rod back and forth, like a ramrod. More sand, more water—he's smoothing out the bore. We'll leave him now, because for several days he'll be at this phase of the operation. I'll fill you in on what will happen next—he's going to make yours far smoother than the normal blowgun bore. He took a rope, tied a large knot in it, and impregnated it with wet, fine, quartz sand. With Tamashyo at the far end holding the cord there, they pulled it back and forth, for hours, every now and then freshening up the knot, with a resulting bore that was glass-smooth, a refinement for you. The two halves fit perfectly; he gums them together with latex from one end to the other, binds the halves with palm fibers, and then spreads a thick coating of latex around and over the wrappings, smoothing it down with a heated slab of flat crockery. The next day he applies a coating of pitch (which you saw, yesterday, right? bubbling up from the ground far to the other side of the *yuca* patch), smoothes it, sets the bone mouthpiece (it's about an inch and a half long), and then, the finishing touch, builds up a small, sighting ridge of pitch from just forward of the mouthpiece to a distance of two feet down the barrel. Done. Your *oom* is finished, your *tseas* pot-ready, and your *tunta*, with its gourd stuffed with cotton from the kapoc tree, laden with *tseas*-dipped *tsenkseka*, whittled from the ribs of palm leaves, is standing by.

All set to join Naita and me for a friendly blowgun hunt? Good. The best time for blowgunning monkeys is early morning and late afternoon. During the middle of the day they're asleep in the trees and hard to spot. But it's about 4:00 p.m. now, and we'll be hearing them jump through the branches in search of food. You'll find a blowgun is a lot easier to use than you thought. It only weighs one or two pounds, so little strength is required to hold it up and steady it with your outstretched left hand.

There, right over there are two or three monkeys in a tree, about thirty feet away. See them? Fine. Walk up underneath the tree as close as you can and get a position for a good clear shot. Move slowly now. Take a dart from the *tunta* that already has a cotton collar on it, put the *tseas*-stained point in first with your right hand all the way till the cotton is inside the barrel. Raise it up slowly and sight down the ridge. No need to allow for wind (there is none) or for distance (the monkey is only fifteen feet up). When you've got the *oom* steady and the monkey in your sights, take a deep breath and exhale it in one explosive puff. "Waft" is a good word to describe the *tsentsek*'s silent and slow flight through the leaves. Don't worry that you missed the monkey on the first try. That's to be expected. But you came pretty close, didn't you? And don't be surprised if, when you hit a monkey right on target, he grabs the dart, pulls it out (it will only go in about an inch or so) and throws it away! Have another *tsentsek* ready. Most often the dart will break off when the monkey tries to pull it out. Remember that *Ramar of the Jungle* show where Jon Hall's friend screams and dies instantly from the nick of a poisoned dart? If you remember that scene as you wait two to five minutes for the monkey to fall out of the tree, you will probably laugh out loud. Don't try to explain it to Naita.

Now you may be in for a rough scene. When you go to pick the stunned monkey off the jungle floor, he will look at you with his enormous round eyes, wondering and pleading. He is far from dead, only paralyzed and fully conscious. You may not have it in you to take him back to the *hea*, kill him, skin him, and eat him. After all, the Shuara have birds, fish, pigs, capybara (a huge rodent), and tapir to catch and eat. These thoughts, of course, carry little weight with Naita. The Shuara love animals—but here is meat on the jungle table, food for his children. This comes first, and he is right. Naita quickly dispatches the monkey, after nodding his approval of your fine shot, and the three of us turn back to the *bea*.

Another important addition to the headhunter larder is fish. But to go fishing Shuara-style is to abandon the line and pole routine for a more thorough substitue: poison. They take large amounts of the roots of the *barbasco* plant, pound them into a thick white fluid, and then, selecting a quiet part of the river, blocking off the upper current, and sealing off a section downstream, proceed to pour the poison on the water.

No, it doesn't kill the fish, it stupifies them, and the Indians pick up dozens of them as they float or sluggishly move about on the surface. To our Shuara, this root has a male soul, so it can be handled only by men. In Jivaro it is *teemyu*, and it is another contribution of the Jivaro to the world, for it is used in airplane crop dusting: *rotenone*.

Everyone—man, woman, and child—can handle fish, however, and as Ralph and I sat on a warm granite boulder one day watching, the whole clan piled into the smooth water to laugh, cavort about, and pick up floating fish.

"Jack, the greatest fishing in the world is right here in Ecuador, and all over the Amazon Basin. I tell you, when the millions of licensed fishermen in the States finally discover it—man alive."

This from Ralph, and he should know. "There are hundreds of kinds, thousands of rivers. River seals—twelve-foot pink porpoises—fresh water sharks—why, two thousand miles upriver from the ocean you can catch by the boatload tarpon, swordfish, sawfish, you name it. One day I'll take you to where you can catch a 500-pound manatee. One thing though, never come here in the high-water season, for most of the fish take off for side rivers and lakes. Of course, that makes for good trips, if you don't mind a few unusual things." He laughed, and I with him. "At that time of year, the piranhas really turn on. They look just like perch, you know, they're only about a foot in length, sometimes a lot less, of course, when they're growing. Ever seen their teeth? Like razor blades. You hear so much about the piranha, how they'll strip a large animal to the bones in seconds. I once saw a movie in the States where the villain fell in a jungle river and was eaten alive by them, the water boiling with blood-thirsty piranhas. But you know, I've gone swimming in piranha-infested rivers all my life and never even been nibbled at. I once threw a big piece of fresh meat into a stream—sure, they came and took bites out of it—but there was no churning, crazed mob of them. I hope we'll catch some here, the small ones with red blotches. Butterfly and pan-fry them. Man, they are fantastic!

"Want to try your luck with some really big ones? I'll hook you up with a pirarucu. Now there's the world's largest fresh water fish. Actually it's a swordfish, and I've seen pictures of Indians cut right in two by one cut of its blade. Ready for a nine-foot long catfish? Manatee come in all the time at over a thousand pounds, and if you want to take home something that Sam down the block hasn't got mounted in his den, boat an Acara: It rears its babies in its mouth!"

"Let's get back to that 'pirarucu' number, shall we?" I asked. "Any fish that can cut a man in two with one *cuchillada*—I want to hear about." A laugh from Ralph and, "One slash, eh? Well, that's right, but listen to this, my friend. Its length averages out at eighteen feet—yes, eigh*teen*—long and beautiful, about 300 pounds or so. Its white scales are so terrific they're made into artificial flowers, and it comes equipped with lungs as well as gills. No, I'm *not* kidding. I'll show you a file made out of its tongue, it's that rough and tough." He avoided a pretty fast left hook, but carried on anyway. "Its flesh is so rich with vitamins that you could make pills out of little pieces, and it's delicious. Want to can it and make a fortune?" (Ralph was correct, of course, in everything— except it is being canned now. It's called *Paiche* in Peru.) "That catfish I mentioned? It's the Paraiba, and he's really a monster. When you go fishing for him, you take along two machetes. Are you ready for a two-foot-wide mouth? Incidentally, the flesh of the manatee tastes just like prime beef. Someday I'll prove it to you. When we get back to Sacua we'll get out a map and I'll point out at least twenty rivers or their tributaries where you can dive for pearls and come up with a beauty every fifth trip. Shellfish? All over, and delicious.

"Jack, the Amazon and all the rivers that flow into it, from here and everywhere, are a fisherman's paradise. We've escaped their attention so far, but the day will come. Ever hear of a man named Agassiz? Well, he's the King of Amazon fishermen. He has personally collected over 1,800 species. Right, and when you think that all the rivers of Europe, from the Tagus to the Volga, have less than 150. . . .well. We have more than the entire Atlantic from pole to pole!"*

*Note: information on Amazon fishing expeditions is on page 207.

That was as far as we got in the fish department, for all of a sudden Sakimbyo, who was carrying a basket of fish up the hill to the *hea*, put down the basket and said something to Tamashyo nearby. Small Tamashyo started running down the hill. Now, normally, Shuara, big or little, seldom do any running unless they're carrying a lance held high, so we both immediately clambered off our rock and started up to meet him.

High-pitched, hurried Jivaro words and he was off again, as Ralph told me, "Sakimbyo is sick; he has sent for Tangamashi. This should be very interesting for you, Jack. If Saki is really ill, you'll see a healing witch doctor go to work, but we sure will have to clear it with Tangamashi first."

We all helped Sakimbyo up the rest of the hill, and there was no question about it, he did not look good. His groans were low, but obviously were being held in. He kept his hands pressed against his stomach. The sweat was pouring out of him; apparently he was running a high temperature, although he was not shaking. As we were about to enter the *hea*, Ralph looked inquiringly at Tangamashi, and gestured in my direction. He received a short nod.

It is getting dark now, and in the darkest part of the *hea* we set Sakimbyo down on a sleeping platform. Atsáyü hands Tangamashi a small bowl of something to drink. He sits down on a stool next to Sakimbyo while Ralph and I retire to stools some feet away. Tangamashi starts to whistle, with long, low notes. After some minutes he then begins to chant, deep and steady. Atsáyü hands both Ralph and me bowls of *chicha* to drink, and now you will watch with us every move of the *uvisheen*.

Sakimbyo lies covered with an *itipi*. Above him now stands the *uvisheen*, holding in his right hand a bunch of bright, green leaves, while to the witch doctor's left stands Atsáyü, holding in both hands a bowl of *chicha*. Chanting softly, Tangamashi proceeds to shake the leaves in his hand, held high over the patient. The rustling sound is loud, for in the warm darkness the jungle is quiet.

The leaves become still, and Tangamashi reaches for the bowl of *chicha* held by Atsáyü. She dips her right index finger into the bowl, lifts it to her mouth, and tastes it, thus signifying that the drink is not poisoned. It is not the patient who drinks, it is the witch doctor, who, upon handing the bowl back to his wife, begins to chant once again, and to wave the fresh, bright foliage with even greater vigor.

Now Tangamashi leans slowly down and, pulling back the *itipi* presses his lips lightly to the bare abdomen of Sakimbyo. Abruptly straightening up, Tangamashi touches his lips with his left hand and then flings it out as he chants, "*tsoooo, tsoooo.*" Again and again the procedure is repeated—the shaking of the leaves, the drink, the chanting, bending down, touching, lifting, the strange wave and call.

"He is sucking out the evil demon that is residing deep in Sakimbyo's belly." This from Ralph, in a low whisper. "It is a *tunchi*, a magic dart sent by an enemy *uvisheen* to lodge inside Sakimbyo. There was something in that small bowl Atsáyü first gave Tangamashi that enables him to see the *tunchi*, so he can then suck it out."

Suddenly the sucking and the chanting stops. Tangamashi leans down and speaks quietly to Sakimbyo, who, to my unprofessional eye, appears vastly improved. He then stands up and walks out of the *hea*.

When I awoke the next morning, Atsáyü and her daughter were already busy at work manufacturing *chicha*. A large bowl of boiled yucca was between them, and each, in turn, would scoop up with her fingers a mouthful of the thick stuff and put it in her mouth. Much chewing then ensued, and finally each would spit the well-masticated material into another large pot. The saliva did the trick—the starch of the yucca meets up with the enzymes in the saliva to come up with sugar, which ferments over a period of some days. *Voilà!* Beer.

This is a task that keeps the girls quite busy, for the amount of *chicha* Shuara—even the young children—consume is really amazing. The men must drink at least a couple of gallons a day.

And sitting nearby—with a bowl of *chicha*, naturally—was Sakimbyo, re-caulking a blowgun. He looked up at me, smiled, took a deep breath as if to say, "Look at me, I am perfect!" then smiled even more broadly and went back to work.

Was Sakimbyo's illness psychosomatic? Very likely. Curses, I suspect, are a form of self-fulfilling prophecy. Cursing, the sending of *tunchi* by enemy *uvisheens*, is going on all the time and all Shuara know this, even though each particular act of cursing is done in secret. This would make Shuara quite vulnerable to psychosomatic ailments, so frequently that these ailments must often coincide with an immediately prior cursing, such that the Shuara perceive a causal connection.

No doubt, then, that the show Tangamashi put on for Sakimbyo was, given these circumstances, excellent psychology. He did not

There is an air of
nobility—there is
a shimmering
passion within her
that feeds you
every step as you
climb to her long,
knifelike crest in
the sky.

Left: *The vast
waves of Alpine
peaks that stretch
in all directions
carefully keep
their distance.*

Right: *Author
and guide, Alfons,
climbing in the
early morning
light*

The Matterhorn is
the classic moun-
tain of this earth.
She reigns and
governs like no
other mountain
in the world.

Left: The steeply
sloped ridge,
appearing vertical
from where I
stood, was never
ending in length,
as it held steady
in its upward
march to the
summit.

Right: "Alfons,
there he is!" A
small plane was
coming to greet
us. It was my
father; he was
keeping his
promise.

Incredibly white,
with a burning
vividness against
an unending,
cobalt-blue sky,
the phalanxes of
soaring rock-fangs
literally stole your
breath away.

There was no
sound on the top
of that peak from
the two solitary
figures standing
there, side by side,
looking down—
only the wind,
which had
lowered its voice
as if its task in
helping us to the
top were finished.

A vast, unending
panorama of
peaked crags,
glaciers, and snow-
fields, all proud
and glistening

Author with Tangamashi, who is prepared to instruct JW in the use of the lance

Left: *Look at that collar around his neck—and those necklaces hanging to his chest— birds on the bottom loop, shells, pods, and bones.*

Right: *The mother, a young girl really, was giving her baby a bath, spraying him with mouthfuls of water.*

Sakimbyo with
son, Tamashyo

Left: *Tangamashi
was giving author
his first lesson
in the use of the
Shuara lance;
author is wearing*
itipi.

Right: *Author
takes his turn.*

Shuar (Jivaro)
with a **tsantsa**
(*human shrunken
head*)

Old and abandoned **hea**, symbolic of Shuara customs and traditions

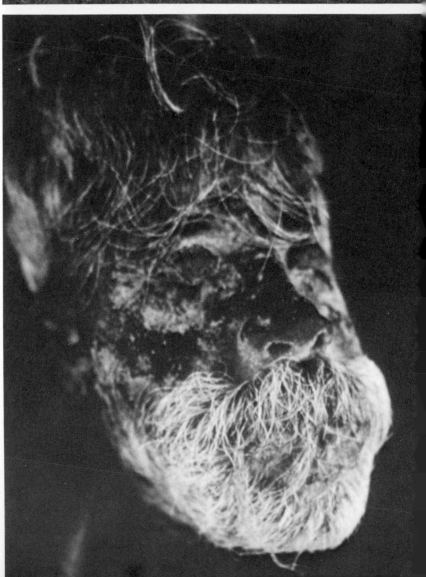

Shrunken head of a German explorer who raped one of the Curaka's daughters

Tangamashi as he looks today, with his wife, Chess-yu

Left: *Author with Tangamashi; Tangamashi has had his hair cut and is wearing a bright red shirt.*

Right: *Tangamashi displaying proudly a key chain given to him by Ralph Edwards for appearing on* **This Is Your Life,** *when author's "life" was done on the show in 1961.*

Atshuara family

Atshuara widows at Pumbuentsa

Atshuara hea-fortress, possibly the only one left in the Oriente

Atshuara man; note balsa wood plugs through his earlobes.

Old Shuar woman

Young Atshuara warrior; helicopter in background

Cooking fire and sleeping platform in Atshuara village

Left: *Jivaro child*

Right: *Young Atshuara boy with a balloon that author had given him*

Waterfall on the Pastaza River below Banos

Quechua women at market on road from Quito to Oriente

Example of the great beauty of the jungle

Walking through the Amazon jungle

Local form of transportation in the Amazon

The Amazon River at Iquitos, Peru

Machu Picchu, the "Lost City of the Incas," in Peru

Namba man working in his taro patch

Tivakuna boy in village on an upper Amazon tributary

Another example of the jungle's beauty

Bunlap, a Namba village on Pentecost Island in the New Hebrides

Chief Bong and family of Bunlap; Chief is wearing the traditional **nambas,** *or penis-wrapping, while his wife and daughters are wearing traditional grass skirts.*

Scene from Bunlap

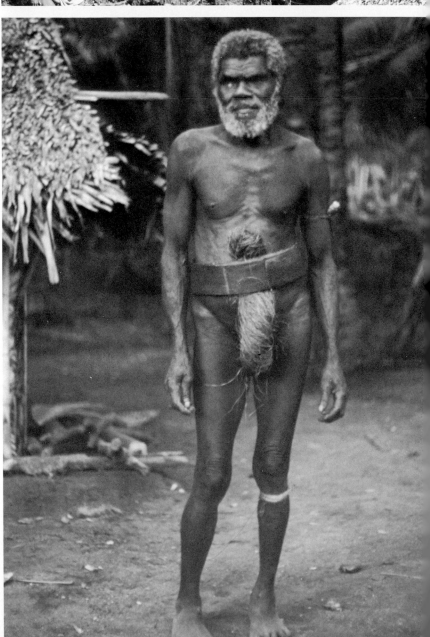

A Namba cannibal in a Malekula village

give Sakimbyo any medicine, and if you ask me why not, I must say that I don't know. For I do know that the Shuara do some quite astounding things with their herbal mixtures and brews.

In the years that have passed since I witnessed that ritual, I have returned more than once to the Amazon, and much of what I have learned about the Jivaros' drugs and medicines will, I think, startle you as much as it did me.

There is a plant the Shuara call *maikiua*. The Quechuas and civilizados who have knowledge of these things also refer to it as *malekoa* or *floripondio*. If you boil the leaves to make a very weak tea, it will relieve pain, like morphine. A strong *maikiua* tea will produce hallucinations, similar to those produced by *natema* (we'll have more to say about this little number in a minute). The Shuara wrap wet *maikiua* leaves as a poultice around a broken bone. They claim the break will heal in one-third to one-half the time. I've heard this confirmed too many times by too many people in the Oriente to disbelieve it.

The Shuara have several ways of preparing an herb they call *piri piri* (run both these words together when you say them and put the stress on the second "i": *puh REE puh-ree*). It is a widespread practice of many Jivaro clans to offer a visitor a woman for the night. While Tangamashi's clan did not observe this custom unfortunately, in those that do, the *uvisheen* gives the girl a preparation of *piri piri* prior to the advent of her nocturnal hospitality. The drug acts as a contraceptive: The Jivaro have had a birth control pill for centuries.

The *uvisheen* gives the guest a different concoction of *piri piri*, informing him that by drinking it he will be better able to enjoy the evening. I realize that the outside world of science declares flatly that no such preparation exists, anywhere, anytime. To find out for yourself, you must go and visit an appropriate Jivaro clan. And how you do that, among other things, is what this book is all about.

If you belt the booze pretty good and have a liver problem, have Tangamashi prepare a gourdful of *huama*. It is the fluid contained in the lower part of a towering grass that looks like bamboo. Drink it straight. If you're troubled with rheumatism, try a poultice of *michá tsuak* leaves. And if you want to prevent tooth decay, rub a paste made of the *nushumbi* root on your teeth and you will never have a cavity again. The only trouble is that it turns your teeth black, but you can't have everything.

The most fascinating drug by far, however, is made from boiling a small vine. It is called *natema*. In other parts of the jungle it is called *ayahuasca*, and you had better sit tight, because what I am going to tell you about it is going to blow your mind. *Natema* is LSD.* That's right! Acid. Timothy Leary and Ken Kesey and Electric Kool-Aid. If one wished to be flippant, he would say that the Shuara are acid-freaks. Are you ready for that? I didn't think so.

The taking of *natema* is an integral and important part of many Shuara rituals, as it is with all of the other groups of Jivaros, and researching anthropologists have determined that its hallucinogenic effects are very similar to those of LSD. Back in 1960, when I was first told of "vision-producing vines" used by the Jivaro *uvisheens*, my curiosity was frankly not too aroused. LSD was unheard of. Only in the past few years did I, along with certain anthropologists, make the connection.

What we call the real world is not that to the Shuar. To him, it is but an illusion, while the "real" world is that which he sees through *natema* and *maikiua*. Only by drinking *natema* (in the small bowl, remember?) could Tangamashi see the *tunchi* lodged inside Sakimbyo, or see and converse with the *arutama* (spirits) that give an *uvisheen* magic power and strength.

The vine *Banisteriopsis* is known by many names throughout the northwest Amazon. While the Jivaro call it *natema*, the Desana, a tribe in the jungles of Colombia, call it *yajé*. The anthropologist Gerardo Reichel-Dolmatoff reports that, "The fundamental basis of Desana religion is the interpretation of visions induced by the use of hallucinogenic drugs" (p. 171)—as it is for the Jivaro. He gives the following description:

> Taking *yajé* . . . is interpreted as a return to the cosmic uterus . . . to the source of all things. It has the objective of reaffirming religious faith, through the personal experience of seeing with one's own eyes the origin of the Universe and of mankind, together with all the supernatural beings. On awakening from the trance, the individual remains convinced of the truth of the religious teachings. He has seen everything: He has seen *Vai-mahsë* and the Daughter of the Sun, he has heard her voice; he has seen the Snake-Canoe float through the rivers, and he has seen the first men spring from it. The voice of the *kumú* has guided him and has explained everything to him in detail. (p. 174)

---

*LSD-25 (d-lysergic diethylamide) is a synthetic substance not known to occur naturally in any plant. Chemically, however, it has an "indole structure" that is quite similar to that of *natema*.

It is crucial, then, that when you go to live with the Jivaros you understand that the world of spirits, demons, and the supernatural is a world they live with and in every day. When a Jivaro baby is but a few days old, he is fed a chewed leaf that is a mild hallucinogen, so he will enter this world at the start of his life.*

Should you wish to enter this world yourself, you must do so with great care. You must first stay with a traditional Shuara or Jivaro clan for at least several days and gain their confidence. You must make sure that the *natema* is prepared properly, not cooked hurriedly in a dirty aluminum pot or simply mashed around in cold water. The vine must be mashed well and carefully on a clean surface, then placed in the bottom of a large earthenware bowl. Clear, pure river water must then be put in to cover the mashed material, and the pot placed over a small fire so that the mixture may slowly simmer for several hours. Only after several more hours of cooling and settling is the clear, dark green liquid—*natema*—ready. Taking sloppily and irreverently prepared *natema* will only result in extreme nausea, vomiting, diarrhea, and a very bad trip.

Thus, you must in no way, physically or psychologically, approach the matter casually, as simply a great trip, getting turned on by the headhunters. For the traditional Jivaro, these drugs lie at the very core of their religion, and their use is sacred.

Due to the hysterical irrationality of our own society's prevailing opinions on hallucinogens, it may be difficult to grasp or accept this. The fact that the distinction between licit drugs—such as tobacco and alcohol—and illicit drugs—such as marijuana, LSD, and cocaine—is a *ritual* distinction only, and that the users of illicit drugs are persecuted in the same way, and *for exactly the same reasons*, as were witches and heretics during the Inquisition and witch trials of the sixteenth and seventeenth centuries, is, tragically, understood by few.**

---

*All Shuara, and all Jivaros, of all ages, take *natema* fairly often; only the *uvisheens*, however, take it regularly, and only they use *maikiua* with any degree of frequency (and with caution, for it is much stronger than *natema*). According to drug researchers, the leaves of *Banisteriopsis rusbyana (natema)* contain the hallucinogenic alkaloids harmaline, harmine, d-tetrahydroharmine, and N, N-dimethyltriptamine (DMT—although some researchers attribute this last to another plant used by the Indians, *Psychotria viridis*); while *Datura arborea* juice (*maikiua*) contains hyoscyamine, atropine, and scopolamine.

**For those who wish to so understand, I cannot recommend more highly psychiatrist Thomas Szasz's utterly brilliant book, *Ceremonial Chemistry*.

Not that I advocate the use of drugs, either licit or illicit. I am neither advocating their use or avoidance. I suggest only that our prevailing views on certain drugs is grossly and irrationally distorted, is morally very misguided (as far as government intervention into the private lives of individuals is concerned), and should not be allowed to get in the way of coming to understand the Amazon Indian's way of life.

With the passing of every hour, I felt that I was drawing nearer to the climax of my living with headhunters—the telling to me of the three great events in a headshrinking Shuar's life: the attack upon an enemy and the taking of his head, the ceremony and process of shrinking that severed *cabeza* (not only the "how," but, more importantly, the "why"), and, lastly the great *Tsantsa* Victory Feast that followed.

These were the things that I had to find out before I left my hosts, for the fact that my anthropology department at UCLA looked with any degree of favor upon but a handful of accounts by explorers of these life-practices continued to prey on my mind. Even here there were decided contradictions in both the descriptions of the acts and the conclusions of the authors. My friend, think about this situation for thirty seconds. There are few people on earth who have not heard of shrunken heads—they represent, to understate the matter, a unique life-style. Yet the astonishing fact remains that there are only a handful of books on the subject that are at all reasonable.

It was very dark in the *hea*, with the only illumination coming from a small fire that was burning with hardly any smoke (wood from the Quinilla tree). There was not a sound in the house; the children and dogs were asleep. Two members of the clan that I could not make out in the darkness entered and sat down without a word. One of them began to speak.

"A Shuar is murdered. His headless body is discovered by the next early riser who comes out of the *hea*. Who did this slaying? The *uvisheen* enters the jungle, drinks *maikiua*, and an *arutama* appears to him and tells him the name of the slayer and his clan who did the killing. The second day, still alone, a vision again, and the *uvisheen* is told when the reprisal should take place. The witch doctor returns to the *hea* to inform his clan, and the preparations begin.

"A Shuar falls sick and dies. The *uvisheen* retires to his *ayamdai* ('vision world'), the *maikiua* or *natema* is taken, and the *arutama*

90

appears to reveal to the shaman who sent the *tunchi* that pierced the victim. The *uvisheen* again drinks the sacred juice, and the spirit again appears to tell him if he will be successful in his blood revenge or not. If the vision is good, he returns to the clan and the arrangements begin, according to the time suggested by the spirit. If the advice is negative, a postponement, and another visit to the *ayamdai* will be forthcoming.

"A Shuaria is attacked just before dawn, the *hea* is broken into, or is rushed when the first member of the clan arises and opens the small door. Bodies are lanced and shot, heads are cut off and carried away. The survivors, escaping by racing out either door, identify the enemy clan. Their *uvisheen* goes to his *ayamdai* to see if the time is right for retaliation. If it is, plans are laid. If it is not, another vision, another time.

"A Shuar is murdered and his head taken, but all attempts to kill the slayer by the attacked clan fail, and the years pass. The murdered man's son, when barely old enough to understand, is told, time and time again: 'The spirit of your father has not rested all these years, he has found no peace. His killers have offered no compensation.* He has been crying in the dreams of your mother for revenge, that his slayer be killed and the head taken and prepared, so that he may rest and be happy. This thing you must do, and then you will find happiness, and have a good, long life.' "

Ralph's voice changed completely with the ending interpretation of the Shuar's last words. He said, quite calmly and dispassionately, "Jack, you must understand that these people have lived by this code of blood revenge and retaliation for centuries. It is the individual's sense of justice; it is directed only towards the slayer of his relative; he never kills for new lands or profit or for pay. What do you think has kept him strong and warlike and preserved his nation while other tribes have been conquered or faded away? You simply cannot compare it with our society where the taking of a life in retaliation would cause a state of anarchy—or can you? In any event, his life is in a jungle separate from the world; he believes in what he does, and this way of life has kept him fearless, proud, independent, self-reliant, and protective of his family and his

---

*Often a clan may offer payment of a shotgun, or several machetes and steel axes (the most valued material items to the Jivaros) as compensation for a killing they perpetrated, especially one done some time before, to avoid revenge. Once accepted, and it quite often is, the feud is ended between the clans.

culture; and above all else, Jack, his nation has endured, this way, for centuries. How long have we endured? Are all of the character traits that I have just named to be found in *our* strange new breed of children? What *is* happening to our 'civilized' life? I'm not talking about the millions and millions of our people we keep killing in constant wars alone; I also think of our personal families. These people never lie, cheat, or steal; they never fail to help or nurse a sick or wounded person, even if he is a white man, who has struggled into their Shuaria, and they never expect a gift or cent for saving his life. They never break their word and no SPCA will ever be needed in their land—their dogs and pets have souls as good as their own. There is so much more, and we call them dirty savages and bloody murderers. They cannot stand even the smell of a white man. You know why—they take at least three baths a day. I'll stop now. Be patient a minute, I shall have to try to explain to them what I have been saying to you. You'd be surprised at how much these Shuara know about our life."

I have recalled his words as best I can; certainly I paraphrased them. But I'm pretty close. His thoughts are not ones to be forgotten when they are spoken in a headhunter house at close to midnight in the jungle with the owners three feet from you. Ralph finally finished speaking in Jivaro. There was stillness again for long minutes and then the Shuar began to speak again, almost in a whisper.

"The clan is told by the *uvisheen* that the dream has been good, and the *arutama* has told him that they will be successful and that the attack must be made in nine nights. A *Curaka* is chosen to lead and be the absolute ruler of the raid; he is the oldest and wisest father in the clan, and he selects the war party. It must be understood that everything they do now has been done the same way since *Pangi* gave us life. For seven nights the warriors perform the *anekma* [the war dance] with their lances and shotguns, and they drink much *chicha* to gain strength and smoke much tobacco, for it has great magic to ward off evil spirits. On the eve of their departure they paint their faces, breasts, arms, and legs black, and you must be told that each wife embraces her husband and they all cry in their fear for them. He, in turn, tells her that the *arutamas* have spoken to him in his dreams (*natema*-induced) that he will not be killed and that he will take many heads. He always speaks to her of the intensive instructions given to him for each of the past six nights by the *Curaka* and the careful planning of each step of the attack by these nightly meetings, that the spies have returned with all information as to traps and numbers of the enemy, and as to how they are armed and the *hea* fortified. See, he says, how well prepared we are, and then he tells her to stay busy while he's gone, making the clay bowls and platters, for they will be needed for the victory feast. A final dance, and a war song sung at the top of their voices by all the Shuara—it has much magical significance, as does the dance. They then file out, one at a time, identical with their line of march, and the *Curaka* shuts the door."

The quiet, impassioned voice, almost monotonous in its tone, ceased again, and Ralph's pleasant, normal, unhurried voice, never faltering, carried on—in that same uncanny stillness in the whole *hea* that had prevailed since the first figures entered and sat down. The flames coming from the small, circular pile of rocks had subsided and there was just a glowing, making the half-circle of shadows even more ghostly. Ralph finished, and the deep voice began speaking again in Jivaro.

"The attack that we are describing took place two days march from the Shuaria. It was conducted, as always, in complete silence, with the warriors maintaining the single file advance. The *Curaka* alone had the power and the privilege of speaking and it must be noted that one warrior was always assigned to walk ahead of the party and one to the rear; when it was necessary for the *Curaka* to speak, he always did so in a whisper. Each of the two nights on the path, when they arrived at the location in which to spend the night, they formed two rows facing each other, and the *Curaka* walked up and down in front of them, going over and over his plan of attack, at the end of which he said the good, true, things: 'Your heart will be strong and your courage great. Have no fear, you will be the victors—you will take many *wakanis*!' [souls.]

"The second night they prepare for the attack. It will come just before sunrise, when one of the enemy leaves the *hea*. We wish you now to look closely to see how they are dressed and how they make ready for the raid. Each warrior is now wearing a cap made of monkey skins instead of his toucan feather headband; his *arusa* [ear cones] are now in place and these are so long they nearly reach his shoulders and will be rich in magic power. His hair no longer hangs far down his back, but is now divided into three pigtails tied with human hair and toucan feathers. Look closely and you see that his necklace is of jaguar's teeth. His belt is of *pangi*'s skin and he is painted black for two reasons: He has the appearance and the strength of an *iguanchi* [demon], and he will be easily identified by his fellow raiders—and I tell you this is important so that you will know that the power is great in all that the avengers wear."

One of the Shuara—I could not identify him for it was now almost totally dark, and since *nanto* [the moon] was but little more than half-full and took a lot of time to climb over the very tall trees at the edge of the Shuaria it gave little light—left the *hea* just as my *compadre* began to speak directly to me once again. "Jack, you will have noted that they are telling you of a raid by a large war party, not one wherein a single Jivaro is seeking the head of the personal enemy who had killed one of his own family. I think I should point out to you, right now, that the Jivaro always does what the enemy does to him. If one head is taken by the slaying of one man, then that will be the retaliation. But if a clan has been attacked in its entirety, and many have been killed, then that will be the objective of the avenging warriors. In other words, what you have done to me, I will do to you, and they adhere to the ancient custom, as they do in most things. Now this is mass retaliation that you will now watch in your—what shall I say?—mind's eye. And remember, these people were, and are, the most warlike Indian nation in the world." His words, coming slowly at the end, coupled with the blackness and "these people" all about me, cast a chill over me that literally made me shudder. Sure, I admit it; and if one day you sit in that very *hea* and. . . .

"The avengers arrived at the edge of the enemy Shuaria as silently as *wakanis*, where they were joined again by the three warriors who had gone on ahead to strangle, one by one, without a sound, the sleeping dogs of the Shuaria—no barks would give the alarm to the sleeping clan. The shadows waited, the dark became grey and then a pale white, and, without warning, the door to the men's side of the *hea* swung open and an enemy Shuar stepped out. After looking about the clearing, he began to walk directly towards the waiting warriors. One step, two, three, and with the speed of the wind, and as noiseless, the attackers broke from the jungle's edge and were upon him before he could make a single cry. Three lances went through his chest as of one. A machete flashed, and the first head rolled over and over on the hard, packed ground.

"With the sound of dust settling, the attacking Shuara entered the still-sleeping great house until all were inside. There they separated, each going to scattered, stretched-out, and curled-up figures on the platforms. All paused, stood as if ghosts, and then each, as if with the same heartbeat, screamed the dreaded Shuara war cry at the top of his bursting breath. In that one room its sound was ear-splitting, and before its echo had even died, high-pitched screams of panic-stricken females were rending the cold, morning air with the shrill screeches of children, the instant wails of babies, the hoarse, feverish shouts and yells of awakening males joining in the horrible chorus—and over all, the constant, never-ending war cries of the attackers. The flashing of lances into bodies, the explosions of shotguns, the death screams, the swishing of machetes, and then the heavy thudding of severed heads hitting the ground to roll around the room. Thrusts . . . screams coming from everywhere . . . headless trunks spouting and bubbling fresh, hot blood, with gouts and spurts striking the painted black bodies to run like thick, red juice down the sweating, ebony-colored flesh. Attackers, blinded from geysers of blood shot into their eyes by headless, pumping necks, wiped with dripping, crimson hands and fingers their brows and eyes, adding to their frightful appearance. Women running, stopped by lance points going through their necks and breasts; old men hacked with machetes, blown apart by shotgun blasts—the ground becomes pools of steaming blood, with warriors slipping and falling until their bodies are no longer human, the splatter of blood clots striking posts and walls, making sucking sounds that bounce around the slaughter house. Blood is dripping from the thatch roof at the low corners of the room—it has spurted that high—the smell of entrails, hot blood, vomit, and split-open bellies is bringing enormous clouds of mosquitoes, and vicious black, green, and gold flies. With a sickening humming they fight their way with a desperate fury to get through the spaces between the poles of the walls; in instants, the stench has brought them by the hundreds and they begin landing and sucking on the bodies that are still twitching and shuddering and convulsing even though they have no heads. The victorious attackers show no mercy; they scream and thrust and blast and cut with great vengeance upon all about them—except very young women, small children, and babies. These they allow somehow to rush outside screaming, but even then some of them in trying to escape run into the path of thrusting lances that are now dripping with so much blood that it seems as if they are springs, gurgling forth a constant flow of sticky, red molasses. Suddenly they are all dead; the bodies, with or without heads, lie everywhere—crooked, bent, with severed necks, crossing each other to litter the red earth. There is now not a groan, not a cry. Even the war shouts are stilled.

"There are no sounds left now except heavy gaspings for air from heaving chests exuding red and black viscous balls of sweat and the sound of meat being sliced in a butcher shop. The deed is done, the steam and the stench is rising off the floor to mix with the masses of feasting insects, the humming is growing louder as the gore-saturated red bodies slide over the soggy floor, stepping over corpses that are nothing but hunks of scarlet flesh, to walk out into the beautiful sunrise that is awaiting them and leave the stench, the buzzing, and the dripping. . . ."

Silence. I looked about me. That *hea*, it must have been just like this one, right where I am sitting. I turned to the black figure of Ralph sitting next to me and said, "I'll be back in a minute." I got up and slowly walked to the entrance, then outside. I held it in until I got far enough into the forest—then I fell to my knees and got violently sick. My stomach kept convulsing far after it emptied itself of all the monkey and yucca and *chicha* it had contained. When it was over I stood up and stared for several minutes at the moon that was just rising over the trees. Finally I turned around and walked back to the *hea*.

Ten minutes later, all of us were seated or lying down again. The flames were now leaping modestly in a new fire, and the shadows were properly jumping around the *chonta* walls and the cone-shaped thatch roof. The faces around me were once again quite expressionless and they continued to stare at me, not rudely, but as if in passive contemplation. While the *chicha* was being drunk a few minutes ago, Ralph told me that for the purpose of telling the story with the meaning that should be given it for my understanding (and also to make it easier for him), sometimes he substituted words and whole phrases that he knew would tell the story more clearly for me. The Shuar began to talk once again, stopping often to allow Ralph to translate.

"Now there was speed and urgency in the victors' every move. Quickly, the weeping, blood-spattered but unhurt girls, seven in all, were herded together in a single line. With nine of the eleven victorious warriors carrying dripping heads wrapped in cloths and hung over their shoulders, the attackers took their original positions and, with the females in the middle, hurried into the jungle along a trail that led completely away from the true direction home. It will be four or five days before they reach it, for the route that will be followed is far removed from the one upon which they came. This is done in order to throw a pursuing war party off the scent, if one can be gathered from neighboring Shuarias. The victorious *Curaka* does not this time fear such a thing happening, for his spies had reported to him that bad feelings existed at the moment between the clan to be attacked and their nearest Shuarias. But he takes no chances, this wise old man; he had left behind the fastest and the youngest of his warriors to watch the silent death house and all the trails leading to it from a hiding place that he had selected just before the attack.

"You are wondering what the survivors did who escaped, and what they thought, when at last they came back to the *hea*?" That was exactly what I was thinking. I nodded my head several times, looking straight at him. He spoke, and I continued to watch him.

"I will answer your questions. Yes, there were, and when they returned they were weeping, and they looked upon the bodies with a fear greater than their sorrow; for to a Shuar to be slain by a *chonta* lance is a terrible thing. His soul races away from the great spiritual weapon as far as it can, and then will begin to seek out its natural home, the severed head. He will find it, and he will do much harm to the warrior who took it if the warrior has not prepared it properly, so that he may re-enter it and be at peace once again. And what of the weeping ones? They buried the bodies as quickly as they could, right in the very ground upon which they fell; and when this was done, they left the Shuaria at once, never to return to it again."

Ralph, his voice changing its quality and rhythm as usual when he finished the Shuar's words and began his own said, "We have talked about the strong feeling that all the Jivaros have regarding their dead, right, Jack? You remember: food for two years for the spirit, the bodies buried in the *hea* with the chief upright. All this devotion goes down the drain when the relative is killed in war and his head is taken: The soul is gone and the headless body killed by *chonta* is an object of horror and something to be dumped, but right now. But the most important thing he has told us yet. . . . *eeh, unta?*" The Shuar had asked a question of Ralph, and receiving an answer immediately began speaking to me again.

"The party and its captives made their way rapidly through the jungle, not stopping to rest the women until *itsa* (the sun) was high. Then it resumed its march until dark and stopped for the night beside a small river where the seven young females (who

97

would become the wives of their captors) went downstream to bathe the blood off and cleanse themselves. The two warriors who had not taken heads did the same in the waters beside the camp, scrubbing their belts and caps, everything, to remove all blood and matter. They then left to go to a field nearby to get yucca. They would announce themselves beforehand to the clan; they would now not be identified with the raid, for they were clean.

For the nine takers of heads a new life had begun, and it would last for much time. Their fast had begun; they could eat nothing but yucca and they would have to prepare it themselves—and only eat it mashed or boiled. They could not remove one drop of blood from their bodies or clothes, even wash their hands or faces, until after the purification ceremony many days from then; even their weapons must remain blood-clotted and stained. They sat admiring their heads, stroking the long hair, and speaking to them—for they knew that *their souls had found them* and were hovering about. For many days, every act of their lives would be devoted to the *securing the soul of the captured head*."

(It was not my imagination that had placed the emphasis upon the eight final words, it was my excitement, for here was a clue to the mystery of the *tsantsa*.)

"They traveled far the next day, finally stopping early in the afternoon after going deep into the jungle away from the old deer trail they had been following. This was the hour for which all young Shuara warriors lived: They would begin to prepare their heads to become *tsantsas*. It is well to remember at this point that the slayer's life from the moment he took the head is governed by the most severe rules that number as many as the teeth in the mouths of twenty *tigres*—and will last for many months. He knows that the spirit of the head is filled with hate for him and desires revenge above all things. Thus he must do as the *whuea* directs and our ancient customs demand.

"Watch as the nine takers of heads stand in a long row waiting to reach the *Curaka*, who has placed a large leaf that possesses much magic upon each head. The warriors, in turn, walk to the chief, stand beside their head, and receive tobacco (which has great power to give strength to the slayer for protection against the spirit of the killed enemy). This is the first of many steps that will be taken to protect him—and I say this with open face; if I were to tell you of all, we would be here until *nanto* rises again.

"Now there were only three who had prepared a head before, therefore the *Curaka* ordered that all watch the eldest of the three skin it. Holding the head between his knees, he held apart the long black hair with his left hand, and with his right hand placed the tip of a long, sharp blade at the very edge of the severed neck. He then drew the blade upwards, cutting deeply from the base where the ragged skin ended to the top of the head. He then began peeling the skin and hair from the skull, moving very slowly and carefully, for the skin does not easily loosen; it must constantly be cut loose or scraped free from the bone. It finally drew free, and the skull was dropped to the ground where it rolled away. It was so useless that no one wanted it, including its *wakani*. The knife moved again, making certain that as much of the matter be gone without piercing the skin once. The young men were surprised to see that with the skinning done the eyes remained, but a thrust of a finger pushed them out. Then the skin was cut and trimmed, for the eyelashes and lids must be as they were when used by the dead Shuar. Moving as slowly as *uyushi* [sloth], he sewed the eyelids shut from the inside, took three *chonta* pins, and, after turning the skin right side out again, made three very little holes on the top and bottom lips facing each other with his knife point. He then pushed the little pieces of wood through the holes in both lips to bind them tightly together so that the lips and mouth were sealed.

"The *Curaka*, while looking at the head once in a while, built a fire and had water boiling in a large pot. He also had taken from his monkey skin bag certain roots, herbs, leaves, and vines. He, being the *uvisheen* of the clan also, knew all the magic of the jungle's growing things, and it was he who placed them in the boiling water, calling out the name of each to the warriors who now were in a close circle around the fire; they knew them all, but this cere- mony would be the first in which they themselves would make a *tsantsa*.

"The warrior tied a *liana* to the long hair and lowered it into the boiling pot. He tied the rope to a stick set across the pot and looked about for three small, round, smooth rocks. He found them and placed them in the fire under the pot. The *Curaka* gave the order and soon there were nine fires burning and warriors were busy with their heads. In time, the warrior Taisha, who had been watching his head in the water, pulled it up and in a few minutes was able to hold it and sew up the back and top of the skin. Scooping up one of the very hot rocks with a hollowed-out slab, he carefully let it roll around inside the now bag-like head. He moved it carefully and slowly around as it cooked the inside of the skin; when it grew cold, in went another.

He this did over and over again. Then he took hot sand that he had kept in piles under the fire and, filling the head, began to spin it around, not with the waving of *chuo* [brown monkey], but firmly. This he repeated time and time again.

"The head has now shrunk to a much smaller size. The head-taker began to mold the features of the *tsantsa* with his fingers—for the *tsantsa* of the dead warrior must look exactly like the warrior when he was alive. In this way, with this pressing, and this bringing to life the features of the warrior again, he was forcing out the water and the oil, causing the head to begin to harden. When the sand came out the knife went in, as it had several times. The last pieces of skin and fat and matter were now gone. More sand and more rocks—then Taisha shaped the face again, and the head grew smaller and harder as the hot sand cooked and shrunk the skin. At last he was satisfied, his head was ready for the smoke of the fire to change the skin color to dark, to seek out and dry the final oil, and harden even more the now firm head. So Taisha had led the way, but his life for many months would be difficult and as demanding as the leadership of a *Curaka*. Look! Nine victorious avengers, each by a fire, each preparing a head that, in time, after a thousand rites, would serve him—and itself. . . ."

I did not get very much sleep that night. It was almost completely black in the *hea*, but through every space in the wall behind me moonlight was entering in single narrow shafts between each lashed *chonta* pole. Hundreds of tiny silver beams all pointing down at the same angle—the rest of the room was black. There was only the sound of breathing, and I could barely make out some of the figures sleeping on the platforms. It seemed impossible that these people, towards whom I felt such an affection, could engage in the kind of bloodletting I had just heard described. Head-hunters. Now I was up against the full reality of that awful word. But what did I expect? The Shuara are the most famous headhunters in the world. Did I expect a birthday picnic in the jungle? To live a dry-cleaned, story-book adventure with the mud, the insects, the savage spear-thrusts and spurting blood conveniently edited out? Maybe so. Well, nothing has been edited for you, Jack. This is an adventure straight into the mind and soul of primitive man: Of course part of the way there is going to be rough and brutal. But I have found a strength and a decency in Tangamashi and the people of his clan that I will probably seldom see matched in my entire life.

I learned, this night, the secret of the *tsantsa*. Pidro had talked far beyond midnight. When he brought that victorious war party home Ralph could not keep up with the flow of words. His voice rose—he was living his life again. See, he had cried, see them enter their Shuaria! All are ready for them—the women in long rows outside, the men inside. See the slayers—they appear as beggars, the blood-encrusted clothes, the lances and shotguns coated with dried blood, their hair hanging loose upon their shoulders, no ornaments, no paint. But the *tsantsas* are placed around their necks—their *whuea* will guide and instruct them in the thousand things they can do and cannot do for the next six months, a year.

It had been a night to remember, and now it had become a morning to appreciate. The sun was just rising and its light was turning all the grey things about me to gold. Tangamashi is going to meet me here for some dark purpose of his own. I was passed the word by Ralph last night. Everyone knows that I come to this same place by the river every morning at sunrise. My thoughts kept shooting back to Pidro and his returning warriors.

That very day of their arrival, each taker of a head passes through an elaborate purification ceremony that is topped by a feast. It is called *numbuimartinyu: numba*, blood. . . . *martinyu*, to paint. From his first entrance into town, the head-taker is joined by his wife and daughter, and for all the months to come these women fast with him, hold him by the hand, go through a myriad number of rites, eat the same food. If he is not married, a near relative takes the role. After a series of entries and re-entries into the *hea* (he is putting to rest the spirit of his head who can harm him upon his first entrance inside), there is a dance by all the women, who, with shells jingling and drums beating, finally dance into the hut where all the men are waiting, lined up in rows. Then the slayer takes off his newly shrunken head, which has been hanging around his neck, and ties it to the top of a *chonta* lance that is just inside the door, this of course to prevent the spirit from entering. The *whuea* is the priest who has been assigned as the avenger's personal master of ceremonies for the next six or eight months; he will be with him constantly, for he is the expert on every detail, and there are over a *thousand* that must be carried out to the letter. He is always an old man, very wise, and he must have taken heads during his lifetime. There is also a priestess {*ohaha*} who is also designated to handle all the ceremonies that have to do with women (and there are many) that are a part in the rites, rituals, and rules that will govern completely the wives of the slayer, and his daughters.

101

From that first day, when the slayer participates in two ceremonies—washed by chicken blood, purified by water, painted with black *sua*—he must follow rules that govern his food, his sex life, his dress, his physical acts; his whole existence has to go by the book. It requires a priest and a priestess to advise and to control everything until many months later, when the great Victory Feast is held that lasts four days and nights. He is at last free to move without danger from the spirit of the head. But that dance the first night he returns is the high-water mark of his life. Even the Victory Feast, that he has gone through hell to reach, cannot compare with the exultation he feels when he dances the *antsemata*—a ring dance with all the women dressed with great care, with their rattles of snail shells about their waists, and the men heavy-laden with ornaments, their faces alive with blacks and reds, with geometric figures, snakes, and butterflies. All friendly clans are invited; the slayer dances all night—everyone does. No one is allowed to sleep, and the shrunken head rides upon the back of the victor every dance.

Do not think of the paint on body or face as mere decorations. Watch them as they dance. See that black *sua*? Direct protection against the spirit of the enemy. There is a demon in this genipa berry paint—and in the slayer's feasts of *suamartinyu* and at the final victory feast it is painted upon the slayer with an elaborate ceremony. At all the feasts and all the ceremonies there is one objective: protect the victor against the spirit of his enemy, the soul of the head. But the hundred and one things that the slayer does to conquer the spirit eventually wins, and the spirit not only has to obey the slayer of its head, it must help him.

But that first night victory dance—it is the great hour. Hear what the slayer says: "I have done what I am here to do in this world. I have killed my enemy. I am victorious over his evil spirit. He knows I have his head. He wishes to return to it and have peace, but he wishes to avenge himself first against me. I will show him in a hundred ways in the months to come that he cannot hurt me. I will prove to him that I can help him, and then he will help me. What has happened to all the souls that have been crying and wandering, unhappy, and with no peace because of an evil man who had killed them? I will tell you what has happened to them tonight. They are free—they are happy—they are at peace—they need wander no more—for I have killed their enemy! Is there any greater joy for any man in this world?"

So speaks the slayer. His first victory night—and what is his dance? Look. See the ring of warriors? They are circling a *tsantsa* that is impaled on a *chonta* lance. Look at them thrust, see them leap at him, stab at him. Three steps towards the *tsantsa*, three steps back. All in unison—then a movement to the side—and then a lunge of the lance forward. And the chant, the unleashed passion and the raw feelings for the enemy—all directed to a tiny head that once was held high. The *tsantsa*.

The four days of the final Victory Feast. The third day there is the washing of the *tsantsa*, the dipping of the shrunken head into a magical solution made from the *sikimuro* root carried in the bosom of the slayer's wife. The comb that is used by the witch doctor to arrange and comb properly the long, black hair of the *tsantsa* has been carried in the bosom of the slayer's daughter. They too will break their long fast this day with the slayer. They have held his hand in all the countless ceremonies, have never left his side. The washing at long last makes the spirit of the head the slave of the victor. Such is the magic of the *sikimuro* root—but only if the devoted wife has carried it in her bosom, only if the whole family has fasted for many months, only if the countless rites in endless ceremonies have been faithfully followed, only if the entire clan has helped in every way, only if. . . .

THE SECRET OF THE *TSANTSA*

The spirit of the slain enemy is seated in the *tsantsa*. It fled from the scene of the murder to wander in fear and hate until it recognized its head. It came home, but from that instant of re-entry it had only one desire: to harm, to hurt, to destroy the slayer. This hate was gradually weakened by the continual rites and conditions imposed upon the slayer. The power of the magic of the slayer's actions was too much for the spirit; it began to converse, to talk to, to even help its enemy. Through the actions and thoughts of the slayer the *tsantsa* becomes possessed of supernatural strength, which the slayer used in many ways. When all was well, and the *tsantsa* was happy and content, being now the possessor of great power itself, imparted to it by the slayer, the spirit of the *tsantsa* was able to leave its host body and become whatever it wished in the animistic world that it and the slayer believed in. Certain Shuara know this; therefore when the moment of departure comes when the spirit begins another life, he recognizes it, and the *tsantsa* becomes nothing but an empty, shrunken head of mere memories. Other Shuara do not know this; they hold to their belief that the spirit of the slain enemy is still within—and must stay in his slayer's *hea*.

Well, I received a surprise that morning alright, no question about it, for there came Tangamashi and Pidro, but where was Ralph? You remember I told you of Ralph's passing the word about the *Curaka* wanting to meet me that morning? Right. What could be on tap that wouldn't require a bit of translating now and then?

Smiles—even from Tangamashi. Now that was really something. I received a beckoning signal from Pidro, so without a word being said, off we went Shuara fashion, single file with the *Curaka* leading. Well, we weren't going far at any rate, for we made a short curve and doubled back to the river.

Pidro stepped over to me and, touching my shirt as if to pull it off, quickly made a swimming motion with his arms. His point was clear: Go for a swim, Jack. Well, no need to explain my thoughts; suffice it to say that I stripped, scrambled over a few boulders and walked in, not dove, thank you, for the water was far from warm, that you know. I swam around for a minute, staring at the two witch doctors on the jungle bank, and they looking at me. You must admit, I do get in the damndest situations, but always seem to muddle along, like this time, for there was Pidro's arm waving to come to shore. Motioning for me to dry myself with my shirt, Pidro then turned and opened a bundle that I already had noticed he was carrying. Deeming it impolite to check his unpacking, I turned myself around and started toweling. I had reached my left calf and was in a bent position, looking down, when an *itipi* was suddenly hanging before my eyes. Obviously I was to put it on, so I made the try and it was easy, a quick wrap-a-round and I was set except for one thing: how to hold it up. The witch doctor tandem had slipped up on this one, but Pidro's quick sentence to Tangamashi brought me one word I knew well: *liana*. He started off and my hand up stopped him, as I reached down and pulled the belt off my pants.

Three minutes later we were in the clearing; one more found us at the *hea*—and in ten seconds I was surrounded by Shuara. There was Sakimbyo, all paint and glory, resplendent in a magnificent vest of glowing vari-colored toucan feathers. Never had I seen the clan in such breath-catching beauty. Out of the whirling and the glittering came Pidro himself, his vest shimmering in the virginal sunlight with a mass of green parrot wings and shining toucan bills. There was the *Curaka*, Tangamashi himself—orange feathers, blue feathers, stuffed hummingbirds of shaped rainbows, toucan bills, monkey bones clicking and clattering by the hundreds. Shuara are everywhere, and they are laughing, smiling. Look at Tamashyo, he's a giant spilled-out paint box! I was swung around by Atsáyü, all smiles and beads, adorned with a new *tarachi*, a new dress, wearing face paint—that could only mean a great feast, a ceremony.

And then I was sitting down, a circle of smiling Shuara above me and the *Curaka* himself painting my face as the clan began to chant. Tangamashi's face is within inches of mine and his lean fingers are busy with lines and designs and animals of reds and blacks. The chanting grew louder and they began to dance—and then Atsáyü, with a conjuration. This is a dream, I said to myself, and the emotion that I felt in those minutes I feel to this day as I share with you this ceremony, that came from hearts, not war cries. Atsáyü was kneeling before me as Tangamashi finished; she ran her finger around the rim of a cup she was holding, touched her lips with it, handed the bowl to me, and I drank. The *Curaka* leaped to grasp his war lance leaning against the *hea*. Flutes began to play, a *tundui* [drum] began to throb, and Atsáyü and her husband-chief began to dance, only the two of them, facing each other, chanting, as the clan in the circle swayed back and forth. The words were to the spirits to gain their blessings and bring happiness to me. The dance ended, and bowls of *chicha* were drunk by all.

I was not aware that the warriors had disappeared and the women had entered the *hea*. I was not seeing well at the moment, and I am not ashamed to admit it. Suddenly—attacking Shuara, lances flashing, ran at me, and past me. I spun around and there, impaled upon a *chonta* lance, was a *tsantsa*. A magnificent one, his hair, glossy and black, streamed to envelop the war lance below. I was seeing the *Tsantsa* Victory Dance, the famed dance that is the climax of a Jivaro's life—his supreme moment of fulfillment. Look at the brandishing of lances—see the thrusts—hear the cries; they are defeating evil, displaying courage, and protecting with their lives, souls, and lances their family, their clan, their religion, their existence.

Tangamashi spins from the thrusting warriors, walks to me, and motions with his dance to follow. He leads me to the circling warriors and, pressing me gently, has me enter and sit beneath the *tsantsa*. With the flowing hair almost touching me, the thrusting spears that nick and taunt and pierce the head above, the gleaming, feather-bedecked bodies moving in trained, wicked quick moves of death around me, with their shouts and cries of defiance, I know why I sit in the circle of death. No evil spirit can harm me more if I show disdain for it and if I have the courage to combat it. That is the message that is being given to me—the message or the *Tsantsa* Victory Dance—and I have received it as an adopted member of a great Shuara clan.

Headhunter Briefing

(Preliminary Note: The Fergusons left Sacua and the Oriente in 1965. Where they are now I do not know, but I hope all is well with them and that if either Ralph or the Doctor happen to read this he will contact me.)

As you know, the Jivaros live in the jungles both of Ecuador and Northern Peru. Details on living with the Aguaruna, Huambisa, or Achuali Jivaros in Peru, as well as other wild tribes in the Amazon, will be in forthcoming editions of *The Adventurer's Guide*. For your expedition to the headhunters of Ecuador—the Shuara and Atshuara—you will secure a guide through Tangamashi himself.

The last time I saw Tangamashi was in Sacua during the summer of 1972. I had not seen him for several years. All Shuara must cut their hair now, according to Ecuadorian law, which is why he looks somewhat menacing. A girlfriend once asked me if I wasn't scared in returning to the Oriente "to live with savages like the Aucas and the Jivaros in the jungle." After reflecting on my emotional response to her question, I told her that for some reason I wasn't, that the jungle was a place of peace for me, and that the *real* and *genuine* savages of this world do not live in jungles but in presidential palaces and government office buildings. When I asked Tangamashi if there was anything he wanted that I could send him from America, the translated answer came back: "Yes. A gun so I can shoot the man who made me cut my hair."

With the torrent of civilizados hungry for Shuara land and missionaries hungry for Shuara souls pouring in to the Oriente, together with the hordes of soldiers sent to "protect" the invaders, many things have changed since those days when I lived in Tangamashi's *hea* and he had long hair and wore an *ititpi*, instead of a bright red shirt. The more a Shuar tries to live by his traditions, it

106

seems the more he is harassed and ridiculed by civilizados and soldiers. It must be admitted, however, that many Shuara have not given up those traditions unwillingly. Buying cloth is much easier than making an *ititpi*, a shotgun much better to hunt a *tsunchu* [jaguar, *tigre*] or *pakki* [tapir] with than a lance. A shotgun is the Shuar's constant companion now, not the lance.

But the Oriente is deep and thick, and within it lie many Shuara and Atshuara clans that have been able to preserve their ways— with varying degrees of success—even against the spiritual on- slaughts of the missionaries, ever-searching to add more notches to their halos. Certain men carve notches on their bedposts, and I strongly suspect some missionaries of similar motives.

I must admit to a fair amount of bitterness on this point, as I have personally witnessed the pretentious, condescending manner of so many missionaries in dealing with the Shuara, and the ravages effected by these dealings. It is not all one-sided, of course. There are many fine people among the missionaries, doing such good work as teaching the Shuara arithmetic and simple contractual matters so they won't get ripped off by land-grabbing civilizados. An example of this is the Shuar Federation, set up by the Salesians at Sacua. But the fact remains that I have yet to meet *anyone* who is not a missionary who has lived in and knows the jungle well and praises them highly. This is so because missionaries are, bluntly and essentially, *culture-destroyers*. It is the most basic and sacred beliefs of the Indian that the missionary must challenge, condemn, and root out before he can supplant them with his own. Thus it is the Indian's *mind* that the missionary poisons and destroys. Fear . . . sin . . . guilt . . . humility . . . sacrifice . . . these are the psy- chological poisons the Indian has his mind filled with to the brim- ming.

Now I'm not going to lay a Rousseau "noble savage" piece of sentimentality on you. A primitive's life in the jungle is brutal and tough: You've certainly been witness to that. But it is infinitely superior, in terms of its *potential for human happiness*, than what is left after the missionaries have worked him over.

Someday, I think, I will form the Wheeler Anti-Missionary So- ciety, which will send Anti-Missionaries, trained in anthropology, to primitive tribes and cultures throughout the world, telling them that their traditions and old ways of life were and are *good*, and that they should look upon the missionary and his teachings as their most deadly enemies. The only problem with this idea is that it is fifty or a hundred years too late. If anthropologists had only spent less time on diagramming kinship practices and more on insisting to govern- ments that all missionaries be thrown out of the countries they were invading on their patronizing ears and banned forever from re- entry, the science of anthropology would today be much less the study of the past.

The situation is blackest in the South Pacific, even more than the Amazon. The missionaries have destroyed almost every vestige of the islanders' traditional customs and mores, and are busy today hunting down and condemning those that are left. It is probably most pitiful in Tonga. There, the missionaries have so much political power that they got a law passed making it illegal for a man (much less a woman!) to appear in public without wearing a shirt. Just think about that: It is against the law on a South Pacific tropical island for a man to go bare-chested.

This is why Chief Bong of the village of Bunlap, on the island of Pentecost in the New Hebrides, is a personal hero of mine. He is the only chief or leader I know of in the South Pacific who has told the missionaries to go hell, and refuses them entry into his village. He considers them morally evil—and he is right. He knows that their claim to *love* him and his people, together with the rest of mankind, is an obscenity. It is no accident that the people of Bunlap—where the women still wear grass skirts (and *only* grass skirts) and the men only a penis-wrapping, and the missionaries' teachings are rejected *in toto*—are the happiest people I have ever stayed with.

Thus, when you go into Jivaro country, and see your first Jivaros, prepare yourself for disappointment. They will be wearing clothes, unwashed and ragged. Their eyes will have a dullness to them, their walk a shuffle while they carry a transistor radio playing a sermon in Jivaro. To find real *Shuara*, with fire in their eyes, pride in their hearts, and a lance in their hands instead of a transistor radio, you must venture into those deep and hidden parts of the Oriente where they have remained true to themselves and their unique existence. It may require an enormous effort. You may have to walk in mud and sweat and rain for days. But you will find them.

Tangamashi now lives within a few hours' walk of Sacua. He chose not to retreat further into the forest but to move closer to town for his children's education; he hopes this will protect them against the civilizados. I hope so too. The civilizados are poor Ecuadorian nationals down from the mountains. They—as does the government—regard themselves as "true" Ecuadorians, while the Shuara are just "los Indios": merely Indians, not true Ecuadorians, you see.

So the Shuar is discriminated against and his lands expropriated, the same disgusting, familiar story. The missionaries raise little hue and cry over this, but they do help in some ways. Thanks to them, many Shuara are raising cattle and competing economically with the civilizados. I wonder, however, how many civilizados would dare venture into Shuara country if the missionaries had not tamed and pacified them first, if they thought there was a good chance they might receive a lance in their chests and their heads end up on a *chonta* pole the size of a man's fist once they tried to steal Shuara land.

The Spaniards, in keeping with their traditions of butchery and lust for gold (which all Indians thought completely insane), at-

108

tempted to enslave the Jivaro during the last part of the sixteenth century. Rather than pay the demanded tribute of gold, a *Curaka* named Quirruba led a revolt. The year was 1599. Tens of thousands of Jivaros simultaneiously attacked the Spanish towns of Logronyo and Sevilla de Oro, both on the Upano River. They took over 25,000 heads.

The brutality that the Spanish Governor had shown to the Jivaro was returned to him by Quirruba. As described by Juan de Velasco in 1842, Quirruba and his followers captured the Governor, and told him that he was now to receive his tax of gold:

> They stripped him completely naked, tied his hands and feet, and while some amused themselves with him, delivering a thousand insults and jests, the others set up a large forge in the courtyard, where they melted the gold. When it was ready in the crucibles, they opened his mouth with a bone, saying that they wanted to see if for once he had enough gold. They poured it in, little by little, and then forced it down with another bone. His bowels burst with the torture, and all raised a clamor and laughter.

Savage, you say? Yes—but sometimes justice is savage. The memory of Quirruba ensured that the Shuara were to be left in peace for almost 300 years. Then came the missionaries.

To this day, no civilizado enters Auca country. Government troops are terrified of the Aucas, and even the mention of the word *Auca* makes most any Ecuadorian shiver with fright. The only enemy the Auca has to fear is the missionary, for once the Auca is pacified the theft of his lands and the end of his culture and independence will soon follow: the same fate that is happening to the Jivaro now.

GETTING IN SHAPE

Now I can't have you trudging off into the forest with Tangamashi without having you in shape. So let's get the physical requirements of your living with headhunters out of the way first. You do not need to be superbly fit (although that always helps!). But you do need to be in reasonably good condition to walk through the jungle for days on end. All those exercises we discussed for your climbing the Matterhorn are the ones to use here too. Jog or run two or three miles a day, bicycle, play tennis, take ten- or twenty-mile hikes on weekends, do deep knee bends and toe lifts, all those things we talked about. Once again, especially stick to the jogging. I know it's boring, but remember: You are going to be walking through mud and rotting underbrush, stepping over vines and fallen tree trunks, bathed in sweat—for days. When you're out there in the jungle slogging away, you're going to be extremely grateful for all the jogging you put yourself through.

Next, I want you to stay in Sacua, your last stop before your

109

expedition departs into the jungle, for a few days. Just as for the Matterhorn, when you had to acclimatize yourself to the altitude, here you will need to do the same for the humidity. Unless you're used to it, the high humidity can make you lazy, listless, drained of energy. The heat will not be that bad—you'll be in the shade most of the time anyway—and if you go around September through November, it won't rain much either. But break yourself in to the humidity, so you won't find yourself exhausted out on the trail. This is especially true if you spend any time in the high bracing air of the Andes prior to your jungle adventure. (And incidentally, if you want to indulge in some fantastic climbing—like of the highest active volcano in the world, Cotopaxi, at 19,344 feet, or where the equator is at its highest point around the world, on Cayembe at 16,000 feet—write to the International Andean Mountaineers c/o the Club Wildcatter, 1022 Avenida Colon, Quito, Ecuador. They'll arrange for guides, climbs, equipment, everything.)

The watchword again, then, is stamina, not strength. Size, sex, muscles? They count for little here. Age? Well, that depends. A young teen-ager fourteen or fifteen will not have much difficulty, but a parent or older friends should, of course, accompany him. There really isn't an upper age limit, for your condition is what counts. There was an eighty-six-year-old man who jogged around Kapiolani park every day when I lived in Honolulu. He'd knock off ten or twenty miles at a single crack. I'll walk through the Oriente with him anytime.

What tricks do I have for the jungle? (Like Persantin for the Matterhorn, remember?) Well, for openers, take lots of vitamins, lots of iron, A, E, C and lots and lots of B, the whole complex. (Iron oxidates the E, so take them a few hours apart). A side effect of B, especially B12, is that it gives an odor (unnoticeable to you) to your perspiration that is offensive to mosquitos.* Forget about uppers, downers, sleeping pills, drugs of that nature. But glucose tablets are good, and absolutely crucial are salt tablets. You must have them. Take two or three every few hours, or else you may very well end up as I did once, floundering in the mud and heat, thoroughly exhausted and unbearably thirsty. It was horrible, but all I needed were a few salt tablets—which I didn't have. You bring them. If you're able to get hold of any limes, sucking on them will also help prevent dehydration and assuage your thirst.

Besides getting the normal shots (smallpox, typhus, typhoid, paratyphoid, tetanus), also get one for yellow fever. Start taking malaria pills (Aralen phosphate) once a week three to four weeks before you expect to be in the jungle. And to keep your intestines in good working order, I have several suggestions. There are few things I can tolerate less than diarrhea, so I follow them all religiously. One: Eat bananas. Bananas are wonderful. They taste

*For suggested dosages, see page 120.

110

good, they're cheap and plentiful, they're nutritious, and they're constipating. You just can't beat that combination. Two: Always use iodine water-purifying pills when you fill up your canteen. You can get them at or through your local sporting goods dealer. Most streams in the Oriente are clean and pure, but the iodine will help kill any evil things inside you. Three: a tiny white wonder of science called *lomotil*, and that good old stand-by *entero-vioform*. You can buy copious amounts over the counter at any large drugstore outside the U. S. The entero-vioform kills the bugs inside you, while the lomotil is an amazingly effective cork. Take them at the onset of any trouble. They are your most valuable possessions.

BEING MENTALLY READY

Now on to the mental requirements for living in the jungle with primitive peoples. The first thing to do is relax. The jungle is not the place of lurking horror that Hollywood makes it out to be. You're not going to get your head cut off and shrunk, you're not going to be killed by a poison dart, eaten alive by bloodthirsty piranhas, attacked by a man-eating jaguar, crushed to death by a boa constrictor or drowned in quicksand. None of these things is going to happen to you. You can't drown in quicksand—although if you panic and thrash around wildly enough you can get stuck in it so deeply that you will not be able to get out without someone's help. Just stay calm and if you can't pull yourself out with an overlying branch or vine, lie down (you will sink only to your knees at the most) and float on it, pull your legs out, and slowly crawl to dry ground. All large animals will do their best to avoid you: they never attack unless wounded, and fight in self-defense. The same applies to snakes. They hear you coming and slither away into the forest. Chances are very large that you will never even see one. Nevertheless, you should wear your boots at all times when walking through the forest (see page 118 re boots), just in case. As for boas, they are not poisonous, and I never even heard of one actually attacking a man. Piranhas and poison darts you already know about. Regarding the safety of your head: As you know, the Shuara are extremely hospitable. If you conduct yourself in a proper and friendly manner you will be in no personal danger from them. White men are rarely accused of witchcraft, of sending a *tunchi* that only an *uvisheen* knows how to do. Thus you should have little fear of having a Shuara machete separating your head cleanly from your shoulders. So relax. Enjoy the jungle—don't be afraid of it.

The second thing is to become mentally inured to the forest's annoyances as quickly as possible. Don't gripe about the mud, humidity, and insects. At every Shuaria there is a nearby stream where you can wash and do your laundry, so you can be clean and have clean clothes every day. Wear long-sleeve shirts and pants, not shorts. Take your B vitamins. Be well smeared with Cutter's insect repellant and your mosquito bites will be few. Get used to those that you do have. The main point here is not to let the lousy insects spoil your adventure. Say to hell with them and all other minor grievances, for you can't expect an adventure like living with headhunters to be all cookies and milk.

Lastly, a few tips on proper conduct among Jivaros. Number one is never call them Jivaros. Call them Shuara, Atshuara, Aguaruna, Huambisa, or Achuali. Never Jivaros. Most civilizados call them Jivaros out of ignorance or discrimination. Number two is to act as a polite guest at all times, for that is what you are: a guest in their forest. Shuara love to shake hands. When you run into a group on the trail, your guide will chat with them for a moment and there will be much shaking of hands. Never refrain from this, saying to each, *puengehr pu-hamuk* (roughly, hello, how are you), to which they will reply *vipuengehr pu-a-hey* (I'm fine, thank you). Distribute a few simple gifts when you spend a night at a Shuaria. Blow up and give the kids some balloons. They'll shriek in delight. Give the adults American cigarettes and small boxes of waterproof matches. Pictures from a Polaroid camera are always a big hit. Salt is highly valued and you can often buy feather headdresses and blowguns, etc., with a pound or two. Give an ounce or two of black gunpowder to the *Curaka* of each Shuaria you visit. At each Shuaria you will probably be offered a bowl of *chicha*. Drink it. Drink it all and don't just take a polite sip. If you can forget how it's made, it will taste just fine. Try to eat as much of the food they offer you as you can. Always ask permission before you take pictures of them. Be polite and smile, never yell and get angry. In other words, use common sense. You will quickly discover what a wonderful and friendly people they are.

You should refrain from asking about shrunken heads—at least until you feel you have gained the confidence of the Shuara that Tangamashi will take you to live with. This includes Tangamashi himself. What the Shuara will allow you to see is in large part up to you. The missionaries have persuaded the Ecuadorian government to pass a law threatening any Shuar who takes a head with seventeen years in prison, thus resulting in a very ugly mess of commercial head-taking for enormous amounts of money, attracting smugglers and criminals to the trade (now that *tsantsas* are outlawed and very rare, collectors in Europe and elsewhere are paying gigantic prices for them). Religious head-taking still goes on, but in great secret. Thus I can in no way assure you that you will witness any *tsantsa* rituals. The last remaining true Shuara are naturally suspicious of all. But if you treat them with friendliness and dignity, as equals, they will do so in return.

112

HEADHUNTER PARTICULARS

How to
get there

In Ecuador, one normally begins in Quito. You can fly to Quito quite easily from any major city in the world via connecting flights. There are direct flights from Miami most every day. You can go by car, bus, or thumb through Mexico and Central America to Panama, then by boat to Esmeralda, and from there by bus to Quito. If your port of arrival is Guayaquil, you need not, however, go to Quito, but take a bus to Cuenca, and from there fly or take a bus to Sacua.

Your aim is to get to Sacua. The air fare from Quito is about $20 (500 sucres: 25 sucres to the dollar). By taking a bus for $2-$3 from the highlands of Quito (altitude 9,200), dropping down through river canyons past magnificent waterfalls into the jungle to Pastaza (Shell Mera), catching a light plane for $4 to Macas (there are no roads from Pastaza to Macas) and from there another bus to Sacua for a dollar—you add to your adventure but not your expenses. (The road from Quito to Pastaza, especially from Baños on, really is spectacular. Orchids grow by it, waterfalls drop on it, streams flow over it, and there are places where, if you dropped a coin out the window, it would fall half a mile. Just don't drive it in the fog in the night, like I did once). TAO and SAN are the safest air taxi companies to fly in the Oriente. You can write to them c/o the Quito airport for fares and schedules. They have daily (well, almost) flights to Macas and Sacua. The buses operate constantly.

Once you arrive in Sacua ask directions to the Shuaria (some civilizados will refer to it as a "Jivaria," but don't you) San José. For a few sucres, someone will take you down the road a few kilometers, stop at the bottom of a small hill, and point to a path on the right leading off into the forest. Take this path down to the river (the Tutanangosa), cross the bridge, follow it for about a kilometer until it cuts sharply to the left and goes up a steep hill. At the top of this hill is a hut on your left where Tangamashi's brother, Miguel, lives. Beyond it, about 200 yards, is the hut of Tangamashi. There you will find him and his new wife, Chess-yü. I am sorry to say that Atsáyü passed away some years ago. You will find Shuara walking on this trail that you can ask directions of, so you should have little trouble. If you wish to write to Tangamashi telling him of your coming, write in Spanish to Shuar Manuel Tangamashi (the Spanish name is to differentiate him from his brother) c/o Shuar Federation, Sacua, Ecuador. He will get your letter eventually, and have someone read and translate it to him.

When to go

The weather stays pretty much the same all year long in the Oriente, since it's right on the equator. During the months of September, October, and November it usually rains less. Go then if you can, for the walking will be easier: less mud.

Language

This is a problem. Many Shuara now speak Spanish and Quechua—but, of course, no English. So the solution is to speak Spanish or go with someone who does. The languages I speak are English, American, Canadian, and Australian. I speak all those languages. Even a smattering of Spanish, which is all I have, will help. If you do not speak Spanish yourself or cannot recruit someone who does to go with you, then your only alternative is to find somebody in Ecuador to accompany you as your interpreter. The most expensive way would be to hire one through Metropolitan Touring. If you write the president, Señor Eduardo Proaño, whom I found to be an honest and capable man, he will secure an excellent interpreter for you—but at a price of about $20 a day. The address is 10 de Augusto 1251, Quito, Ecuador (phone 524-100). Ask if Walter Cruz is available.

There are always a number of Americans floating around Ecuador, most all of them in Quito, a scattered few hiking around in the Andes. The trouble is finding the right one, the one who speaks Spanish fluently, is able and adventurous enough to accompany you, and—this is most important—you can get along with. Quite by chance I run into just this sort of fellow quite often. You may too. Normally, he's elated to find someone who has plans and contacts for going into the Oriente and living with the Jivaros. Your best bet is to go to any of the gringo-owned bars and restaurants in Quito. The most popular are the Silver Slipper, the Townhouse, and the Club Wildcatter. Any taxi driver knows where they are.

I know of a group of young Americans living in Gualaceo, near Cuenca. One of them is fluent in Spanish and has a good knowledge of the jungle. His name is Dale Ray, although everyone calls him Seah. I tramped through the Oriente with him once, along with a friend of his named Randy, his dog Koa, and his monkey Toka. It was an experience, let me tell you, and if you can get him to go with you, you'll have quite an experience too. Write to him c/o the Hotel Cuenca, Cuenca, Ecuador.

So don't appear in Sacua some bright, sunny morning without someone who speaks Spanish! (Preferably yourself, of course: How about a night course in conversational Spanish at your local *escuela?*)

114

Now, how about speaking Jivaro? Well, if you write or drop by the Gospel Missionary Union, at Vozandes 186 in Quito (write c/o Cassilla [Box] 5), for thirty-five sucres they'll supply you with a Spanish-Jivaro dictionary. The official title is "Vocabulario del Idioma Shuar." For thirty-five sucres it is a very wise investment.

Guide

When I saw Tangamashi last, he agreed to secure a guide for anyone I sent to him. They will be his kinsmen, thoroughly trustworthy. Figure the cost, after some bargaining, to be around 100 sucres a day ($4), which includes their food, per Shuar guide. You should have one guide for every person in your party—unless you plan to carry your own pack. Ask Tangamashi specifically for Cruz, one of his sons; Ku-kush, his brother-in-law; or Tsangusha, married to the daughter of his cousin. I've been through the forest with all three.

Your Shuar guide will be very unhappy if your pack weighs over thirty pounds. Also, you should have some room in it for the small number of things he will take with him. If you would like to spend a few days with Tangamashi's family, ask him if that is possible (it may not be) and offer to pay him for his hospitality (a few sucres at most is what he might request or an ounce or two of black gunpowder; make this offer at every Shuaria you sleep at, and for their food as well). If not, you can stay at what functions as Sacua's only hotel, the Rio Upano, for a dollar a night. Before you leave, take Tangamashi and your guide(s) into town for a few beers. But be prepared: Shuara can drink a lot of beer.

Tangamashi loves to talk now, and you can spend many fine hours listening to him regale you with legends, stories, his personal adventures. He will tell you all about Disneyland and Los Angeles, for he and Naita are the only Shuara to have visited the United States (to be on "This Is Your Life"). He may not tell you about the time we were all taking the jungle river cruise at Disneyland. As we passed under a big plastic boa hanging on a branch, my father got carried away, grabbed the *Curaka* by the arm, pointed, and yelled wide-eyed: "Tangamashi! Pangi! Pangi!!" I thought the old fellow was going to jump out of his skin.

There are few people on earth I love more than Tangamashi, and I am trusting you, as a fellow Adventurer, to treat him with all the respect and kindness he deserves—which is quite a lot.

Where to go

Now you're in Sacua with your guide and ready to take off. The Oriente is a big place and you must have a specific goal in mind.

Here are my suggestions:

1. Take a bus or taxi to Macas, and walk to Macuma. Your goal is the Shuaria of the *Curaka* Uñungar, about halfway or more to Macuma. You can walk it in two or three days easily; from there to Macuma is about two more days. Your guide will walk back to Sacua and you can fly a mission plane to Pastaza. (Macuma is the headquarters of the missionary Frank Drown.) Uñungar is making the best attempt in this area of heavy missionary influence to stick to Shuara ways. He will take you blowgunning and hunting, and tell you stories all night long by the *shirikep* [pitch] fire. Be sure and tell him that you are a friend of the young American who told *him* stories all night long about visiting the Aucas.

2. Take the bus down to Mendez and walk to Miazal (a Salesian mission), then on to Taisha. This is quite a ways, the first part of it over steep trails through the Cordillera del Cutucu (few take it for this reason; all the better for you). A week of walking will get you easily to Miazal, another four days to Taisha. This area has little missionary influence, which is what you want. The most genuine Shuara in the Oriente live along the Patuime, Cangaime, and Casuime rivers between Miazal and Taisha. These Shuara are called the *chumapis*, and you should allow at least a month for this route, for you'll want to spend a few days at several of their *heas*, I'm sure. You can fly a mission plane (or a military plane—there's a military camp in Taisha) from Taisha to Pastaza, while your guide will walk back. (Remember: You must pay your guide for the days it will take him to walk back as well. He can walk from Taisha to Sacua, via Macuma, in two or three days.)

3. Take a TAO or SAN plane up to Pastaza, then a mission plane to Taisha. (A note on mission planes: They are single-engine Cessnas operated by MAF, the Missionary Aviation Fellowship. They carry mostly cargo, but if you're nice to them they'll give you a ride when they have space—which is most any day. It is the only way to get around in these parts, except on foot.) In Taisha, there are a number of ways to go. Here are three:
a. Walk to the Pastaza River. It will take you two to three days, but en route you will see some very legitimate Shuara. Your goal is any one of a number of Shuarias on the Pastaza. From there you may want to paddle a dugout canoe up or down the river visiting other Shuarias. The river is navigable only sporadically, so there is a chance you would have to portage. I have seen *tsantsas* in several of the *heas* on the river, but I don't want to pinpoint them for fear of government reprisals.
b. Walking southwest to the *chumapis* on the Patuime, Cangaime, and Casuime rivers I mentioned earlier. My comment on reprisals holds here also. About two to three days one way.
c. Southeast of Taisha is Atshuara country. The missionaries are thankfully having great difficulty taming them. Because there is

116

widespread resistance to their efforts, by visiting the Atshuara you will witness a rare primitive culture in a state of (albeit precarious) preservation. Atshuara live in bigger villages than the Shuara, and there is one a day's walk out of Taisha called Pumbuentsa, another two days further called Wichimi. Even though a Salesian priest, Father Luis Bolla, has been working with them for years, they still retain most of their old ways. Many of the women at Pumbuentsa, for example, are widows, their husbands killed in raids.

I wish I knew how to get you to a village of Atshuara who also call themselves chumapis, but I don't, short of chartering a helicopter (see page 117 on this). They are extremely remote, on the Peruvian border, and are practically untouched. The only large *hea*-fortress, complete with barricades, I've ever seen is here. It may be the last in the entire Oriente. I was flying with a pilot friend of mine, Eddie Rodriguez, in an oil exploration chopper when we got off track and blundered on to it. They hadn't seen a white man for years and years.

Be sure and bring the map on page 52 and discuss at length with Tangamashi and the guide(s) he selects for you where you want to go. You needn't limit yourself to my suggestions. How much time you spend at any given Shuaria is up to you, your guide(s), and especially your host. I have given you walking time only. A couple of final notes:

(a) re MAF: They will not charter their planes, so you must depend on their space availability. No one will rent you a small plane in Quito to fly around the Oriente, as it's just like flying over the ocean: a vast green carpet with no landmarks. Getting lost is enormously easy, and there's no real advantage to it anyway, as you can usually catch a MAF flight to any place that has a strip. Your object, though, is to get away from these strips as far as possible.

(b) re helicopters: The ideal way to travel in the jungle is by helicopter, but chartering one is *very* expensive. There still is a certain amount of oil exploration going on in the Oriente, so if you prowl enough in the gringo-owned bars in Quito, you may be able to make friends with chopper pilots flying for the oil exploration and drilling firms. It really is a fantastic experience, skimming over the treetops, flushing flocks of parrots, spotting toucans and monkeys in the branches below, landing in remote Shuarias and Atshuarias that would have taken days and days of walking to reach. Should this not work out, and you really have that much of an aversion to walking, you can charter a Bell G-4 three-seat helicopter (including pilot) for $200 a day, plus $200 an hour flying time. If this has not taken your breath away and you are still considering it, contact Ecuavia Oriente, Casilla [box] 3418, Quito. Please say hello to Gloria, the pilot's secretary, for me.

117

Cost

If you've been noticing, the costs are pretty minimal (except for the helicopter!). The main expenses are in getting to Quito, and your equipment (next topic). You might want to stay at the beautiful, but expensive, Hotel Colón while in Quito, to savor the last luxuries you'll be enjoying for a while (no hot showers in the jungle!). But $8 to $20 gets you to Sacua, $4 a day for a guide, $1 to $2 a day for food at various Shuarias, a few dollars per MAF plane ride. . . .so don't tell me that you can't afford *this* Adventure!

Equipment

Once again, the first order of the day is your boots. Forget about those magnificent mountaineering specials you just bought for the Matterhorn. They will not do in the rain forest. You want a light but sturdy boot good for the mud. For this, you can't do much better than the U.S. Army's Tropical Combat Boot. The official tag says "combat, tropical, mildew resistant," and it costs from $10-$15 at most Army-Navy stores around the country. It was designed for slogging through the jungles and swamps of South Viet Nam, and will resist bacteria, mildew, and penetration from bamboo spikes and snake bites. Wear them with wool socks, and, as your feet will swell up slightly, get the boots in a size a little longer and wider than shoes you normally wear. Double-lace the boots at the third or fourth eyelet. Use a shoe polish containing silicone, and dry the ventilating insole that comes with the boot in the sun. Never dry the boots (or any boot, for that matter) next to a fire.

I have tried all kinds of boots in the jungle, including those calf-high numbers. Most Indians use rubber boots, when they can get them. If you're interested in rubber boots, check what Eddie Bauer has to offer (page 51). But believe me, the Army's tropical boot can't be beat. Especially at that price.

To keep you dry, get a quality poncho. It should be overpack, knee-length, lightweight, made of urethane-coated nylon, with hood and drawstrings. Ski Hut's Trailwise Nylport overpack model is such a poncho (page 51).

For sleeping, I avoid lugging around a sleeping bag in the jungle. I use a combination of a nylon mesh hammock that rolls into a pocket-size ball, and an aluminum space blanket. Together they weigh nineteen ounces. They are inexpensive and compact, yet keep me warm and comfortable. Get them at any sporting goods store, or through Ski Hut.

Next, you need a backpack. Probably your best bet here is one of the new frameless, wrap-around "soft packs." Pick out a good

118

mid-priced one from Ski Hut or REI. You want one with fully padded shoulder straps, lower back padding, and waistbelt, coated (waterproof) nylon, and large outside pouches.

To put in the pack: a good, compact flashlight with spare batteries and bulbs; waterproof matches; two or three candles; a good pocket knife; a compass; first-aid kit (suggested: Recreational Equipment's Mountain First Aid Kit); personal toiletries (minimal, especially you girls!); chapstick; several bottles of Cutter's insect repellant, or Jungle Juice, billed as "the most potent repellant made, used in Viet Nam"; a roll or two of toilet paper (this is most important!); dish soap; a set of eating utensils and a small cook kit; an extra long-sleeve shirt and pair of pants; two or three extra pairs of undershirts, undershorts and socks; a light sweater; some dehydrated food packages and dried beef jerky to supplement the yucca, bananas, and monkey. Don't forget room for lots of American cigarettes, waterproof matches, balloons, black gunpowder, and some salt—and save a litt e space for your guide's small belongings. One more thing: Wrap everything in plastic bags. Oh, yes, I assume you'll want to take a camera and film. Plastic bag these especially. Remember your vitamins, glucose tablets, salt tablets, water-purifying pills, lomotil, and entero-vioform!

Other

All you need now is a good pair of sunglasses—the same as for the Matterhorn—a small hiking hat, and a light canteen, and you're set for backpacking through the Amazon jungle. After the Jivaros, you and I will go off to visit the Naked Aucas, "the most murderous savages in the world," as the missionaries call them. Actually, you'll find them quite friendly—except to missionaries. We'll live with Pygmies in the Congo, Bushmen in the Kalahari, and cannibals in New Guinea. There is so much Adventure in this world. But now—It's off to the Amazon to live with headhunters. And when you shake Tangamashi's warm hand, please say to him *Puengehr Pu-hamuk* for me.

Books

1. *Amazonian Cosmos*, by Gerardo Reichel-Dolmatoff.
2. *Ecuador—Andean Mosaic*, by Rolf Blomberg. A fine introduction to the wonderful country of Ecuador.
3. *Headhunters of the Amazon*, by F.W. Up de Graff. The first (1925) study of the Jivaro by a trained anthropologist.
4. *The Headhunters of the Western Amazonas*, by Raphael Karsten. The classic monograph (1935) on the Jivaro.
5. *Historical and Ethnographical Material on the Jivaro Indians* (Bureau of American Ethnology Bulletin 117, 1938), by Matthew W. Stirling. One of the finest works on the Jivaro by a justly

renowned anthropologist.
6. *Historia Moderna (Toma 1 Años 1550 a 1685)*, by Juan de Velasco. Biblioteca Amazonas, vol. 9. (available at main library in Quito).
7. "Jivaro Souls." *American Anthropologist*, Vol. 64, No. 2, 1962, 258-72. Michael J. Harner. A recent, detailed, and accurate discussion of Jivaro religion.
8. *The Botany and Chemistry of Hallucinogens*, by R.E. Schultes and A. Hofmann.
9. "Native Use and Occurrence of N,N-dimethyltriptamine in the Leaves of *Banisteriopsis rusbyana*." *American Journal of Pharmacy* 140: 137-47. A. Der Marderosian, H. Pinkley, and M. Dobbins.
10. *Manual of Pharmacology*, by Torald Sollman
11. *Ceremonial Chemistry*, by Thomas Szasz
12. *Envy*, by Helmut Schoeck

Suggested
Vitamin
Dosages
(Daily)

A	20,000 IU	PABA	75	MG
D	800 IU	Pantothenic Acid	75	MG
E	800 IU	Folic Acid	300	MCG
C	1000 MG	Lecithin	76	GR
	(with bioflavanoids)	Calcium	1000	MG
B_1	75 MG	Magnesium	500	MG
B_2	75 MG	Phosphorus	1000	MG
B_3	150 MG	Iron	60	MG
B_6	100 MG	Iodine	200	MG
B_{12}	500 MCG	Zinc	50	MG
	(in jungle, 100 mcg normally)			

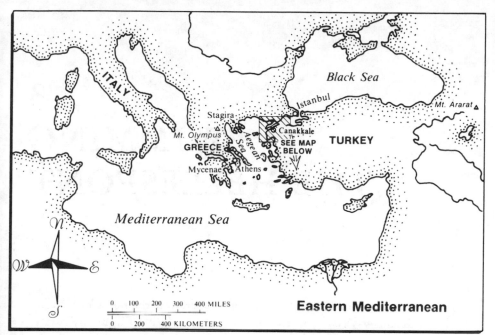

Black Sea

ITALY

Istanbul

Stagira

Mt. Olympus

Canakkale

SEE MAP
BELOW

GREECE

TURKEY

Mt. Ararat

Aegean
Sea

Mycenae   Athens

Mediterranean Sea

N
W   E
S

| 0 | 100 | 200 | 300 | 400 MILES |

| 0 | 200 | 400 KILOMETERS |

Eastern Mediterranean

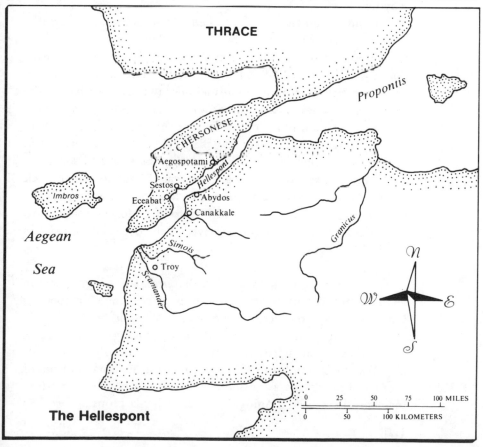

THRACE

Propontis

CHERSONESE

Aegospotami

Hellespont

Imbros

Sestos

Eceabat   Abydos

Canakkale

Aegean

Simois

Granicus

Sea

Troy

Scamander

N
W   E
S

| 0 | 25 | 50 | 75 | 100 MILES |

| 0 | 50 | 100 KILOMETERS |

The Hellespont

3

SWIMMING
THE HELLESPONT

Like a scimitar carved of purest alabaster, the moon of Genghis Khan was rising in the black Turkish night to light my way to Abydos.

A night of romance, with a veiled, sloe-eyed, sinuous, breathtakingly beautiful creature beside me? Thank you. I was in a taxicab with a Moslem fanatic at the wheel. Hunched over, with flaming eyes and twitching hands, this crazed defender of the Faith was either out to do an infidel in or to prove that he had the best damned axles in Asia. Either way I was done for. I thought it then and I think it now: If I can do these things, anyone can. There I was, racing across a great rocky plain, close to midnight, driven by this unlicensed idiot in the flowing robe who had somehow convinced himself that I was a reincarnated Crusader out to sack Mecca. How quickly one embraces the fatalistic philosophy of the East, I reflected. Now what had I heard of a Moslem service? Ah yes, friends give presents to relatives of the deceased. My sisters would like that.

Three hours ago I had landed at Bandirma at twilight, having left Istanbul's Yesilkoy airport late in the afternoon. My throbbing brain carefully considered the question: Had it been this very morning that I had been attending my psychology class at UCLA? Yes, I finally concluded, yes it was. I inhaled deeply—and it hit me. The smell. His breath! The breath of this madman in front of me, and I saw to my astonishment that he was now half-standing up over the wheel, leaning forward with his crimson face and

122

bulging eyeballs actually pressed against the windshield. His fumes were filling the cab, and I thought wildly that he must have one hell of a waterpipe.

The groaning, shaking, shrieking, gyrating vehicular thing was now literally throwing me from one side of the seat to the other. There were no straps to hang on to; they were probably some horse's halter now. I had long since tried to roll the windows down. No good. No handles.

I began to talk to myself again, as is my wont, as well you know. "Now, Jack, remember Greta Anderson's last words to you: '. . . .and remember, Jack, before you enter the water, rest quietly in bed, without a sound to disturb you, for at least eight hours. Sleep—and let not one single thing disturb you. Absolute relaxation is a vital necessity.' Yes Greta, yes Greta."

A vicious lurch, as the right front wheel happily discovered still another two-foot-deep rut, sent me spinning to the floor. I tried to focus my eyes on the now cracked crystal of my wristwatch but my contact lenses had slipped far out of position, so that it was in a dark blur by snatched moonlight that I managed to see that in twenty-seven minutes I was due to start swimming.

Why can't these matters go smoothly, I said again to myself as I crawled up to the revolving seat. Where, oh where, do I go wrong? I had planned every detail so carefully, and here I was, a complete wreck before the damned thing had even started!

A marrow-deep surge of self-pity and ineffable sadness suddenly engulfed me as I hung on with even greater desperation. Seven short weeks ago I had been living in the jungle with my beloved headhunters. I had been so happy and contented and, above all, safe. I had slept in a ten-head *Shuaria*, and with my pot of curare, blowgun, and darts beside me, had been completely satisfied with life. No problems. And now this.

Quick, I said to myself, set up a plan that will work when you face the midnight delegation of confident Turks who will surely meet you—a quick, blurred look at my watch—in twenty-five minutes. Now first things first. When you fall out of this death trap, they will look for your luggage, at least a flight bag containing your gear. And what will they see? *You*, swaying there with a used jar of rancid Vaseline in one hand and a pair of gigantic red shorts in the other—unwrapped.

I was on my way to swim the Hellespont, the churning, myth-laden waters of the Iliad and the Odyssey, naked as Leander, midnight in the dead of winter. No place on earth has raised more

123

legends and given birth to more history than this racing course that neatly divides two continents: Europe and Asia.

On the Asian side, there was in times of ancient Greece a village named Abydos, wherein dwelled, the story goes, a youth called Leander. On Europe's side, there was the village Sestos, wherein dwelled—you guessed it—a beautiful maiden: Hero. Forbidden by the high priestess of the cult of Aphrodite, of which Hero was a member, to see her lover, Hero lit a torch atop a tower. Leander swam to Hero in the black of night, with the beacon as a guide. One night a storm came up and blew out the torch, and the swift currents of the Hellespont carried Leander out to the Aegean Sea, where he drowned. Upon learning Leander's fate, Hero threw herself off a cliff into Helle's Sea.

For thousands of years, the story of Hero and Leander was looked upon as a myth because the feat of swimming the Hellespont was thought to be impossible. But on May 3, 1810, Lord George Gordon Byron swam from Abydos to Sestos, gimpy leg and all, to prove that Leander could have been. To celebrate, he wrote his famous poem *The Bride of Abydos*.

"Since Byron's time, the feat has been achieved by others," reports *Bullfinch's Mythology* in recounting the legend of Leander, "but it yet remains a test of strength and skill in the art of swimming sufficient to give a wide and lasting celebrity to any of our readers who may dare to make the attempt and succeed in accomplishing it."

I had brought a copy of *Bullfinch* with me to South America and you can easily guess what I thought when I read this paragraph. Yes, others had swum the Hellespont since Byron. But Leander, according to legend, was sixteen when he suffered his fate. Had anyone swum the Hellespont at sixteen, at night, during the winter when the storms come up like the one that cruelly blew out Hero's flame? No. No one.

I was sixteen. It was August and I would turn seventeen on November 9. Could I make it? Well, I would try. When I got back home, I swam, and I swam, and I swam, and I worked at every odd job I could find.

I wrote Pan American World Airways to see if they could help me out on the airfare. I told them of Leander, but added: "In my attempt to follow in the wake of legendary Leander, my primary wish is not to suffer his fate, as it would be extremely unfair to Pan American." Pan Am contacted *Life* magazine, and they assigned a young correspondent, Shana Alexander, to write the story. Once

Life was interested, Pan Am said they could offer me assistance.

My parents were worried about how much school I would miss (it was my first semester at UCLA), so it was Pan Am to the rescue again. They told me they could get me to Turkey and the Hellespont, and back, in *one weekend*. I would leave Friday, after classes, be at the straits for the swim Saturday night, and be back in Los Angeles late Sunday evening. I was all set to go.

I was in great shape. Pan Am had made all the arrangements, and I was leaving in a week. I decided to toughen up by swimming in the wintry Pacific off Malibu instead of a pool. I should have stayed in the pool. Sister Fate presented me with her medial extremity and slipped my bod the bug. The day I was to leave I had all the vibrant, bursting energy of a dead battery.

But this weekend was it. In five days I would turn seventeen. It was now, or, as they say, never. My sisters packed my bag with trunks, towels, bathrobe, a two-pound jar of Vaseline (to smear on for insulation against the cold water), vitamins, and various drugs to combat my racking cough, chest and head cold, and strep throat. Yes, I was in great shape.

Somehow, I made it to and on the plane. In New York, I saw my bag go sliding down a ramp and was assured it would arrive in Istanbul as if it were the Dead Sea Scrolls. The bag, of course, was not on the plane when I arrived at Istanbul's Yesilkoy Airport. Peterson's Law of Inevitable Failure had struck ineluctably once again.*

After a frantic and expletive-filled search with the *Life* reporter and photographer sent to meet me, we got on our plane to Bandirma. Since there are no landing lights at Canakkale (near the site of Abydos), the DC-3 must land at Bandirma. The pilot told me not to worry about a thing. The merchants in Bandirma will supply all my essentials and there will be a new limousine waiting for a luxurious, restful ride to Canakkale. . . .

Another quick glance at my watch. We should be arriving in twenty-three minutes and I still had no excuse for the shorts and grease acquired in Bandirma. I noticed that since I had now adopted the Moslem faith in the past half-hour in sheer defense— or could it be the fumes?—I was still crashing and careening about but facing the East.

*Formulated by John K. Peterson, brilliant but unrecognized in his own time: "The probability of attainment of a specific object in view is decreased proportionately by the urgency of its need."

Twenty-three minutes. To think and wonder on the incredible background of the Hellespont. But we must hold on, face the East, and not inhale too deeply.

The waters of the Black Sea exit through a narrow channel called the Bosphorus, now straddled by the city of Istanbul. The channel widens into the Propontis, or Sea of Marmara, and the waters, gathering momentum, then race through slender straits forming swift and treacherous currents, before emptying into the Aegean Sea and the Mediterranean.

Whosoever controlled the heights, called the Troad, above these straits, controlled all traffic between the Mediterranean and Black Seas. So a fort was established at the Troad, which grew into a city rich with ancient splendor, and richer still with the stuff of epic history and legend. The city was Troy. The straits it controlled was the Hellespont.*

Did Troy really exist? Did the Trojan War actually take place? When Alexander of Macedon crossed the Hellespont on his way to conquer Persia, his most treasured possession was a copy of Homer's *Iliad*, the story of the Trojan War, given to him by his teacher, Aristotle. He slept with it, along with his dagger, under his pillow every night. According to Alexander, the *Iliad* was "the perfect portable treasure of all military virtue and knowledge."

Near the Hellespont were ancient ruins, revered as Troy. The first thing Alexander did upon stepping foot on Asian soil was to go directly to the columned tomb of Achilles. In full view of his entire army, he divested himself of all clothing until naked. He then anointed both the tomb and himself with oil, ran naked three times around the tomb, and placed a jeweled crown upon it. The sacred armor of Achilles, Alexander's idol, lay in the ruined Temple of Athena. He exchanged parts of his own armor for the shield of Achilles. It was to save his life eight years later in a battle near the Indus River. Did Alexander the Great believe in Troy—in Achilles and Hector, Paris and Helen, Menelaus, Agamemnon, Ulysses, Ajax, and Diomedes? I rather think he did.

The epic poem of Rome, Virgil's *Aeneid*, tells how Aeneas escaped from the sacking of Troy by running across the plain to the Hellespont (four miles away), carrying his old father on his back. Stealing a raft, he made his getaway across our water. Adventure piled upon adventure befell Aeneas, until he arrived at a place of

*Also called the Dardanelles, for Dardanus, father of Ilus, legendary founder of Troy (or Ilium, hence Homer's *Iliad*).

126

seven hills near a river called Tiber. His descendants, Romulus and Remus, there built a town called Rome. Julius Caesar thought so highly of Troy and his ancestor Aeneas that he officially declared Troy a free and open city, forever free from any form of taxation. Ah, paradise.

In modern times, however, there were many scholars who thought that the city called Troy, or Ilium, in Caesar's day, had nothing at all to do with the city of Homer, "well-walled" Troy with its Trojans "fond of war" and "bronze-clad." They dismissed the *Iliad* as fanciful legend, pure fiction with no basis in fact.

And nobody could dispute them, until there came along a small, strange man who had risen out of utter poverty to become a millionaire, and devoted those self-made millions to proving Homer was real and no illusion.

An amazing and admirable man was Heinrich Schliemann, and I strongly recommend you read the biography of him listed on page 157. He had committed to memory all 26,000 lines of the *Iliad*, in the original Homeric Greek, and, using Homer as a guide, started digging operations at a large mound next to the Scamander River, an hour's walk from the Hellespont near the Turkish village of Hissarlik. With 150 villagers he hired and instructed himself, and with no formal archaeological training (the science had not been invented yet), he uncovered the ruins of one fortress and ruined city after another, each lying beneath the other. Then, in late May of 1873, Schliemann, digging alone with the help of his wife, Sophia, found the Gold of Troy, a mass of gold, silver, and copper treasures that proved to the world he had found the city of Homer.*

The leader of the University of Cincinnati excavations of Troy, C. W. Blegen, acknowledges that "the glory of discovering Troy and making it known to the world" belongs to Schliemann. It is thanks to him that "it can no longer be doubted, when one surveys the state of our knowledge today, that there really was an actual historical Trojan War in which a coalition of Achaeans, or Mycenaeans, under a king whose overlordship was recognized, fought against the people of Troy and their allies . . . furthermore, that a good many of the individual heroes who are mentioned in the poems were drawn from real personalities as they were

*It was taken to a museum in Berlin, where it was stolen by the Russians at the end of World War II.

observed by accompanying minstrels at the time of the events in which they played their parts."

Seventeen minutes I make it for our *ETA*. I am happy to report that the Defender in front has calmed down considerably. Without question, my absorbing the Faith has done the job. It's either that, or no recent pulls on the old waterpipe.

Soon I will be among the ghosts of Homer. I will run my hands over stone walls that watched Achilles chase Hector of the flashing helmet three times around the city and then plunge his bronze spear into noble Hector's chest.

I would see Achilles depart from the war, and earth, with an arrow in his heel, leaving an expression used in every language today.

I would see Paris, husband of Helen of the beautiful hair, who shot the arrow that killed the son of Peleus, dispatched by Menelaus, King of Sparta, from whom Paris stole Helen.

And what of sweet Helen, she of the face that launched a thousand ships? Did she mourn for Paris and wait for Menelaus to breach the walls and rescue her? Hardly. She opted for Number Three, Deiphobos of the white shield. Brother of Paris, he was brother of Hector, too—all sons of good King Priam, King of Troy.

I would hear Cassandra, daughter of Priam, doomed by Apollo to have her prophecies ignored, intoning, "beware of Greeks bearing gifts," as the Trojans pulled on the thick ropes hauling a massive wooden horse within their gates.

I would watch Odysseus, Menelaus, and ten others slip out of the horse's belly that night, open the gates of Troy to the attacking Argives, head straight for the house of Helen and Number Three, and, after a horrendous fight, see our beautiful vessel-launcher once again in the arms of her still-adoring Number One.

Standing in the ruins of windy Troy, I *would* see these things. And so will you.

You will see Diomedes of the loud war cry filled with so much *hübris* that he actually attacks the goddess Aphrodite, wounding her on the wrist so that her *ichor*, the blood of the Gods, spills to the ground. And the colossal figure of the mighty Ajax will loom in front of you, cutting his way through the masses of bronze-helmeted Trojans to rescue the body of Achilles. But then you will see Ajax defeated by the trickery of Odysseus of the nimble wits, in a contest over the armor of Achilles.

The defeat caused Ajax to go mad and kill himself, but he had the last laugh, right up to this second, for now he's a soap, which is more than you can say for Odysseus, who ended up as a trip, a word not even breathed in straight circles these days (straight circles? By gad, that's right, but it had me for a moment.).

Actually, that's not being fair to Odysseus (who became an Odyssey—a journey, filled with notable experiences and hardships) who was an extremely clever and enterprising chap, and happens to be a great favorite of mine. His adventures you and I perhaps will never have, but we'll keep trying.

Not only King of Ithaca and one of the heroes of the *Iliad*, he is the protagonist in Homer's other epic poem, the *Odyssey*, wherein our boy takes ten years trying to make it home after doing his bit for Helen. Odysseus, known to the Romans as Ulysses, was also Kirk Douglas out of Tony Curtis, a psychological novel from the pen of James Joyce, a town in Kansas, and the given name of a president of the United States. Now put them all together and they don't spell Mother but they sure as Hades beat out a foaming cleanser.

Twelve minutes I now make it for our *ETA*. There has been one happy change. The Defender has now taken to singing. I figure that either he is simply nearing his destination and will be well rid of me, or he has a second waterpipe stashed in Canakkale. (By the way, Canakkale, in case you're wondering, is pronounced *Sha-NAH-ka-lay*).

Is it any wonder, then, that I have always been fascinated by this water, this storied strip of wetness, sanctified by more great adventures, heroes, historical and legendary events than any other place on earth?

The Hellespont! The Sea of Helle. And who was she? The sister of Phrixus, that's who. Together they were fleeing on a great swimming ram to escape from their stepmother, Ino. Sadly, sister Helle was not seated firmly on the wool, for off she went into our waters, and brother was sisterless. This meant the deep six for friend ram who, upon arriving in Colchis, gave up his hide, unwillingly, to Phrixus in sacrificial revenge. The hide became known as the Golden Fleece.

The official custodian of the Golden Fleece was the King of Colchis, Aeëtes, who is unimportant except that he had a beauteous daughter, Medea, sorceress extraordinaire. It was love-stricken Medea that enabled Jason, with his Argonauts, to capture the hide of gold, return from a mission his Uncle Pelias thought was sure death, and claim his kingdom. Pure trickery and magic on the part of daughter to father. Aeëtes was "fleeced," and that's why we use that expression to this day. (Note: Pelias is not to be confused with

129

Pelleas, a knight of King Arthur's Court, who loved Ettarre. Yes, Ettarre.)

Now it may interest you to know that there really was a Golden Fleece. The inhabitants of Colchis, on the eastern shore of the Black Sea, extracted gold from streams running down from the Caucasus Mountains* into the sea by placing sheepskins into the streams, pegging them so that the water would flow over them. Gold dust would then collect in the wool, ergo: a Golden Fleece.

Caenis. Ah, beautiful she was, the Greek maiden who bathed so frequently in the Hellespont that she attracted the attention of Poseidon, God of the Sea. Now, speaking frankly but delicately, friend Poseidon, being a God and brother of all-mighty Zeus, had all the privileges that such an exalted station commands—and promptly took advantage of her, as the saying goes. Now this lad was also the creator of earthquakes; he could not move in the water without causing an upheaval somewheres. So I am forced to accept the fact that the resulting experience for sweet, lovely, virginal Caenis was somewhat more than normal.

Eventually, after a considerable length of time, she was able to speak, if not to stand. And her first thought, expressed to Poseidon standing proudly by? Simply put, it was to the effect that if that kind of action was the order of the day and night between girls and boys, she wanted to be on the sending side, not the receiving.

Up went the magic trident and lo, the lovely Caenis was instantly transformed into Caeneus, destined to sail with Jason and be known as the Invulnerable Argonaut.

So why then is the nuclear missile that affords the Free World protection from *attack* called the Poseidon?

Our *ETA* is now about eight-plus. The Defender's voice is still going strong. I suddenly think of my sisters. What were they doing at this very moment? Probably going through my personal effects and dividing them up.

My thoughts returned to history. Perhaps the most fantastic scene in the whole history of the Hellespont was staged by Xerxes, King of Persia, son of Darius.

According to Herodotus, the Father of History, 674 rafts did Xerxes have constructed to bridge our water in order to transport

*The Caucasus are a range of mountains between the Caspian Sea and the Black Sea, in Caucasia, recently conquered by Russia. The highest peak is 18,356 feet, Mt. Elbrus, which you and I will climb someday.

his vast army to Europe and to the eventual victory through treason that was to be his at Thermopylae. Completed, the signal was given for the advance over the bridge by the Persian Horde. At that instant, a devastating storm hit without warning and every raft was swept away and destroyed. Xerxes, in a maniacal frenzy of which despots are so capable, had every single engineer in his army executed on the spot. And then he ordered the Hellespont to be lashed three hundred times as punishment for daring to rise against him.

Look at that scene.

Four mightily muscled Persian giants, each gleaming with sweat and panting fiercely, taking his turn at striking the water with all his strength with his monstrous, flailing whip—as 50,000 Persian warriors watch in awe and deadly silence.

It was the spring of 480 B.C. Some seven months later would see the once-proud King, and the remnants of his mighty army, who were now suffering from famine, disease, and cold, being ferried in retreat across the Hellespont to Abydos. Two months before, on a pretty September day, Xerxes had watched in horror and rage as a small band of Greek ships, led by the Athenian Themistocles, cut his gigantic navy to pieces in the bay of Salamis.

The Hellespont witnessed the retreat of the barbarian horde, and would now witness the rise to power and glory of the victor: Athens. Only 75 years were to pass before the Hellespont saw her eclipse as well. On a cloudy August day in 405, the Athenian fleet was moored at Aegospotami, north of Sestos. Down from his nearby fortress rode the single most outstanding personality and military genius Athens had ever produced: Alcibiades. He advised the Athenian generals to immediately move their fleet away from its weak position and down to Sestos—but Alcibiades was in disgrace and exile; the generals paid him no heed, and he rode away.

The next day, Lysander and the Spartan fleet attacked from across the Straits. The Athenians were utterly destroyed, and with that, the Peloponnesian War was lost, the Athenian Empire collapsed, the greatest achievement of the ancient world—fifth-century Athens—was no more, and the Hellespont had seen it all. Like an explosion of fireworks, the brilliant display of passionate enthusiasm for and commitment to reason, freedom, individualism, and justice that characterized the Periclean Age blazed and vanished, leaving only burning remnants in the minds of those who remembered.

I need something to pick me up after that and all of a sudden a thought strikes me. In very short order I will dive into these famed straits, touch bottom, thrust upwards, break the surface, and start stroking for Europe. Is it possible that the very water that will soon envelop me once caressed the breasts of Cleopatra, cooled the warm loins of Byron, and glistened on the golden chest of Alexander? These were real people, they actually lived and they all indeed entered the waters of the Hellespont.

Not one drop of water has been added to the earth since its birth. All the world's water is continuously re-cycled by Nature, over and over again, the same, and only, water on earth. The water drawn from the tap for your own tub may contain, in part at least, the same water that Caesar used in his Roman baths. Not very probable, but possible.

But with Mother Nature's personal attention to re-cycling as to region, the odds are somewhat lowered. The Hellespont has been the birth of watery history before civilization began, and there does exist the very real possibility that tonight, when the magic waters of these straits touch my body, the same water could have laved the lovely, sensual body of Helen of Troy herself.

The thought indeed picked me up.

For every single crossing of the straits, every swim, be it Leander or Byron, was made at the exact same area on the Hellespont: the narrowest, less than two miles wide. All the events of the Trojan War evolved at, or around, that one crossing, for Troy, before the siege, had always been the fortress that controlled it. All the events I have been thinking of took place at or near the precise location where I am about to swim. Will ghosts by the legions be beside me? Or rise from the depths to greet me in the moonlight?

The taxi, born of the devil and nurtured by a madman, screeched to a tooth-cracking halt. I had arrived in Canakkale. Two minutes to midnight; I must start swimming within a half hour.

A man stood there to greet me. He was short and lean, with a toucan's beak and a copyrighted accent. Black hair, mustache to match, with elk's teeth gleaming in the moonlight, he bounced and quivered like a courting wildebeest. I swear that, in three deep breaths at most, I knew that here was a good man genuinely glad to see me. Charisma dipped in 100-proof sincerity is a hard commodity to come by—I have discovered it in the Gobi Desert and lost it on Park Avenue, but if I ever needed it in my life it was at that moment of descension from Satan's carriage onto Homeric soil. What I required was a bed, not glory and 53-degree water, holy or not, and failing that, a brother spirit filled with life's flowing juices. What I got was the latter, and he had a name: Hüseyin Uluaslan, and he was indeed Allah's messenger making the scene, juices and all.

So this was it. I looked about me. A cluster of smiling faces in the moonlight—soldiers, police, civilians, and, upstaging them all, the Hellespont herself, not fifty feet from where I stood, and, I must admit, looking more than a little ominous in that witching hour as she raced past a darkened, sleeping Canakkale.

In a firefly flash a hubbub of vocal Turkish rose in a wave about me, and suddenly all eyes seemed to be riveted upon a pair of flaming red trunks of Atlas proportions held loosely by a twitching hand—mine. And, as always, your boy came up with an intelligent, all-explanatory answer: "How about that?" Collective eyebrows on the wing brought forth animated explanations by my two *Life* companions to the goodly group about me. In Turkish, of course, so not a word, or few at least, did I understand, but their gestures and facial reactions were magnificent and all-revealing. A spreading of wildly waving arms and hands, accompanied by incredulous expressions, informed me and the open-mouthed gentry clustered about that they were describing the scene at the airport in Istanbul when it was discovered that my all-essential kit was missing (at that very moment, by the way, it was resting comfortably in Frankfurt, Germany). Frenzied, knocking motions in the dry-ice air then revealed to me that they were describing my repeated efforts in Bandirma, running hither and yon, up one narrow street and down the other, in a vain attempt to open closed doors of off-duty merchants in order to obtain almost anything, but with no success whatsoever, except for those double-damned red trunks hand-made, obviously, for the 360-pound, six foot nine, super heavyweight champion of Asia Minor—and a half-filled jar of well-fingered Vaseline.

Sympathy flooded the scene, but no suggestions. "Time is *not* our ally, Mr. Uluaslan," I said to my new juice-filled friend, "as you know, I must make this swim and be airborne before dawn." And, in that captivating accent of his, and one-of-a-kind English, he replied, "Ah yes, you are true, but Yali Hamami, she wait for you. Think I that that you must have Yali do what she do else plane cannot fly for in a seat you will not!"

Now, quite frankly, I was impressed. "By Gad," I said to myself, "this man *does* have complete service!" With assumed nonchalance, and almost complete recovery from utter exhaustion and multiple ills, I enquired, "Yali Hamami?"

With eyes glowing even more fiercely he cried out, "Yes! Yali Hamami! She finest Turkish Bath in all the country of mine!"

The gangplank was shaky and thin, but in seconds I was standing on the deck of the *Turker*. An instant judgment: thirty-five feet long, diesel, fishing boat, with a hand tiller at the stern and a small cabin lit by a single yellow lantern. In the dim light, a tall, thin man with outstretched hand. "Captain Necati," this from Yali's booster, and an instant firm grip followed by a quick gesture to four men standing in a row beside him. "Vedat—Hasan—Ismet—Celal." Four hard handshakes, with Hüseyin saying, "These finest swimmers in all Turkey. All swim Hellespont, but summer, not winter, and in day of bright light, with music of the soft, and food and drink, and boat to hold on when tired. If get in trouble you, all jump in but all say please not to do, for perhaps cannot see in dark but all think no worry for come a long way to meet her." And he turned and motioned towards the black water as it hissed its way beneath the wooden hull.

And then—thirty seconds, the like of which only true Adventurers can share. On the weathered deck, holystoned beyond count, those four wide-shouldered men gathered about me, slapping my back, speaking to me in their language as if I could understand them, smiling broadly, and then, collectively, each hugged themselves with corded arms crossed, nodding at the dark, fast-moving current, and then shook themselves as if freezing to death. All four began to cleave the almost frigid air with clean, sharp strokes, with a constant jerking of their heads towards the racing wetness beneath us.

It was a clear message, "Don't stop swimming. It's too damn cold and dark for us to join you!" And they all laughed and motioned for me to enter the cabin.

I stripped as the *Turker* cast off. The bow of our boat began to dip and rise. The throbbing of our diesel was muffled, but the deck beneath me shuddered with every revolution of the single screw.

(For the sake of accuracy, I must now take leave of you in describing, in the first person, the swimming of the Hellespont. From the first second that I dove into the Hellespont to touch bottom, surface, and start swimming, the extreme temperature of the water took, literally, my asthmatic breath away. I gulped magic water into a strep throat, the current seized me like an animal and my body began an instant, unrehearsed, twisting slide down to the Aegean Sea. From that moment on, I remember little.

Halfway across the Straits, I recall nothing. Period. Therefore, the accurate account can only be given by the two trained professional observers aboard the *Turker*: the *Life* reporter and the *Life* photographer who had met me in Istanbul. Having received permission of Time-Life Inc., I shall now quote, verbatim, an excerpt from the *Life* feature story as it appeared in the December 12, 1960, issue. So, we're off together again, but this time through the eyes of two *Life* staff members and the writing of Shana Alexander, then of *Life*'s staff).

". . . .Shortly after midnight, under a full moon, the *Turker* hove to a few yards offshore on the Asian side of the Dardanelles. Jack undressed and put on his Bandirma trunks. They hung almost to his knees. He kicked them off in disgust and decided to swim naked, like Leander. After smearing his body with Vaseline and some engine grease contributed by the captain, Jack dropped over the side into the black water at 12:15 a.m., touched bottom, rose to the surface and started swimming.

"The water was the coldest that Jack had ever felt. He shook his head to be sure his contact lenses were still secure and began to swim the crawl, a stroke with which he can usually cover a mile in 24 minutes. Soon his face and sinuses began to ache unbearably from the cold, and he was forced to turn over on his back. He swam cross-channel until incomprehensible yelling in Turkish from the boat told him he had drifted too far downstream. He turned north and dug in for the Black Sea. His ears grew numb, the sound of yelling grew fainter, and after about 45 minutes in the water he discovered to his horror that he had gone completely deaf. After that he guided himself by glancing at the single swaying yellow lantern above the pilot house and occasionally at the moonlit cliffs of Sestos on the European shore.

"At 1 o'clock Jack suddenly screamed and disappeared under the water. 'A searing, tearing pain paralyzed my right leg below the knee,' he recalled. 'Waves of agony gushed up my body and I slid beneath the surface and deep into the Hellespont. It was like a dream. But my hand clasped itself around my calf. It was like holding a large frozen rock. I forced myself to the surface, and there was my little old fishing scow about 20 feet away. I thanked the Lord I hadn't come up into its screw, because I couldn't hear a thing. I saw the mouths of the Turks working and I knew they were shouting, but I heard nothing.'

"The captain moved his boat alongside and tossed a life preserver. He urged Jack to give up, and several pairs of hands reached over the side to haul him aboard. Jack shouted, 'no,' and forced himself away. Treading water with his left arm and leg, he massaged his knotted calf with his right hand, as Greta Anderson had advised. 'Don't panic,' she had told him. 'Close your hand around the lump and squeeze it like an orange. Always knead it upward toward your heart.'

"The cramp went away, but when Jack resumed swimming he found that unless he kept his right leg straight and motionless, the cramp would return. He turned over and began a modified breast stroke, trying to keep his face above water and dragging his right leg. The cold made his jaws ache. There was a bare 100-yard stretch of smooth water in midstream, then Jack encountered more heavy currents on the European side of the channel. Though he was barely aware of it, sea traffic was heavy that night. A big Russian cargo ship came rumbling down the channel. When Jack failed to respond to the frantic yells from his escort, Captain Necati threw a line which landed on top of his body. Jack grabbed the rope and was towed about 200 feet until he was clear of the suction of the churning propeller. Then a huge wave engulfed him. When he fought to the surface, swallowing black, greasy ice water, he saw his own boat far up channel toward the Sea of Marmara while the current drew him farther and farther toward the Aegean.

"Jack continued to swim for another 30 or 40 minutes, but he made slow progress because the towing had further stiffened his chilled muscles. Though he does not remember the last part of his swim clearly, the Turks report that he continued to paddle forward weakly like a run-down mechanical toy, shouting incoherently every time they tried to make him give up. When Jack was a bare 200 feet from the cliffs, the captain grew afraid that his boat would break up on the jagged rocks. He ordered his rescue team to remove Jack from the Hellespont. It is likely that the captain's action saved not only the boat but Jack's life as well. What the crew fished out of the water was a frozen, shuddering, grease-smeared creature, babbling incoherently. His arms and legs continued to twitch in convulsive swimming motions long after he had been wrapped in blankets.

"Jack regained consciousness at 2:45 a.m. He was lying on the floor of a Turkish bath back in Canakkale, and the admiring Turks were pouring warm water over his head. At first he was bitterly disappointed to learn that he had not set foot on the European side, but when his friends assured him he could have swum the last 200 feet but could not possibly have climbed the rocks, he felt better.

"When Jack said good-bye to the Turks, he thanked them all in formal Turkish. Captain Necati replied in not-so-formal English: 'Great display guts. Fine young man came from America swim Dardanelles which had not seen daytime and especially this late in year. I say *"Yashaa!"* to this young man.' *Yashaa*, Jack learned, means hooray, or long life."

At 11:45 that Sunday night I was back home in Los Angeles.

And now you are going to learn how you can swim the Hellespont. Where I went wrong, you will go right, for it was a lot rougher for me than it will be for you. Soon, then, *you* will stroke your way from Asia to Europe, to join the glowing ranks of Gods and Kings, Poets and Lovers, Heroes and Armies, all looming tall and straight through five thousand years of history.

Hellespont Briefing

If you are muttering to yourself, "Jack must be crazy if he thinks *I* am going through something like *that*....", don't worry about it. You aren't going to swim the Hellespont at night in the winter. That is definitely crazy and I ought to know. *You* are going to swim the Hellespont under a hot Turkish sun, in the summer, when the currents are less swift. And in good health.

This is just what I did in the summer of 1973. I swam the Hellespont again—this time all the way to the shore of Sestos—and I have a large surprise for you:

It was easy.

Hüseyin and I discovered Leander's secret: how to make the currents work for you instead of against you. With the help of a wonderful old gentleman, Ibrahim Soydins by name, who has fished the Hellespont for over a half a century, we found a peculiarity in the current at a certain spot near Abydos Point. By utilizing this peculiarity just right, *the current will help carry you over to the European side*, instead of sweeping you into the Aegean or back to Asia. How about that?

Notice, however, I said, "will help to," not simply, "will." The current is not going to make it *that* easy! You'll still have to fight it powerfully part of the way, at the beginning and right near the end, and do a fair amount of strong swimming. But swimming the Helles-

137

pont is a superhuman feat no more—and can become, in fact, more pleasurable and exhilarating than exhausting.

The summer sun was shining, the waters of the Straits were as smooth as a lake, Ibrahim instructed Captain Torkes to maneuver his boat, the *Müjgan*, around 'till we found the right spot, the water was warm, and the swimmer Hüseyin asked to accompany us, Ali Gözücik, swam along with me for a ways just for the fun of it. Hüseyin and I talked and joked back and forth every so often, I felt myself getting stronger with each stroke, and, as the shore of Sestos got closer and closer, I realized I would soon be standing on it, not to be fished out 200 yards away from it, frozen and babbling. Then I felt the bottom that was Europe beneath my feet, I waded ashore to stand and wave to the little boat 100 yards away with the yelling, cheering people on board. I stood there for some time, in the warm sun, as it was one of those mirror-looking moments we talked about in the Introduction. Finally I swam back to the boat, and once returned to Canakkale, we headed straight for—you guessed it—Yali Hamami.

This is the way you will swim the Hellespont. And now you and I, together, will make sure it will be as easy for you as it was—the second time!—for me. I must confess to you, however, before we begin: I was (for once) in very good shape. Most anybody of reasonably good health, if they follow thoroughly the advice of the *AG*, can climb the Matterhorn and live with headhunters. And in the upcoming chapters, there are many Adventures that *anyone* can do if he's not in an iron lung. The Hellespont, however, is a different matter.

The younger you are, the better. Olympic swimming champions are rarely in their twenties, most are teen-agers. I would say the ideal age for this Adventure would be—for both men and women— between fifteen and twenty-five. The ideal age varies greatly from sport to sport. For mountain climbing it is the middle thirties. Hillary, for example, climbed Everest when he was thirty-five years old. But swimming belongs to the younger set.

This doesn't mean you should abandon all thought of swimming the Hellespont if you're in your thirties or even late forties. What it does mean is that you are going to have to think seriously about your desire to swim the Hellespont—and you'll have to be in the best shape of your life.

And even for the teen-agers it will not be easy. Being in good general condition is not going to cut it. Long-distance swimming takes specialized training. I have a friend who was once in the Marine Corps. While in boot camp he was selected as being in the best physical condition of any Marine in the camp. Jim is in fantastic shape and yet in a swimming race he's exhausted after 100 yards. To get in shape for swimming you have to swim. All the jogging and push-ups in the world won't help you.

I hope by now you aren't scared away. If you are under fifty and in normal good health, I'll make you a blood brother of Lord Byron and

138

Leander, believe me. But you must follow the training program I'm about to lay out for you *to the letter*. I don't want Hüseyin fishing you out halfway across.

GETTING IN SHAPE

First, you must find an ocean, lake, river, stream, or pool to swim in. An Olympic-size pool is best, and there should be one in a local high school, college, or gym near you. If you are a student at a school that has one, fine. If not, call the recreation department of your city, and ask when and where you can practice. An Olympic pool has a length of twenty-five meters, and you should definitely practice in a pool of this length if at all possible. Family-size home pools are simply too small for effective training. And oceans are too big. But use whatever you have available. Perhaps you can find an appropriate section of a lake, river, or ocean bay (between 25 and 100 yards wide).

So far, I've assumed you know how to swim. If you don't, it's about time you learned! Any competent instructor can teach you in a couple of weeks. From then on, it's just practice for a few months until you feel ready for the training program.

Now, what you're going to be involved in for your training during the next couple of months is what the coaches call *interval training*. Instead of swimming for a long time and taking long breaks in-between, what I want you to do is swim 100 meters (four laps), then rest for 20 seconds, swim another 100 meters, rest for 20 seconds, and do this five times. Take a short break. Relax, fool around, talk to a friend—for about five minutes. Then repeat the 100-meter/20-second rest routine for another five rounds. Take another five-minute break, then go at it again until you've completed the circuit five times.

You will have swum a total of 2,500 meters and it will take you (when you start getting in shape) less than an hour and a half. If 2,500 meters sounds like a lot, remember Australians swim *14,000* in Olympic practice daily.

There are two key items to remember in your interval training. No. 1 is to swim through your program *every day*. No excuses. Every single day for two months. At the end of these two months you'll be ready to swim the Hellespont.

No. 2 is *pace*. Work to develop a strong, steady, consistent pace—you're not worrying about setting any records, you want staying power, *stamina*, that good old watchword once again. Swim with a waterproof watch, and try to keep to the same time for each lap, or for each 100 meters.

Don't speed up, then slow down. Keep the same pace and get into a groove with it. About 25-30 seconds per lap, 90-120 seconds for each 100 meters, is a good, steady time. Work up to where you can consistently keep up this speed throughout the entire 2,500 meters.

One more thing: Don't push off strongly at each turn. You are not going to be able to push off every twenty-five meters in the Hellespont. Push off as gently as you can.

To liven things up, swim 100 meters in each 20-lap circuit *kicking*, with your arms straight ahead of you, holding on to a float board, and another 100 meters *pulling*, swimming with your ankles tied together.

During the second month, swim the last 500 or 1,000 meters of your daily program straight, with no breaks. And even if you are training in an Olympic pool, do some sustained swimming in an ocean, large river, or lake (if you can) about once a week as well. Swim for a half-hour to an hour with no breaks or push-offs.

This constitutes your basic training for the Héllespont. All the jogging you did for the Matterhorn and the jungle will do you little good here. Jogging has no "carryover value," as the swimming coaches put it, from land sports to water sports. In addition to the above, however, I suggest you develop a program of weight training.

For this, you need access to a weight room—the high school, college, or gym you're swimming at should have one. Go through the program three or four times per week.

For men: do three sets of each exercise with 8 to 12 repetitions (reps) per set. If you cannot do 8 reps with the amount of weight you select per exercise, reduce the amount; if you can do more than 12, increase the amount.

For women: do three sets of each exercise with 25 to 30 reps per set, using a small amount of weight.

Here is the program. Stay with each exercise until all three sets are completed. Be sure you have an instructor in the weight room show you how to do each one (see pictures, pages 141-150).

1. Bench press
2. Upright rowing
3. Leg press
4. Lower lat pull
5. Arm depressors
6. Arm dips (3 sets of 10 for men, 5 for women)
7. Arm curls
8. Front leg extension
9. Sit ups (work up to 100 reps)
10. Pulleys (100 reps, 35 pounds for men, 10 pounds for women)

If you adhere to this program, and the interval swimming program, for two months, I *guarantee* that you will be physically fit for the Hellespont.

1. Bench Press

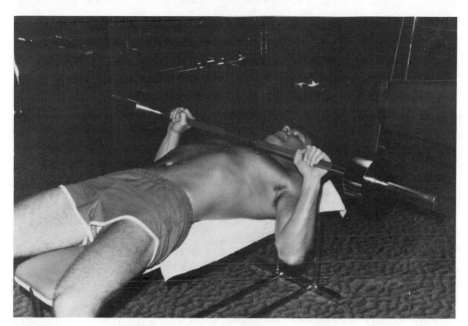

a. begin

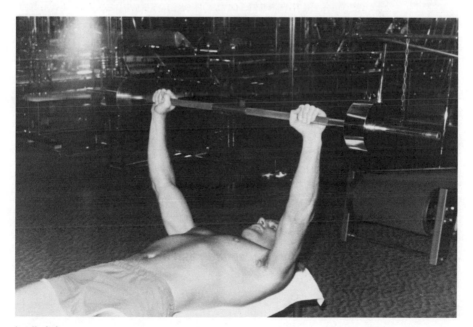

b. finish

2. Upright Rowing

a. begin

b. finish

3. Leg Press

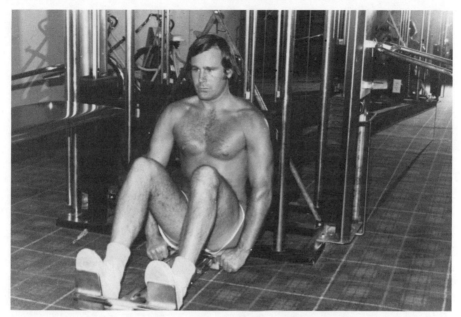

a. begin

b. finish

4. Lower Lat Pull; keep legs straight!

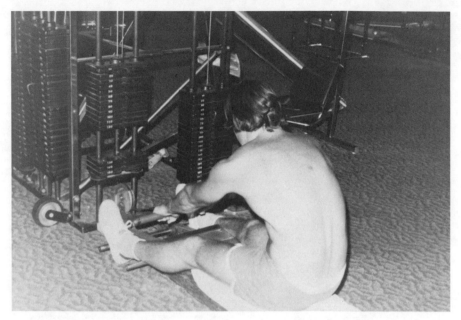

a. begin

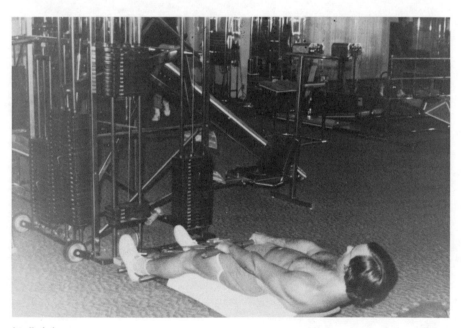

b. finish

5. Arm Depressors

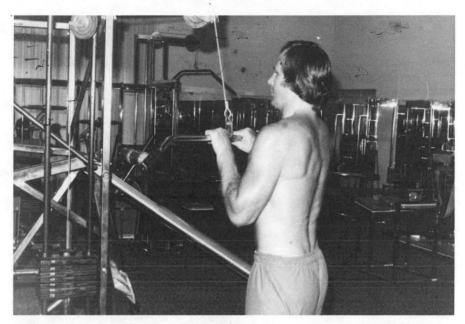

a. begin

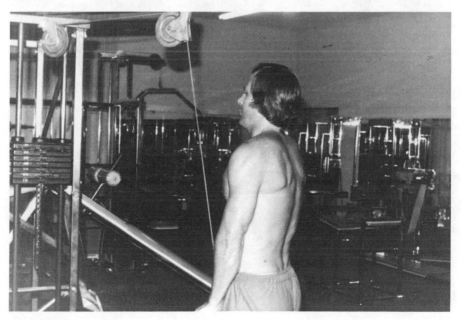

b. finish

6. Arm Dips

a. begin

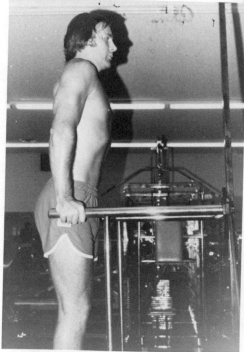

b. finish

7. Arm curls

a. begin

b. finish

8. Front Leg Extension

a. begin

b. finish

9. Sit Ups; always bend your knees.

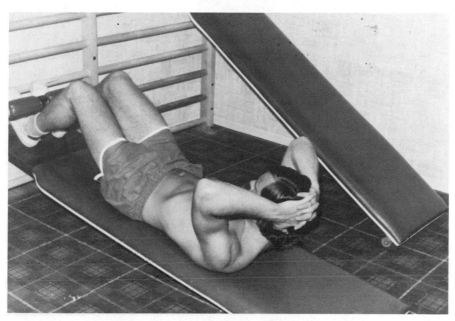

a. begin

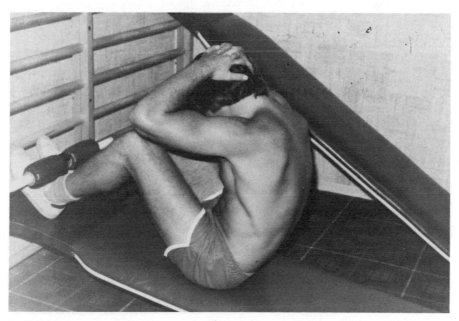

b. finish

a. begin

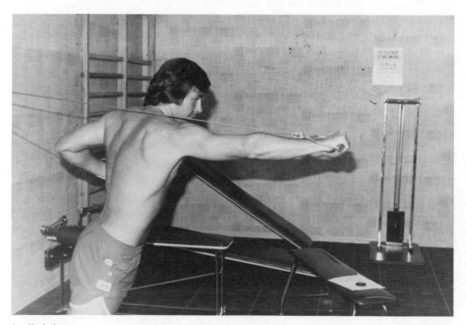

b. finish

But being mentally fit is just as important, as I'm sure you know by now. Going through the programs above will give you the knowledge and self-confidence that you can swim the Hellespont. When you slip into the waters of Leander you will have no doubts as to your ability.

There will be no danger as Hüseyin and his men will be watching over you. What you need now is strategy. And that turns out to be very much like the Matterhorn: Forget about the other side.

This is extraordinarily important. Just take it 100 strokes at a time. Concentrate on finishing the next 100 strokes, and nothing else. Hüseyin will make sure you don't stray off course. You'll wind up on a beach at Sestos, not rocks at night; you won't go deaf: you'll be swimming in warmer waters, so you need only think of the next 100 strokes.

Monotony and boredom can be exhausting. There is nothing to look at or concentrate on when swimming, as there is on a mountain, to help you forget about the end. Therefore, it is crucial that you: (1) remember that the entire swim will only take you two to two and a half hours or so,* (2) completely forget about reaching Sestos, and (3) concentrate entirely upon swimming the next 100 strokes.

Try not to rest by switching to another, easier stroke than the overhead crawl. But, if you want, every 1,000 strokes, turn over on your back and swim 100 easy strokes with an inverted breast stroke, coupled with a frog-kick. Don't goof-off, though. After 100, turn back over and get into the crawl again—and wait at least another 1,000 strokes before doing it once more.

A long-distance swimming friend of mine says he makes up musical rhythyms while swimming and strokes to the beat—says he can swim for hours that way. Try it: You might just like it.

Some other strategy tips. Once you arrive in Canakkale, relax for at least two days. Lie around in the sun, practice-swim a little bit, perhaps visit Troy (but no extended trips, such as to Pergamum; save that for after). Have Hüseyin take you to Yali. Feel fully relaxed and refreshed before your swim. And get a good night's sleep!!

Stay away from things like uppers, of course, but take plenty of vitamins. Preferably you should be neither constipated nor have the runs (remember the bananas, the entero-vioform and lomotil?). You should be wearing racing trunks—tight-fitting, no baggies (the naked-as-Leander bit is reserved for nighttime). Wear a pair of eye-cup swimming goggles to protect your eyes. Using fins, though, is cheating, and if you're going to swim the Hellespont, you might as well do it legitimately.

*The straits between Abydos and Sestos are about two miles wide. But because of the currents, you must swim in an arc, upstream for the first half, covering about four miles.

I have a good friend, a Homeric scholar, who swam the Helles-pont while on a pilgrimage to Troy. But he did so making numerous pit stops at the small boat following him, taking short respites at the side with another refueling of *ouzo*, the local Turkish firewater, each time. Now this is one way to do it, a fun way, and that's great. But it wasn't Leander's or Lord Byron's. I trust it won't be yours.

Your hair should be cut as short as possible—aesthetically pos-sible for you, that is. This may make you edgy, but body hair does create a drag in the water, and it will grow back. Champion swim-mers shave all their hair off (some men shave their legs, and their heads bald), but you needn't go to these extremes. If you have long hair and can't part with it, wear a cap. And if you guys with shoulder-length hair complain that wearing a cap makes you look like a girl, well. . . .

In the summer the water will be much warmer than in November, so you won't be going delirious because of the cold. But the waters of the Black Sea racing through the Hellespont are never warm enough to take a bath in. The best time is August and early Sep-tember. The water temperatures should be in the middle to high sixties. If you think that is still a mite chilly, then, like Persantin for the Matterhorn, I have a little something for you.

It is called *Cold Guard*. It is an insulating cream developed for scuba divers, and it beats Vaseline flat. It is not greasy, will wash off with soap and warm water, is perfectly safe, and is really quite effective. By rubbing a healthy amount all over your body, you will insulate yourself against the cold water. Divers swear by it and I highly recommend it. Please be sure you put it on before your skin is wet. Get the large size, eight ounces, for $3. It is made by Scubapro, and any dive shop or sporting goods store can get it for you.

Another benefit with the insulation of Cold Guard: There is very little chance you will get a cramp using it. You know what to do with one: Don't panic, knead it like dough, moving it upwards, towards your heart. But with Cold Guard, warmer water, and your being in shape, have no worries about cramps.

One final suggestion: Read Homer. It should provide you with an overflow of inspiration. Besides, it is the finest epic literature of Western Civilization.

Well, you are now set to swim the Hellespont. One life. That is *all you have*. Isn't your life *worth* having the adventure and heroic victory of swimming the Hellespont?

I think it is—*The Adventurer's Guide* was written because of that conviction.

152

Hellespont Particulars

Below is a letter from a man whom I am proud to say is a dear friend. It includes details and prices for your swimming the Hellespont.

All you need to do is: (1) Write Hüseyin, telling him when you want to come, and (2) upon confirmation from him, show up at Istanbul on the pre-arranged day, with your trunks, vitamins, lomotil, Cold Guard, et al., and copy of the *Iliad*, and Hüseyin will take care of the rest.

As you know, the *AG* is not a travel guidebook, so I strongly suggest you get a good one on Turkey—I recommend Fodor's, published by David McKay—as there are an amazing number of fascinating places throughout the country. See them *after* your swim, however, not before: Don't let your two months of training go to pot.

You can easily catch a bus (Turkey has an excellent bus system all through the country, using modern, air-conditioned coaches) from Canakkale to Izmir (the ancient Smyrna) and thence to Pamukkale and Goreme, two of the most extraordinary natural wonders in the world. If you want to climb Mt. Ararat,* the legendary landing-place of Noah's Ark, you must make your way to the Turkish Iranian border. You can hire guides at the village of Dogubayazit. But be careful: You stand an excellent chance of being attacked and robbed by the Kurdish villagers living on Ararat's slopes. Climbing with a group of four or more, and dispensing some medicines to the villagers (such as antibiotics for their chronic bronchial ailments), will help to minimize the danger.

Climbing Mt. Olympus is, thankfully, another matter entirely. At less than 10,000 feet, it is easy, safe, and fun. Take a bus (after crossing over the Hellespont on the ferry to Eceabat) to the Greek Turkish border in Thrace, and on to Salonika (you might want to make a side *hadj* to the birthplace of Aristotle at Stagira), then down the east coast of Greece to the village of Litokoron. There, you can get someone, for 200 drachmas, to drive you up into the foothills to the road's end, and two hours' hike from there will bring you to the rest hut, a good meal, and a nice night's sleep in a real bed. Charging off at dawn, clad only in shorts, sweater, and lightweight climbing

*At 16,945 feet. Best time to climb is August, coinciding with your swim.

153

boots, you'll be up on Zeus' Throne by 9 or 10 in the morning, back off the mountain and on your way by late afternoon. A few hours' drive away is Meteora, a valley where ancient monasteries perch dramatically on top of weird rock pinnacles. And be sure to make your way down to Mycenae, in the Peloponnesus, south of Athens, where Agamemnon once ruled the bronze-clad Achaeans, conquerors of well-walled Troy.

In reading Hüseyin's letter, you can see how he has worked out a fairly complete program for you. Any questions you have, on costs or whatever, please write to him directly. And when you read his letter, just ask yourself how wel l you speak and write Turkish!

CANAKKALE
Phone; 1200 - 1449
Cable; TROYANZAC
Canakkale

My Dear Jack:

Here are detailed answers according to the lines of your letter.

a-As you say upon receiving a letter or call from your readers expressing a desire to swim the Hellespont, you may have confidence in me that, I can handle every single detail to insure their effort-With our best possibilities -, It is also possible to arrange side-trips after swim Hellespont. As Troy and Pergamum, world famed ancient sites.

b-As you will state the list all costs in your book, here are the services for one of your readers arriving by air to Istanbul, Yeşilköy airport.

Our interpreter-guide will meet the clients at the airport and after a while rest on the coast of Bosphorus they will be proceeding by a private car or a pullmann coach to Canakkale which takes 5 Hrs. Overnight at Canakkale at the Hotel Troy or Tusan first class, overlooking Hellespont.

Swimming Hellespont, as you noted in your letter our team is not only experienced but also selected on a basis of their personality and manner of behaving to your clients. Be sure that, they will be warm welcomed to Hellespont and we shall do our best for them. As you have confidence in me, all arrangements no doubt will be successful. After 16 years experiences on this business I know what is necessary in order to have pleased our clients.

The price list for swimming the Hellespont.

Persons—by private car—	1	2	3	4
$	175	125	100	75

Persons—by pullman coach—	15-20	21-35
$	60	50

Prices fixed above are based upon your idea as close as humanly.

154

These prices include:

Meeting the parties at Yeşilköy airport in Istanbul with interpreter-guide.

Transportation from Istanbul to Canakkale by a private car
or by a pullmann coach.

Hotel accommodation at Canakkale, Hotel Troy or Hotel
Tusan first class.

Motor-boat, will be at disposal during the swim Hellespont.

Escorts, chosen among the best swimmers- 3 or 5 -

Turkish Bath, will be engaged for the clients as privately.

Services of guide for the whole trip from and to Istanbul
Yeşilköy airport.

Equipments, will be supplied.

Special police protection.

Meals and drinks during the whole trip swim Hellespont.

Transportation from Canakkale to Istanbul by a private car
or a pullmann coach and to see off the party from
Yeşilköy airport.

In the re-creation of your swim, I have researched my old files
and 12 years later, I have collected some information as follows.

On that memorable night your taxi came to Canakkale from
Bandirma at 11.45 p.m.

About half an hour later motor boat TURKER came alongside to Abydos on the Asiatic side.

At 12.15 you leaped over the black water of Hellespont.

Captain of TURKER was NECATI

Your escorts were VEDAT, HASAN, ISMET, CELAL.

At 1 o'clock your right leg was cramped.

At 1.45 AM. you have been taken on board by escorts far
from 200 feet European coast as the motor boat would
break up on the jagged rocks.

You came yourself at Turkish Bath 2.45 A.M. The name of
Turkish Bath is YALI HAMAMI.

You slept only three hours at Hotel DOGAN PALAS in
Canakkale

You left Canakkale shortly after dawn by your chartered
plane for Istanbul.

This memorable night is arranged by our Agency and I am
HUSEYIN ULUASLAN "pronounced as king of Jordan" still acting
as Manager of Agency.

Side-Trips are recommended -after swim Hellespont- TROY:
32 Kms. far from Hellespont "Leander's Passage," the land of
Homer's Heroes, The subject of the world's first and greatest War
novel ILIAD. The biggest war-trick-Wooden Horse of TROY- and the
site where king Priamos Treasures found. Troy is one of the most
glamorous of all the ancient places that that men still remember. It
was poetic genius of Homer that immortalized the legendary city.

155

PERGAMUM: "Where Satan dwelled" said the Bible -Revelation 2:13. of Pergamum, where Rome's priests martyred Christians. Yet Christianity took root and bloomed, making Pergamum the site one of the original Seven Churches. The city's alliance with Rome won it riches to splurge on a marble acropolis, whose beauty rivaled Athens' -240 Kms far from Hellespont-

These two side-trips takes one day, after leaving Canakkale in the morning visiting the ruins of famous Troy and lunch at a summer resort AKCAY sea-front restaurant. Afternoon visit Pergamum, dinner also in another summer resort DIKILI sea-front restaurant. Arriving hotel at night.

The price list of side-trips "Both Troy and Pergamum"

Persons "by private car" $	1	2	3	4
	125	100	75	50

Persons "by a pullman coach" $			15-20	21-35
			40	35

Above prices includes, transportation, services of guide, hotel accommodation, meals, entrance fees.

I think, I have given you necessary information in connection with your letter, but if I had missed and forgotten anything ask me, then in a short time I'll write you.

"This is your life" it was very interesting programm. I'll never forget it. Because in this programm also my life dream came true. As my life dream was to cross Atlantic Ocean by a Transatlantic. Then it became true.

Now many years later, my second dream is about to be realized to make collaboration on Tourism Business with a close friend in United States.

Yes, I am waiting your book and your readers desire to swim Hellespont.

With great affection

HUSEYIN ULUASLAN

156

Books

1. *On Swimming*, by Forbes Carlile.
2. *The Science of Swimming*, by James E. Counsilman. This and the Carlile work above are the best texts extant on competitive and long-distance swimming.
3. *Bullfinch's Mythology.*
4. *Fodor's Guide to Turkey*.
5. Homer's *Iliad*. I recommend the translation by Richmond Lattimore.
6. *The Gold of Troy*, by Robert Payne. A thoroughly engrossing biography of Heinrich Schliemann.
7. *Troy and the Trojans*, by Carl W. Blegen. A scholarly history of Troy from Schliemann to the present, by the leader of the famous University of Cincinnati excavations.
8. *A History of Greece to 322 B.C.,* by N.G.L. Hammond. The best history extant, written by the editor of *The Cambridge Ancient History* (Third edition).
9. *Paideia: The Ideals of Greek Culture*, by Werner Jaeger. The *magnum opus* of the twentieth century's greatest classicist. See in particular the following chapters of Volume One: "Nobility and Arete"; "Culture and Education of the Homeric Nobility"; "Homer the Educator"; and "Ionian and Aeolian Poetry."

4
HUNTING
A MAN-EATING
TIGER

North of Singapore, south of Hong Kong, east of Siam, and west of the Philippines lies a womb-shaped jungle that daily gives birth to world headlines, murder, political tyranny, and sheer terror.

It is Viet Nam in Indo China, and it became two countries, the Communist North and the Republican South, when, in 1954, Russia and England laid down a geographical ruler over the wounded and dead bodies of a quarter of a million Frenchmen who had tried and failed to keep it whole.

I had come to Indo China as a hunter of tigers and leopards and rogue elephants, animals that yearly take a terrible toll among the primitive Montagnards living in the central highlands of South Viet Nam.

It was growing darker by the minute and the monsoon drippings were increasing by the second. It was 4:30 in the afternoon, the 26th day of August, 1961. I was seventeen years old plus nine months, and quite possibly the only American within a thousand miles that distant day, years ago, in the deep reaches of that almost impenetrable maze of Central Highland jungles.

To my left stood a tall Vietnamese, the legendary Ngo Van Chi.

To my right, a short, burnt-orange naked figure, wearing but a black strip of hand-woven material about his waist, with a single strand disappearing downwards beneath his thighs.

My *Chao Ong* had been wasted upon him but breaths before, for he was a Montagnard, a crossbow-bearing primitive, whose lands I had now entered, at his request. Vietnamese he did not speak, but his pointing finger spoke for him.

Look at the setting with me, as but minutes before we had burst out of the jungle into a fair-sized clearing. There had been a scattering of houses, sitting like pregnant storks upon spindly legs, five feet or so above the wet, sucking mud. Of bamboo and thatch, they had, at the sudden moment of our appearance, become the target of scurrying, naked figures, running to the ladders or notched logs that led upwards to their elevated rooms.

One man, the Chief, advanced to meet us.

Now, please study, even more closely, the physical layout. Behind us, and to our right, the cluster of huts on stilts. In front of us, extending some three hundred yards, both to the left and the right, cleared fields, hacked and burned from the jungle. Concentrate if you will upon the vista to our port. Almost smack in its middle, there is a strip of matted, interlocked, demented jungle growth, extending for a distance of, say, a half a mile. Beyond it (for it appears to be several hundred yards deep), there appears again cleared land. A rotted Devil's Garden that even thousands of years of primitive cultivation could not conquer.

And what of the pointing figure? Directed straight towards that flourishing ribbon of green hell: What message was his finger delivering to me?

It was in there—it was as simple as that. Thoughts, like passed batons in a relay race, shot through my brain.

"Okay, son, you're bucking the odds. You're the Christian in the Arena; the Bull at the Moment of Truth. Inside that quarter-mile-deep corridor of instant screams waits for you the most deadly animal on earth—a wounded leopard, fear-crazed and pain-wracked. He has, in his frenzy and desperation, darted out of his last retreat three times in the past twenty-six hours to seize a child, a young mother, and a youth just turned warrior, to smother their cries with efficient tearings and rippings." Bad scene, but suddenly the quiet, accented voice of Chi. . . .

"Jacques, it is expected of us. We have answered their call. Our course is clear. It grows dark; the rain, she is falling more heavily; it must be done now. He must not be allowed to escape, to attack another villager. We will enter, and look. I remind you: A leopard climbs trees, he crouches upon a limb above the trail, he looks down, and if your eyes meet his, he leaps, as of an instant, upon you. To me, it is a sad thing to inform you that no creature on earth is as bad as a wounded leopard in great pain and hatred for all about him. A tiger at least waits for you upon the ground. Alright, friend Jacques, it is time to find out, are you Number ONE or Number TEN?" And he motioned for me to step across the clearing towards that rapidly darkening labyrinth in whose clotted depths awaited a man-, child-, woman-killing, wounded leopard.

I have no recollection of any movement forward whatsoever, but advance I did, for the wet earth was moving beneath me, and I do remember vividly my saying to myself, "That poor bastard lost his left paw in a Montagnard trap seventy-two hours ago. He chewed most of it off, he did, to get his leg free. He's made three kills that we know of, and now he's in there. Waiting. For his enemy. His next victim. Me."

Furrowed brow was bending contact lenses, teeth were grating at C above high C, and sweat was out-flowing the drenching rain. But like the feeling for Dr. Fell, one thing I knew and knew full well: Once I stepped into that blackening, steaming trap across the clearing, force of habit and self-training the hard way would command concentration to the exclusion of everything else on earth save the job at hand—Viet Cong, man-killers, and seeping guts notwithstanding.

Side by side, but with Chi as point by a full foot, we were at once engulfed by greenness, blackness, and wetness. The hissing of the massive monsoon discharges splattered upon our bodies, even the air to breathe had disappeared, and in its place were iron-heavy smells that you tasted and swallowed. Rotted vegetation embraced our legs to the knees, vines with life battled with the licking, holding mud for possession of our boots and gaiters, while plants and trees and bamboo shoots and all manner of moving things whipped our faces and distorted our vision. But of most concern to me was the absence of space above us; the limbs and branches were entwined, that was to be expected, but so low! A hundred, strike that, a thousand leopards could be crouching up there throughout our stalking route and their leap upon us would take but a fraction of a second. How in anybody's name could we spot him first? For the greens, and especially the yellows and browns above, all enmeshed, gave him the distinct camouflaged advantage. And the quickly gathering darkness lengthened the odds in his favor. Oh, we could still see alright, but it was now a matter of shadows and murky movements. To be quiet was to live, but fallen tree trunks and vines as big around as the clenched fists of Atlas tripped and flung me. And the staring, the constant straining of the eyes—this way, that way, up, down, sideways, never stopping. . . .

We were through. We were standing in deep mud, but the rain was hitting us cleanly and directly, the reaching spaces about us were clear, and I looked straight up at the scudding black clouds with wet barbs striking my eyeballs, and smiled. But for about two seconds, then Chi was off, making a circling motion with his hand, and I got the message: We would circle the egg-shaped strip to the other side. My sweat dried quickly, if not my clothes, for it was getting cool indeed—say, that's right, I haven't told you that the weather in Saigon, and the Mekong Delta, is as different in the Central Highlands, especially Dalat, as milk and booze. It's blankets at night in one, and implanted heat and humidity in the other.

We turned the corner and headed for home base. About fifty yards from our initial penetration, we saw the Chief. He was jumping up and down, and as we forced our way through the now glazing slough towards him, his yells meant nothing but his wildly jerking arms, as they indicated a location beyond our original entrance, assuredly did. As we reached and passed him he took off towards his village, which by now was merely a vague outline, and since I'm always receiving instant impressions, the sounds of his bare feet smacking the mud and then sucking their way upwards sounded much like horrid retchings. Which figured, in my mental and physical state. Retchings.

Reborn by emotion and desire spawned by hope, Chi picked his spot and swerved. I followed, and we entered again into instant entrapment.

The strain is now intense, make no mistake about that. There is a leopard on every branch, behind every log, in every matted clump or bamboo stand, and I am convinced that only the calmness, imperturbability, and *presence* of Ngo Van Chi prevents me from firing at things I see but are not there.

Suddenly, without warning—Chi's hand upon my arm and a nod of his head forward. My heart leaped to my eyes, and I stared with every fibre of my being—and saw nothing, only that wet, moving mess of jungle garbage ahead of me. My head twisted to Chi. He nodded again, straight ahead. I could not see into the great hunter's eyes, his head was in profile, and motionless. I have regretted many times since the lost opportunity to see into his soul at that moment.

Even now, more than a decade later, as you and I live together this adventure, it is difficult to restrain my emotions, much less my meager descriptive powers to adequately describe what I saw at that fateful moment when I turned from Chi and discovered it. It was a physical blow, I mean that, and in a flash, my body, every inch of it, was tingling, vibrating. There was no leopard; no body, no head, no form. Only an eye.

A single, enormous *eye*, glowing, I swear, with greenish-yellow brilliance. But the extraordinary discovery-factor was a blink! Countless times I have relived that fractional second and each time the conclusion is incontestable: My eyes had passed the beam of yellow light and stopped, arrested by the flicking of its shutter. The release was slow, totally unrelated to a human twitch, and then the shining held, suspended several inches above a fallen, black, rotting tree trunk. There was no outline of a head, only that luminous, single eye.

A whispered word, hardly audible in the sound-filled rain forest, came from the tall, shadowy figure to my left.

"Shoot!"

I slowly raised my rifle, and at that instant—two eyes! He had turned his head slightly and, with the movement, had also disclosed the darker outline of the uppermost hump of his back as he crouched behind the log.

A sibilant, "He's waiting for us to get three steps closer, then he jumps. Shoot!" from the darkness to my left.

A silent movement, a raising, an aiming, a squeezing.

A tremendous roar in the close, confined jungle area pressing in and around us, a single, small blue-white cloud in the rain and gloom, and the eyes vanished.

Ten, perhaps twelve, careful strides through the clutching vines and mud, and we were at the place of the eye; there he lay, the village raider, the eater of human flesh because he could no longer hunt his natural, but harder to obtain, prey, with his grievous injury—killed instantly.

Ngo Van Chi dropped to his knees deep in the jungle bottom and, raising the leopard's head with his hands, carefully held it and stared into its still open yellow eyes. Thirty seconds passed, and more, until:

"I have been a hunter and guide in the jungles of all Asia for thirty-five years. In all this lifetime, I have seen but three such animals."

It was a Cloudy Leopard, rarest big-game cat in the world. His suffering was over—and so was death by his fangs and claws in the Montagnard village.

With this realization, and with the strange discovery at the end, we silently shook hands.

There are few rewards in this life as good and as sincere as when one is fortunate enough to do a service for a people whose very existence is at stake. Especially it is enhanced, this simple feeling, when the humans involved are in no position to help themselves, and when they know, as you know, that neither has anything to gain, except life and the joy of bestowing it, or assisting in its continuance. But then, that's gaining quite a lot, on both sides, isn't it?

There will be deep snow in simmering Saigon before I forget the faces of those primitive Montagnards as they carried the leopard out of the jungle and, in an ever-increasing procession, followed us to our jeep close by the village. As we drove away into the now complete darkness, with the farewells of the Montagnards following us, Chi said to me, "It has been a good day and a good hunt. The story will go far beyond this village. For your country and mine, I say again, this is a good thing that has happened today."

Back at base camp—another Montagnard village several miles away—before cleaning up, we skinned the leopard; that is, Chi and Khim and Brum did—I took a lesson. As I write these words, I am looking into the eyes of that very same Cloudy Leopard. My good friends, the Pendl brothers, taxidermists extraordinaire, when mounting the beautiful killer, cleverly concealed the missing foot by placing it behind a log. So you see, he never did die, but lives—with me.

"Ask him what animal is the most dangerous to his people." Binh, my interpreter, cocked his head in concentrating on the Chief's answer, and no wonder, for from tribe to tribe—there are over thirty—the dialects vary to a marked degree. Finally, "He speaks of several; each different, cannot say one. The elephant destroy many houses and much crop, like rice, corn, and manioc. He say all his people ask spirits please help to bring elephant meat to village. He says that wounded leopard like you shoot is very, very bad, also. Gaur he hates. He speaks of many times he see gaur charge elephant, sometimes whole herd. Elephant run. Montagnards run too, he say, if not, die. But he and his people are afraid the most of *Ong Bang Mui*: Lord Tiger."

The three of us were sitting in a most unlikely setting: under the Chief's house. The stilts about us supported the structure, and this area is normally used for storage, or children playing out of the heat and rain or gaining some degree of protection from tigers, snakes, or whatever. We were eating some sort of tapioca pudding made from manioc, just like the Shuara's *yucca*, so many thousands of miles away, and shoveling it into our mouths with hard-baked pieces of bread (also made from manioc). Between gulps, "I don't want to be out of line with this question, Binh, but can you ask him, if it's okay with you, what he and his people think of the Vietnamese, both South and North." Binh is a Vietnamese himself, a friend of Chi's who had come up for a few days from Saigon to visit him and enjoy the resort of Dalat, three hours' drive from here. He looked at me with a marble-sized smile and said, "Jacques, I tell you now his answer, and to make clear I use American. He will say—and watch his face when ask question—they stink!"

Binh waited till the headman had the tobacco in his pipe going well. (They grow their own and even the women are forever lighting up. I cannot report on the quality of the tobacco for I was then, and am now, a nonsmoker, as is Chi himself, and since I cannot smell anything, as you know full well by now, its fragrance, or lack of it, is lost upon me; but I have seen a family of bird-carrying mosquitos fly into its smoke—and nose-dive onto the deck in one second flat. I have decided against importing it into the States in order to make a quick bundle.)

I studied the Chief as Binh, his glee in putting the question scarcely concealed, leaned forward in a near-toppling position. If you have ever seen an Hawaiian beachboy sitting on the sands of Waikiki, then you're looking at another one with me at this particular moment. (These people must have traveled by outrigger to this vast jungle. I reminded myself not to call him "bruddah.")

It came. The reaction. And Binh had called the shot. The smooth, tanned-colored, not-yet-old face froze, still as death. The rather round head remained at twelve o'clock high, but the brown eyes swiveled to meet mine. There was a series of grunted words, two of which were spat. I was later to learn that they translated as *acay* and *nxeng* ("child" and "fat-grease"). What the Chief had said in launching his diatribe was, "This child has a head filled with fat-grease." Why? Directed to sweet, innocent me? Simply that friend Binh had put on display the rather unique Vietnamese sense of humor. In asking the loaded question, he had put it in terms of a statement of mine to the effect that I had said that the Montagnards had great affection for the Vietnamese. And quite naturally, the house fell on top of me, stilts or no stilts.

The Chief's attitude was not that difficult to understand. Most

164

Vietnamese—I was going to start the next phrase with "including," but I think I should change it to: especially the educated or sophisticated Vietnamese that you will meet—fall generally into the category of children. Now this is important for Americans to know, for should the yoke of Communist imperialism ever be thrown off, South Vietnam is going to be the tourist's dream, and rightly so. For hunters, an absolute paradise.

Quick to take offense; an obsessive desire never to lose face; excitable to the nth degree; creatures of self-serving pleasure; susceptible to any bribe, gift, or token, in return for favors; sybaritic to the end of time; sycophants of the first order, bar none; masters of the set-up; bearers of smiles that mean absolutely nothing; values of an oversexed rabbit; and, while it serves their self-rewarding purposes, the most charming, convivial, interesting, delightful, and boon companions that you could ever imagine acquiring. In short, for your purposes, either as a hunter or a tourist, you will have an extraordinarily good time—except for taxi drivers, waiters, and policemen, among others.

Many of these character traits are strictly Oriental in nature, not limited to the South Vietnamese, and I have always found myself somewhat in sympathy with their psychological and pathological make-up, for they do have an excuse for the weight of the chip on their shoulders. A thousand years under the Chinese, a hundred years under the French, domination for a decade and more by the American, and now the full horror of Communism: These things do add up to a self-defensive mechanism. And yet, under all this, they have maintained to an admirable degree their own dress, language, customs, and mores.

"Chief says he not like or trust Vietnamese. South better than North, for VC very bad. Come village, take everything. Say to my people, you not help South; if do, return and kill everybody. This thing they have done many times." I nodded, and then said, "I understand, but ask him why he does not like South Vietnamese. After all, they are all citizens of this country." The reply was long but it boiled down to this: Vietnamese are "foreigners," meaning that any one not a tribesman is a foreigner. That their only real dealings with the "foreigners" stem from tradesmen and soldiers. The former cheat them, and the latter sometimes act just like VC. "We want just let alone. No one make fun at our spirits [gods], steal cooking pots and wine jars and crossbows from graves of tribesmen. The French Number Ten—he very, very bad."

"Are there any Vietnamese that he likes?" I asked. No waiting for this reply. "Chi—he very good man, brave man, always keep promise. Always give meat to Co Ho, and not cheat Co Ho trackers and scouts. He also learn Co Ho tongue, and like us. Lord Tiger very afraid him. He save many tribesmen and villages by shooting Lord Tiger as many times as trees in forest. He good man." I can think of no better epitaph for any man on earth.

Through Binh I told the Chief of Chi and I attending a party given by the mayor of Dalat in honor of our taking care of the wounded leopard. I told him that the mayor and his wife, both of whom I liked very much, had some very kind and good things to say about the Co Hos. Upon hearing this, the Chief actually smiled and clapped his hands. It startled me—it was so unexpected. I also told him of the several tiger skins I saw on the walls of the mayor's home. "Mighty hunter," I thought of the good mayor, until Chi informed me that they were all from the Dalat zoo! We all had a good laugh, and the Chief called for someone to bring us a jar of rice wine.

At this point we were joined by Chi's top two trackers, Khim and Brum. They were both Montagnards, and of our tribe, the Co Ho. Khim has killed thirty elephants with his crossbow and poison-tipped arrows. Brum has killed an even dozen with—are you ready?—a spear.

Brum's method is to float down a stream on a tiny, makeshift raft to where an elephant is bathing. Maneuvering the raft right underneath the elephant's left shoulder, he then rams a poison-tipped spear through the beast's armpit and into his heart. The elephant is not able to extricate itself quickly as its feet are stuck in the deep mud of midstream, thus giving Brum time to dive off the raft, swim like mad for the bank, and escape until the poison does its work.

I learned much of the Montagnard that afternoon simply by asking questions. For example, why do the tribesmen call the tiger "Lord"? Out of fear and admiration, I was told, and furthermore, I was made aware that in their animistic religion, the tiger and the elephant are divinities, and rank just below the major gods such as Bok-Hoi-Doi, the Creator.

Bok-Hoi-Doi, I learned, lives far, far beyond the clouds, at an unreachable distance in the sky. He created all things, the sun, the moon, the stars, and man and woman. He is the master of the universe, and governs all the gods, major and minor. He is pictured in the minds of all Montagnards as a patriarch with flowing white hair, just like a wise old Montagnard sage.

166

A slit-gong (traditional log drum) in a Namba village on the island of Malekula, New Hebrides

Another scene from Bunlap

*Canakkale,
Turkey, on the
Hellespont*

*The Hellespont,
looking across to
the European
shore, above
Canakkale*

*Abydos Point on
the Asian side,
where the swim
begins*

*Author near
Abydos Point,
about to enter the
water (1973)*

*Author swimming
the Hellespont*

*End of successful
1973 swim, at
European side
near Sestos*

Huseyin Uluaslani, a messenger from Allah

Street scene in Canakkale

*Yali Hamami
Turkish Bath in
Canakkale*

*Sunset on the
Hellespont at
Canakkale*

Pamukkale, Turkey: the "Cotton Castle"

The ceiling of an old mosque in Konya, Turkey

Seljuk fortress overlooking Dogubayazit, at the base of Mount Ararat, Turkey

Mount Ararat, legendary landing place of Noah's Ark

Left: *Mount Olympus*

Right: *Closeup of Mount Olympus taken near the top*

The Acropolis of Athens in late afternoon sunlight

A monastery at Meteora, Greece

The Lion Gate at
Mycenae, city of
Agamemnon, in
the Peloponnisos,
Greece

The "wine dark
sea" of Homer, in
the Greek Isles

*Author with the
"Man Killer of
Dalat"*

*Author, Chi, and
Montagnards
transporting the
"Man Killer of
Dalat"*

Left: *Elephants
at East African
river*

Right: *Giraffe at
Lake Manyara,
Tanzania, Africa*

Left: *Bambuti Pygmy boy, Ituri Forest, Congo (Zaire)*

Right: *Two Bambuti Pygmies, with the hard and brutal life of the primitive written on their faces*

Author with Bambuti Pygmies in the Ituri Forest

The Great Mystery of Africa: the ruins of Zimbabwe, in Rhodesia, South Africa

Sunset on the Zambezi River

*The Well of Job,
Bukhara, Uzbe-
kisten, Russian
Central Asia*

*The ruins of the
mosque of
Bib-i-Khanonm,
mistress of Tamer-
lane, Samarkand,
Uzbekistan, Rus-
sian Central Asia*

Two views of the "Treasury," carved 140 feet high into the cliffs at the "Rose Red City" of Petra, built by the Nabtaeans 2000 years ago in southern Jordan

The 175-foot-high Great Buddha, carved into the side of a mountain 1400 years ago at Bamyan Valley, Afghanistan

The entrance gate
to the famous
ancient University
at Timbuktu

Left: *Rivermen
poling into an
approaching sand-
storm, Niger River,
Sahara Desert*

Right: *Bora Bora
seen through reef
islets of Tahaa,
French Polynesia*

*View of the lagoon
of Huahine,
French Polynesia*

*Sunset behind
Bora Bora*

Sunset in Tahiti

There are lesser gods who do the bidding of the Creator, such as the God of Thunder, the God of the Rice Fields, the Water God, and the God of the Mountains.

One step down are the Lords—Lord Tiger, Lord Elephant. The Montagnard believes that *Ong Bang Mui*, Lord Tiger, is able to imitate the calls of all other animals and human speech.

Lord Elephant is a mighty ally when he chooses, and this is why so many are captured when young and trained to carry the Montagnard into battle against man and animal.

Fear governs every single act of the Montagnard, and the signs and omens that come in dreams from the gods are all-important. Rites, rituals, and taboos are legion. It is a spirit world in which they live, and, again, every tribe has its religious deviations from the other.

Chickens, pigs, and dogs have joined the meeting at various times and domesticated water buffalo have sniffed us out. With all this for the tribal larder, why not meat on the table more often, I reflected. I gained the answer in a private chat with Binh the next day or so, for I had a hunch that such a question wouldn't do in an open meeting. I was right. Sacrificial rites and taboos and customs prohibit the normal sitting down to roast pig or fried chicken. That is why elephant meat, and gaur steaks, and roasted banteng liver, along with every other part of these animals, is eagerly sought and properly appreciated.

The Montagnard.* The aborigines of Indo China. The tribe I was staying with, the one that occupies the region of Dalat, is called the Co Ho. Scattered throughout the Central Highlands there are thirty-two other tribes, each distinct and separate, each speaking a different language (with a limited amount of common understanding), each differing in religion, customs, and mores, each having a different name, but all living in the remote and mountainous areas composed of dense jungle and deep rain forests that completely dominate their environment, where they have remained aloof from civilization for centuries.

Neither in appearance, language, religion, nor culture do the Montagnards have a single thing in common with the Vietnamese (of both North and South, for they are culturally distinct as well:

---

*Pronounced *Mon-tahn-yard:* French for "mountain people." The Vietnamese name for the Montagnard is *Nguoi thuong* (pronounced *Newy tung*), meaning Highland Citizen. Those that are ignorant or disrespectful call them *Moi*, which means "savage" in French.

167

Annamese in the South, Tonkinese in the North—although several million Tonkinese live now in the South, having fled the North's tyranny, albeit now to no avail).

In appearance the Montagnard resembles the Filipino, the native of the Philippines. There is a dash of South Sea Islander and a spot of Indonesian. This makes sense, because the Montagnard is not an Oriental at all—his racial stock is Malayo-Polynesian. His ancestors, originating from what is now southeastern China, filtered down through Indo China forgotten eons ago. While some stayed, others continued to migrate east, populating the islands of Indonesia and sailing their outriggers as far as Tahiti, Easter Island, the Philippines, and Hawaii. A far cry from a sleepy lagoon, with swaying palms, white beaches, and azure, coral-studded water to snarling tigers in a can't-see-twenty-feet-in-front-of-you jungle. This common ancestry explains why the Montagnard's language is closely related to those spoken in the South Seas—and why I thought the Chief looked like a beachboy.

As for clothes—the Vietnamese wears them, the Montagnard does not, at least from the waist up. Maiden Form couldn't give its product away, even with free rice wine.

The Montagnard is a simple, inherently child-like person with a stoic, passive acceptance of life as it is about him, with no desire to change it or challenge the system of nature in which he is immersed. He dislikes the South as well as the North Vietnamese simply because they are not Montagnards and he does not trust them. But his feelings rarely erupt to killing or violence, only a child-like querulousness when rules are invoked that interfere with traditional tribal customs. Above all, the Montagnards are a kind and gentle people. I am sure I was not the first American, nor would I be the last, to develop a very strong, almost fatherly, affection for them.

Suddenly there was a roaring from the nearby jungle and a jeep careened wildly into the village clearing, driven by Chi. He quickly got out and started gliding toward us. Ngo Van Chi, the legend, the greatest hunter Asia has ever known. Destroyer of over 200 tigers, countless elephant, gaur, banteng, and even the rare kouprey, famed for taking on a herd of elephant with but four rounds of ammunition in his rifle. When an entire herd charged him once, he cooly brought down four elephants: a single shot for each.

Tall for a Vietnamese, with a smooth, round, unwrinkled face, his eyes are almond-shaped, and he wears a small, loose smile, with no teeth showing, almost as if it were a badge. It is sincere, for his eyes are alight, and he does have much in life to be happy with: money (he owns a string of movie-theaters throughout Southeast Asia), health, a world-wide reputation as Asia's premier hunter, and a most productive and rewarding love life. He looks like Dr. Fu Manchu, or a Chinese Mandarin. Chi habitually keeps his arms folded across his chest. Not slumped over, mind you, but erect. Ramrod stiff. Even when tracking a spoor through the jungle or across open country, there he glides—and that is the correct word—with arms folded. His gun bearer is always at his heels, for he never carries a weapon until the very second comes when he must shoot—except when he is engaged in extremely dicey work, like a wounded leopard or tiger stalk. An astonishing character. Damn—it is a shame that Hemingway never trekked with Ngo Van Chi. What bonds would have cemented their lives together.

I hoped Chi would be bringing word about our search for the Montagnard's public enemy Number One: the Royal Bengal Tiger. *Ong Bang Mui*—or "Mr. 30," as he is called—is the scourge of the Montagnard's life, for the toll he takes, day in and day out, is ghastly. The French started it all out by never allowing the Montagnards to possess firearms, only crossbows, two-handed blades, and spears. It is not uncommon for a tiger to enter a Montagnard village, run across the clearing scattering the villagers right and left, seize a woman, man, boy, or girl, drag the living, screaming victim into the jungle, and eat it. There is no question of a Montagnard's bravery, for countless times the victim's family has beaten at the tiger with their fists as he was pulling the struggling figure through the village, even the women; the men and boys jabbing at it with their spears, hacking away with their knives, shooting their bolts into it. But the action is so swift, and the efforts, although heroic, so puny, that there is seldom a saving of human life when the man-eater strikes.

Every few years, for some unknown reason, a disease strikes and kills many of the deer in certain parts of the jungle. When this happens, the grisly menace of "Mr. 30" is hugely magnified, for the deer are the tiger's main source of food. This was just such a time in the forests of the Co Ho. Chi and I were after a man-eater of such bloody proportions he was called the Man-Killer of Dalat. His distinctive pug marks had been his signature in the jungle mud upon which he had spilled the blood of over twenty human beings.

In India you hunt a tiger by resting comfortably on a platform thirty feet high in a tree called a *machan*, or riding atop an elephant, with beaters out in front of you doing the dirty, hard work. In Africa, it's chilled dry martinis and washed and pressed bush jackets every evening, and, when stalking your game, you stride along open plains after alighting from your custom Land Rover. But in Viet Nam, it is a little different.

Chi stooped under the Chief's hut, walked in a crouch, and sat down next to us. "The Man-Killer of Dalat, he come to bait. We go mirador tonight. We quiet. Wait for tiger." Sure, no problems, Chi. Just relax in the dripping, sodden jungle with boon companions close beside you, like eighteen-foot King Cobras, regular run-of-the-mill cobras of only four feet or so, leeches, mosquitoes, bamboo vipers, and a few more assorted good fellows. I get along fine in the Amazon, but this is one jungle you can have.

"Tiger come to bait again tonight for sure. We listen. If stay and eat, you shoot. If tear piece out and run, you no shoot. No time aim." If the tiger does stick around, though, I'll have plenty of time to aim—about a second. I must be sighted in on the bait, guessing of course where it is in the dark, and when I flick the flashlight on my rifle barrel, I must correct my aim and fire instantly, for he'll be off in a blur when the light hits him.

"He close to you. No can miss." Close? Thanks a lot, Chi. About fifteen feet, maybe twenty. But we do have protection, don't we? In a mirador (French for a blind) on the ground, not a safe machan up in a tree. Gossamer-like ferns and feather-like brush with touches of *dao* leaves here and there, all put together into a small box with a round hole in front but inches big through which my rifle barrel will extend, along with my sure-to-be-bulging eyeballs.

"No go sleep in mirador, Jacques." Drop off, just like that, eh Chi? With the constant rain slithering down, those double-damned huge red ants crawling all over and through me when I can't move to crush them, not to mention a man-killing Bengal tiger prowling about a few feet away in pitch blackness? Go to sleep? "Think time now cut big boil."

The next thirty-five minutes I prefer to forget but can't. I had developed a gigantic carbuncle in the middle of my back—it was all of three inches in diameter, believe it or not. (Everything grows big in the Indo-Chinese jungle.) Chi had followed its development with undisguised admiration until he told me, "You look like you are pregnant on the back." A very amusing fellow.

Up the ladder to the Chief's house with Chi carrying his first aid kit. I was handed an earthen jar sealed with mud, holding, at the very least, ten gallons of anaesthetic in the form of Montagnard jungle juice made from rice. Now let it here be established that these primitives in the Central Highlands really put the sauce away; they come close to my Shuara in this noteworthy respect. With all of my living with quaffing primitives about the world, it is a wonder that I haven't by this time joined the A.A., for it is more than a simple insult not to match them belt for belt. But ten gallons?

With several of Chi's trackers, and a full circle of the naked villagers about me, I thrust several bamboo straws into my alcohol jar and sucked away. Into the fire went the formidable blade of Chi's hunting knife, then out it came and into me. I can well believe, as I was told afterwards, that my scream was heard in Saigon 180 miles to the south, and, to say the least, scared the living hell out of the closely packed Montagnards about me. My master hunter-surgeon aborted my ersatz pregnancy, patched me up, stood back, and proudly proclaimed, "Now ready for Tiger!"

Disdaining my impassioned appeal for the last rites, Chi had me half-carried through the jungle to the mirador, where for long hours in the evening and night I lay, hardly moving a muscle, much less making a sound (like groans). Fruitlessly, as you will discover, for it took more than one night in our nocturnal stake-out, while in the daytime my attending physician would cut away time after time in post-operative care, thus gaining much practice and growing admiration from the ever-increasing native audience, while to me it simply became a question of who was to die first, the tiger or me.

The next day—dish-toed tracks, a charging monster, and near disaster.

"Nam find tracks to gaur. Nam say great bull. He loner, no cows. Not know why he so close. We go now. Track spoor. Bull, he sleep in middle day. I think find in thick place. Must walk, after take jeep, maybe three, four hours. Find 'fore dark. Must be very bad, this bull. Alone, no cows. You shoot my Magnum." (He was referring to his .378 Weatherby; mine was a .300 Weatherby. So this was heavy-duty time, a 300-grain bullet.)

Chi was obviously puzzled, and that took some doing, but he turned to me and said, "You lucky Nam find."

With these four words, a death warrant was issued to me. All it needed was a signature—that of a cloven hoof. I do not wax melodramatic. In five hours, just at sunset, it was going to be a very close thing.

171

We made quite a stuffed package in the jeep: Chi, Khim, Brum, myself, and, most importantly at the moment, Nam. What with five high-powered rifles, canteens, machetes, oversized hunting knives, etc., I remarked that we looked like a circus act. No response. Nobody knew what a circus was except Chi, and for once he wasn't talking. I got the message very quickly; there was serious business at hand. The great gaur stands seven feet high at the shoulders, weighs 3000 pounds, and has the disposition of Dick Butkus. No wonder elephants run at the sight of him.

For centuries, throughout South East Asia, from Thailand through Cambodia, Vietnam to Burma, the gaur has killed thousands. After goring to death, he will rub, with fanatic determination, his horns against a tree trunk to remove the scent of man. Regardless of the most cleverly planned and executed operations against him by trained hunters of lifelong experience, the gaur will survive year after year, simply by outwitting his enemies. Many die in combating him because they underestimate his speed and fail to throw themselves flat on the ground in the face of his charge. (I was told that the gaur always jumps over a man in the path of his charge if he is lying flat, and, strangely, takes care not to trample him. "You 'member, Jacques. Not forget!") The gaur, times beyond the telling, has circled around behind the hunter who is tracking him, charged and killed him, striking with blinding speed from behind without warning. He will continue his charge even in the face of blazing guns, fired repeatedly, never flinching, never stopping or swerving, until he either overruns his attackers or falls dead. In almost all cases relative to his defeat, multiple extremely high-caliber bullets are required to do the job. He engages in another tactic that no other animal employs. After being shot at, and either hit or missed, he will many times start running away into thick bamboo or brush or over a hill where he cannot be seen. After him race the hunters, but, if they are not wise in his ways, they will suddenly come face to face with him, and he charges. Running till his attackers cannot see him, he suddenly stops, turns around, and waits. They appear, he charges. The great gaur: with his hatred of the human race, his awesome size, his ferocious expression, his cunning, his skill in combat, his uncanny knack of survival—he is the only beast that can panic an elephant into cowardly retreat.

I looked at the four faces bouncing about me; these men had faced disaster hundreds and hundreds of times together throughout the long, deadly years, had saved each other beyond count.

172

How many lives and villages had they saved by the shooting of man-killers and rogues? Over a period of more than a quarter century, the mayor of Dalat stated flatly to me, the figure ran into the thousands. Think of that. I thanked all the gods for the privilege of being one of them. (Chi was to tell me a few years later, at the start of our second expedition, that, "All boys worried you. Never have hunter young as you. They know must do Number One job for me. You too. All time ask Bok-Hoi-Doi help keep you safe. They good boys. We together all life—never fail. Good boys." Primitives and savages, eh? I think not.)

Chi's Weatherby was cradled between my legs. It was a gift from Herb Klein, unquestionably one of the world's finest big-game hunters. It was through Herb Klein that I learned of the man-killing tigers of Viet Nam, and of their great nemesis, Ngo Van Chi.

Over the years we would hunt often, Chi and I, and eventually be in business together, exporting cinnamon from the Central Highlands to spice brokers throughout the world. Then one day Chi would be captured by the Viet Cong. He would never be seen again.

The mountains ahead were much closer now. For hours, since leaving the jeep, we had been following the spoor, through bamboo thickets, across streams, up hills, down hills, clearings left abandoned by the migratory Montagnard (who would return in three or four years to burn and clear again for their crops, for by this time, the earth would be fallow again, revitalized by non-use), deep jungle, thick, ten-foot high grass, past a small rice field —no sign of a village—and by a watering hole. There, by the tracks of the guar's dish-toed hooves, were the imprints of a large tiger, who had braced his front feet deeply in the mud to drink.

It was a time to raise a hand to Bok-Claik, the Montagnard God of Thunder and Lightning, and Yang-Dak, God of Water, for these two had combined forces to hold back the rains of Lang Bain (the plateau we were now on) from falling on my first gaur stalk. A miracle, third class, I reflected, as I made like Groucho, bent low over the spoor, moving forward in crab-like fashion. The lowering sun was in my eyes; for many days and nights it had been the monsoons, and now, stalking almost due west, it was a matter of squinting eyes, glare, and sudden sweat. "He very close now." Nam. Two feet behind me. "I think he in bamboo there. We go in." Behind me, Chi whispered in quick, sudden Co Ho Montagnard. I felt, but could not see, four bodies move very close to me.

173

Without warning, out of the bamboo crashed a gigantic steam-roller—or was it a locomotive?—a massive, charging bulk not thirty feet away. From behind me, "Jump!" Five bodies flung themselves as of one to right and left. I, for one, simply cannot remember which way I leapt. We rolled, we rose, we looked. He was gone; he had not stopped.

On the spoor. Ten minutes, fifteen minutes. Heart pounding, breathing shallow. Vital signs damned near gone. I speak for myself; for Chi and his Varsity, old stuff; no sweat, no strain.

"You look. He through trees there." Nam again. I parted branches, and there he was, staring directly at me. No movement. I raised Chi's .378, released the safety, aimed at his barn-door chest, and fired at the upper hinges. He shuddered, he fell to his knees, and, without a sound, he lunged upwards and, so help me, charged! I fired again. At twenty feet now, his fantastic bulk pounding the earth so that it vibrated the ground beneath my feet, I was suddenly without thought, without reaction. The roaring of the Weatherby, the smashing of the hooves, the approach of death itself; I was lost in limbo. I fell to my knees, this I remember; I worked the action of my rifle, but before I could fire a fourth time, there came from behind me, blasting my eardrums, three shots as of one. Chi bore witness to this fact; that colossus fell motionless, not ten feet from where I knelt.

The next morning I had a guar steak for breakfast—and so did every one else in the village. Chi and the boys were enjoyably relating the details of how the meat came to be on the Co Ho table to a group of wide-eyed children, when suddenly a strange Montagnard burst into the clearing at a dead run.

Chi translated: "He Stieng tribe Montagnard, live close by Cambodia, run last day, all last night to get here. He say, from village high in mountains, that he and tribesmen hear of killing wounded leopard even far away him. Say that elephant destroy rice crop, maize fields, and last morning throw old woman in air. She not live, he say. All Stieng Montagnard no leave houses, no work fields, all 'fraid. Say to us: Come kill bad elephant. If do, spirits take hold us, make happy. What say, Jacques? You like go?"

The circus act again—an encore. Except for the added passenger—Koko, I think his name was—I was that uptight about the coming action that I can scarcely remember the four-hour jeep ride that then ensued; and that, old friend by now, is a very long four-wheel ride in the jungle.

Forced to park our vehicle at long last, it was still another hour of walking through mud and across rice paddies till we finally reached Koko's town. It was a village living on stilts and fear, clutching at the skirts of a range of mountains thrusting up from Cambodia. Silence greeted us as we walked into the clearing. No songs, no flags, nothing human appeared to adrenalize our systems; results were obviously required, and, as Chi observed, "If no get rogue bull, maybe so you catch crossbow arrow."

No trophy ivory quest this, no glory-swollen leg to be placed proudly for the photographer upon the body of the most imposing animal on earth. This was a good guy gone bad we were seeking at the fervent request of its victims. Why? What makes a rogue? Strange, I reflected, each of Chi's legendary team favored a different answer. Nam gave the edge to infections that would not heal and gave the bull increasing agony. He spoke specifically of an anus disease that spawned maggots and copious bleeding, and when passing excrement the pain was ghastly. Khim stated flatly that an elephant that breaks off a tusk suffers extreme agony that does not lessen with time, and the resulting bad temper almost matches that of the infection that seldom cures itself. Brum held out for the old bull cast off by his harem as inoperable, and the resulting lonely life keeps him in a state of perpetual fury. It was left for Chi to astonish me. Ingrown toe nails. That's right. Ingrown toe nails. He told me, and his team nodded in complete agreement, that the pain from this affliction is intense for the Tusker; he has no way to remedy it; and if it continues, it grows steadily worse, matching his temper and frustration. Ergo: a rogue.

We moved rapidly through the village, wasting no time in picking up the spoor. All about us were smashed houses, leaning precariously upon crippled legs; dark faces were here and there peering from corners, while dangling bare breasts hung motionless over the chopped edges of bamboo platforms. No huzzahs, no flower-tossing natives; obviously these children of the high jungle had seen a rough time.

Nam quickly picked up the spoor of the invader; it lead to the edge of the slashed and burned clearing. He motioned to us. We followed. Up one timbered hill after the other, hour after hour. Nam, at point, was now a hundred yards ahead; we lost sight of him, time after time. When we approached a steeper hill, we at the base stopped as Nam made his way to the top, looked, waved, and we marched again, onwards and upwards and downwards. Chi, of course, is tireless, he's a mandarin strolling in his garden, but with me it's a different story. My rifle was gaining pounds by the minute, my leg muscles were beginning to bunch up, and the old Matterhorn quiver was coursing up and down my calves and thighs.

It was now late in the afternoon. I reckoned we had covered at least twenty miles during the last five hours, and after working our way through still another deep stand of bamboo, we emerged finally into a series of undulating, grass-covered hills. This growth was extremely tall, in places far above our heads; it made for very eerie going. Chi and I were constantly climbing up a rock to look ahead when the grass grew spotty. There was certainly no sweat nor strain in following our friend in this stretch of country; it was as if a bulldozer had preceded us. Up to this stage in the chase, I had found myself cataloguing my newly acquired Elephant File. Three adjectives had kept repeating themselves: fascinating, mysterious, and unpredictable. Why do herds suddenly take off, for no apparent reason, traveling great distances, crossing rivers, climbing mountains, passing through jungles, not aimlessly, but with, seemingly, a definite goal? Why are there so few great bulls with heavy ivory? Seldom do you find them in herds of even forty or fifty cows, calves, and young bulls. They do not use the regular waterholes used by the herd, they do not feed or rest in the bamboo with them. Why do elephants never lie down?

I kept seeing in my mind the vivid picture that Chi had painted for me wherein two bulls place themselves on either side of a wounded or sick member of their herd and, by exerting pressure from both sides, prevent the cow or bull from falling as the three travel for miles on end till they find sanctuary in a thick bamboo grove. Why is the cow, with or without calf, the usual sentinel, the guard, the look-out of the herd? Maternal instinct? A delegated duty, or by choice of the distaff side? A hunter spots a herd; he pursues it; to get really close his best opportunity is while they are resting and not eating; this, invariably, is at noontime. He approaches down wind; he enters the herd, literally. The huge bodies are almost camouflaged by the bamboo, trees, bushes, vines, and grasses. Suddenly the wind shifts, or his wending and winding about has changed his course a few degrees; his scent is in the air toward the herd, and whose trunk at once shoots up? Right: mother or daughter, sister or aunt. Instantly, all the girls join in, trunks extended like tapered funnels directly at the hunter. Two things can now happen: If the lead cow has her child in tow, it's two to one she will charge the hunter; if she is alone, it's ten to one she'll take off in the opposite direction with the whole herd in her monstrous wake. Broadly speaking, why?

We topped a ridge, and there, fifty feet below us, was Nam, Khim, and Brum, together for the first time in hours. They were staring at a herd of elephants not a hundred yards to our left. The herd was moving slowly away from our position, and since the slight wind blowing was at our faces, they had not discovered us. Chi and I joined the trackers and, without a word said, we moved, crouched over, down the hill and to the left. Through sparse trees and low growth, we came to within fifty feet of the fifteen or twenty giants, and I was beside myself, in excitement and anticipation—within feet of wild elephants. But even in that moment of joy and wonder, my whole concentration was almost instantly diverted to the tiny miniature elephants trotting about, perfect replicas of the towering animals above them, but only about three feet high and four feet long. The damndest little people I had ever seen.

Our rogue, of course, wasn't among them. Thirty minutes later, we climbed once again atop a large rock, shaped, I remember thinking for no reason at all, like Mt. Olympus. Fifteen minutes or so before, a waving of Nam's wide-brimmed hat with one edge rolled up had signaled the news that the spoor had been picked up. I promptly sat down, and, due to the fact that I was almost done in, beat beyond telling, I dozed off, sitting upright.

A sharp blow to my face brought my eyes into focus on Chi's extended arm and pointing finger. Looking down, and then to the right, I saw Khim making a circular motion above his head, rapid, high, and full. In three minutes we were at his side; Nam and Brum were already there. "Wind right; if no change, we okay. He stop eat, maybe just over side second hill there. I think go ro ind right; be sure of wind, come up him on open place I see. You alright?" I nodded.

Khim was now leading; he had made the discovery. Chi and I, side by side, a yard behind, Nam and Brum on our heels. The first hill. Negotiated. At the base of the second, Chi halted us with an uplifted hand, then brought us to ground with the flat of his hand in a downward motion. In our customary circle, his voice was very low, almost a whisper; no laughter in his eyes now as he spoke in Montagnard to his trackers. A question now and then, and a whispered reply. Finally, "Jacques. I go alone. See bull. Come back. You wait boys." And he moved up the hill and over the top; he made not a sound, he was a ghost.

Silence in his absence. The leopard and the gaur, I kept saying to myself. You are lucky with them; they're under your belt; you can do it again. The leopard, the gaur. . . .I looked up and he was back. Again, quick, sibilant words, lasting not thirty seconds, in Co Ho. Then, "Jacques, he biggest bull I think see Asia. Biggest teeth. Find much food. He eat, no move. You lucky. Do differen' hunt now. 'Cause you. Send Nam right. He yell at bull if he see charge you. It mix him up, give time us. Send Brum left. Same same. They no shoot. No need. I shoot if must. 'Membah, I kill more one thousand elphunts. Most one shot. Bull he dead no matter anything. See? You no get trouble." And he smiled. "I go first, Khim follow, now you. Must get close, maybeso thirty feet. He high above you. Like house. You sit if can. Rifle barrel he point to sky. Rest elbows on knees if can, but hold rifle strong in shoulder. We work 'round for behind shoulder aim. Shoot big wrinkle. But if charge, must shoot base of trunk. You all time say to me 'no sweat.' Okay, I say—you, 'no sweat.' All got? Good. We go."*

Up the hill, and at the top Nam and Brum faded away. I saw nothing ahead and down except Khim's back. Khim crouched low to the ground; I did exactly the same. We were working our way through heavy bamboo, which, as we both know by now, is a procedure fraught with danger, a prime source of warning to the bull in front of us. I reached forward over or just behind Khim's back to grasp the stalks at a place just above or below his hands; I

---

*To stop the elephant from the front or the side, the "brain shot" is the ultimate; it is not for the novice. Ideally, in the former, you aim at a point just above the base of the trunk and in line with the orifices of the ears. There lies the brain, behind the nasal cavity, and deep. Now—if your bullet expands too soon upon bone, he keeps coming, and you must fire again, and even again. But if the bullet adheres to its course, penetrating the bone in, or just behind, the brain, he will drop in his tracks, but it is a difficult shot, calling for consummate skill and poise under the circumstances. Remember, once the issue is joined with a frontal attack by a great tusker, there is no withdrawing. In an open area, you cannot outrun him; in a bamboo thicket, where most of your action will take place in Asia, you do have a chance, slim though it may be. You can dive aside, and roll, or run, to a thick clump. He'll check his charge, turn, search you out, and charge again. Beware his trunk, he uses it like a broadsword. In these close quarters he has another advantage over you: his sense of smell. He'll travel about, trampling here and there following it, and every second his rage increases and his frustration mounts till his screaming and bellowing is unbelievable. At least this helps cover your movements, as you change position to get off a shot or hide, for his eyesight is far weaker than his sense of smell and hearing.

In the latter, the bullet entering the orifice of the ear, which is roughly the size of a quarter, is fatal and should drop him. But even for the experienced hunter, the heart shot is desirable. This is the "ivory shot"—where you aim for the "big wrinkle" of skin just behind the shoulder.

178

could not let them strike my face or body in rebounding, which might draw an involuntary exclamation or cry of instant pain from cutting or blows, or by sounds of impact as they struck me, which could also signal ahead. We then moved into deep and thick brush, then in trees: my whole world was Khim's body, his movement of hands, arms, legs, and feet. Now he was moving slower, crouched even lower, now he stopped, then he moved, one carefully placed step after the other. I tried to control my breathing, to my own ears the sound of it was incredibly loud, and coming in deeper and faster gulps. It was quite cool, between the altitude and the lateness of day, but I was perspiring; the burning sweat was running in my eyes. I took advantage of the snail's pace to dash the sleeve of my shirt across my eyes and forehead to wipe off the dripping and, at that very second, Khim stopped and was on his hands and knees. My right knee dug into his back, the rifle's heavy barrel struck him on the head, and I fell upon him. Such was his self control, sense of balance, and strength, although I have six inches and forty pounds on him, that he supported me without even swaying, and made not a sound. He rose without even a turn of his head; I disentangled myself and gingerly eased up and back, and we moved forward again, very slowly, very low.

As quick as a slide change we are in thin brush; I could not avoid looking forward now, and there stood Chi, leaning forward and motionless. His left hand beckoned me; I passed Khim, bent beside the great hunter and looked up and ahead. I caught my breath and it held. I was a swallow away from yelling. I was saved by Chi's grasping hard my right bicep, and was not aware that the .378 which I was holding across my chest was shaking. It was the unexpectedness, the suddenness, the instant chilling of my blood at the sight of it—a monster. All of my mental preparation was shot to hell in a flash. A huge grey mass filling my eyes: its four legs were enormous tree trunks rising from the ground to make puny the trees about them, into tall branches its colossal head was moving, and its ears were flapping with a hissing and a smacking. No bullet made, I thought wildly, projected into that huge anatomy would ever bring it down. I caught a flash of long, gleaming ivory high in the green branches—the length of a tall man? Six feet? Impossible. His grey back arched and loomed like some great burial mound, and from his cavernous belly came the rumblings of gas erupting like molten lava in the cone of an active volcano—they were that loud with obscene suckings and pop-pings. Ah, his head is emerging; why it—there was at that moment increased pressure in squeezes on my arm and I turned my head to see Chi pointing to our left with a long, brown finger placed against his thin, dry lips.

Like a king cobra he writhed his way around and past me, and the three of us, in single file again, but with me in the middle, began the slowest of bent-down slitherings around the left perimeter of that half-forested clearing. My mind was ablaze with nothing and everything—and then, a stop. A slight movement to the edge, a peering forth, and there was the great rogue tusker, fully disclosed for the first time. I pass in describing him now. He was simply a grey mountain, less than eighty feet away, facing towards the other side of the tree-studded area. To my left Khim tossed a pinch of his pipe tobacco into the air. The particles wafted straight down; there was not a breath of air. Chi touched me, and his eyebrows lifted slightly with a question. I nodded, and he smiled. There was no haste, no tension about the men; just quiet, assured confidence that flowed to me like a physical thing.

Chi moved—and I was his shadow—towards the monster. From tree to tree, bush to bush; and with every slow-motion step we took my heart and pulse jumped a notch—I could not hold them. Seventy feet, sixty feet, fifty, forty, and he still had not seen or heard us; those stomach eruptions and heroic belchings would cover a 747 take-off. Thirty-five feet, thirty feet—and it happened. He turned with amazing agility for being so impossibly huge, and from a circus type he became in a blink a creature possessed. His massive trunk shot up to point directly towards us, his giant legs braced, his whale's head rose high, and I was so close that I could clearly see the burning, the flaming, the pure malevolent hatred in his eyes. A tremendous blast, a trumpeting that was deafening in that small arena—and so near. It would have frozen the blood of a god. He's going to charge. I know it—he's going to charge.

"Jacques—shoot!"

Without my consciously knowing it, the .378 was leveled at the monster, the safety snapped off, and through the scope, with the light so strong, and the distance so short, that top ridge of his skull loomed like an over-filled ditch. All this happened in a swallow; I do not remember a single move I made until the base of that giant trunk loomed as a bullseye and I squeezed the trigger. The report was sharp, loud, and penetrating; that I heard, but I did not feel, nor was I conscious of, the jolting recoil. As I worked the action, the target held in the scope but I had to lower as I squeezed off the second shot. With that crack I remember thinking instantly: He didn't keep coming, he didn't drop like a rock—he sagged. A hand closed on my rifle, and a voice said, "Jacques, look."

He had fallen on his knees, and his great head, in falling, had been cradled by two larger trees that had surged outward with the titanic weight—but held. There was yelling in my ears, and hands were pounding my back, but I had eyes only for that enormous head, the two incredibly long and perfect ivory tusks that stretched down and down, unmarked and glowing. When I have finished writing two more sentences, I am going to walk fifteen feet and stroke that smooth ivory for the thousandth time, for they are in front of me now, and always will be as long as I live. And with my constant memories of this greatest of creatures on earth, rogue or no, go my gratitude and respect for four magnificent gentlemen of South Vietnam: Ngo Van Chi, Khim, Brum, and Nam. . . .

For three straight evenings turning into night, Chi and I sat, side by side, in the mirador. Motionless, waiting. The first night he did not appear, but the second he did; and then with a rustle, he left. The third evening he came again, at 6:30 p.m.—and stayed. Fifteen minutes passed, or fifteen years. Not a sound. Chi knew he was there still, and not more than thirty feet from us, if that. I did not, though my head throbbed with the trying, the staring, and the listening of it all.

The man-killer just stood there, Chi was to tell me later. Why? He could not see us—and he could not smell us, for tigers can smell little better than I. But he held back, he did not tear the waiting flesh. Why? Then, from Chi, "He gone. But come tomorrow night." He had spoken in a normal voice, and it was shocking, that sudden, human sound.

The fourth night. Sunday, the third of September, 1961.

At 4:30 in the late afternoon, we began our last, silent, lonely vigil. As the greys fled, and the blacks appeared, there came with them—fear. To me, it was not the first time, and I know it will not be the last, for this emotion comes to all living beings, and if a man does not own up to it, he is either a liar, insane, under the influence of drugs or alcohol, or mentally deficient.

Aroused by impending danger, either real or imagined, it is as natural a sensation to man as exultation in victory and anguish in defeat. It comes bearing different labels. Call it apprehension, and you've got a friend calling. It becomes a good thing, this sudden or growing sense of fear. I swear to you—there *is* a time for fear. It

181

sharpens your senses. It quickens your reflexes. And then, after victory, comes the sweet knowledge that you *do* have the courage to extricate yourself from a problem, a situation, or an emergency that caused your mouth to taste of bile, your breath to race, your heart to pound. There is a smell to fear; animals detect it in a man and act accordingly, unless the mental brakes are applied and you put fear to work for you.

Call it consternation or dismay—and it's simply providing a warm-up for your brain to go into high gear and your guts to unwind.

Call it terror, panic, horror—and you've got a stronger challenge that you can still beat by putting it to work, again for you.

When does fear become an outright enemy out to do you in, difficult to control, much less conquer, to turn to your advantage? When it is born and nurtured by an unchecked imagination in facing the unknown, the unseen, or the unnatural that you have never encountered or even imagined. No friend here—kill it by realizing that the unexplainable does not exist, by knowing that reality makes sense, and that there is *nothing* about the world or the universe that is unknowable to reason and the mind of man.

Such a firm realization will force your mind to think, and enable it to think with confidence, about what you fear, which automatically dissolves the void and starts a counterattack that is sharpened and quickened by desire and necessity. Fear *is* your helper. When he comes, bearing whatever label, fool him, *use him*, to put your brain to work. He hasn't any; he is an emotion that you yourself are siring and as quickly can abort—with your brain.

I glanced at Chi; at two feet he was only the barest outline of face, head, and body. Ngo Van Chi, the legend, was sound asleep. I was not surprised, for I knew that thirty-five years of almost daily hunting or tracking or tiger-waiting had so sharpened his senses that the faintest untoward sound would find him instantly awake, alert, and without noise or drastic movement. Surprising, I thought to myself, how many outstanding men can, or could, fall instantly asleep, and as quickly awake, refreshed, whatever their surroundings. I recalled a few to myself: Thomas Edison, Bob Hope, Harry Truman, Winston Churchill. Strange, too, that all should live to a great age—and Hope, go, go, go at over 70. How extremely tall Chi is for a Vietnamese, actually a Tonkinese; he's a good six feet and more. I leaned down close to his head, holding my breath: Even in repose there was that slight smile on that unlined face, not patronizing, mind you, just a damned pleasant and happy expression, which is still another Chi trademark. The long, loose poncho he was wearing concealed the leanness and toughness that gave the man his great staying power on Shikar.

There was no sound, except the rain. Even Chi's breathing was noiseless as he slept. Chi has staying power, I reflected, in other directions as well. An outstanding characteristic of Chi's is one that he possesses in common with all able-bodied, red-blooded Vietnamese of accomplishment and success: They sure go for the broads. I apologize for putting that rather crudely, but what I think at a certain time and then report to you, is accurate and not gilded or rephrased. They go for the broads; that was the thought and those were the unspoken words. Multiple marriages are the order of the day and night. Would you believe that Chi has had as many as twelve wives at the same time? And children? Pick a number. Wrong. Twenty. I repeat: Twenty. Why, this man of many talents had at this very moment a baby four years old and a son forty. And no proxies. Both his. Guaranteed. And on the side, a stable of fair Vietnamese, Chinese, and Eurasians to break the monotony. Well, Chi, I concluded to myself, you are a rich man, you can afford them all; your children, your wives, and your friends—they have the best of everything, with love, compassion, and understanding for all. But one thing is for sure, I said to myself, as I gazed upon him with genuine affection, all the tigers in this world are not four-legged.
8:05 P.M.

Chi was awake. The man-killer had returned. A slight touching of his right hand upon my knee had given me the warning. I knew that the *next* pressure would be the signal to shoot— it had been so arranged. The blackness of the night was complete. I was in a closed closet with a tiny roof that leaked, and had not a wisp of air to breathe. My rifle, as I raised it unseen to enter the small hole and extend outwards, was as wet and slippery as my hands. No trouble in finding the aperture; I knew it now like a light switch at home. But a dripping trigger finger was something else again. I had had much concern for this seemingly trivial matter, and had been keeping my hands inside my poncho to the last possible second. Was this the moment? Would a tearing and then a crunching of huge jaws and teeth hold in the night? It came. The ripping; but with it a confusion of sounds, all-revealing. A scuffling, a series of smacks upon mud, a crackling of wood, then silence. He was gone.
8:30 P.M.

The tiger returned and repeated his performance. So did I.

183

9:50 P.M.

We had been in the mirador for eight hours, straight. In utter silence, and hardly moving a muscle. It was a good thing our kidneys were in great shape. We could not talk, so—I thought, as you would. There is a time, there *must* be a time, when a man's nerves break, and his senses reel, and he cannot breathe, and he is paralyzed, immobile, frozen. Not fear, not the fear of fear, but the cracking, the collapse, the shattering of a man. Final. It has not yet happened to me, this breaking point, but come it may, someday, some night, somewhere. Will I be able to control it? Will you? We'll try, the both of us. And that's the ballgame: the trying.

But at seventeen years, ten months, and six days of life for me, I almost reached the point of no return to normality. Twenty-three collective hours in that trap, with a movie-script setting and conditions, had taken its toll—and brought me head-on to confront the phenomenon of instant wipe-out: derangement in the actual face of imminent and deathly peril.

9:55 P.M.

A touch from Chi. The system is back in operation. The tiger is back. The next slight pressure on my left knee—and I shoot. And this time, I *knew*, with absolute conviction, that this was it.

There it was, the tearing. Now the crunching. It continued. Up went the rifle and through the hole. My whole being, all things on earth, were concentrated on a touch, a flash of light, an instant aim, a single squeeze.

It came. A feather brushing my knee. The thumb of my left hand holding the barrel moved forward of its own accord. The shaft of pure, white light was a slap in my face. A huge head swiveled to look directly at me. It was all in brilliant orange and black, with a glint of white fangs, and two enormous eyes, flashing a bright and bloody red—my rifle was aimed at its left. It swerved to the right, and exploded. A searing pain in my eardrums, a roar that enveloped me like a vise, a scream from twenty-five feet, a flinging back of a tiger's twisting, falling body, all pinpointed in a stab of burning white surrounded by ebony black. My field of vision was a peephole, and in it fluorescent colors gathered together, rose, spun, and collapsed into the jungle cavern.

And I did the most stupid thing I have ever done in my life. I jumped to my feet, my head smashing a hole through the tinsel roof. I leaped forward, splintering the mirador about me, and started running into the jungle, following the roars ahead, the beam of light, now shaking and jerking, leading the way. I did not hear him, but Chi was screaming behind me, "Jacques, Stop! Stop! Stop!" I never heard him. I did not know until much later that I myself was yelling at the top of my voice.

Stumbling, falling through the wet maze, my only illumination from that thin, bobbing pencil of light, screaming over and over and over again, *I got the son of a bitch! I got the son of a bitch!"* I was no longer a hunter, but a creature unrecognizable as human. My face, hair, arms, clothes, poncho, were ripped and caked with dripping mud. I was gulping thick air in massive doses. I was bleeding from a dozen cuts. But I remember only forcing my way through the jungle to reach that man-eating bastard, the source of insane screams and roars that came from someplace in the blackness.

Suddenly, I faced the Man-Killer. He was on his side, struggling ferociously to rise. The light hit his eyes, and their flash blazed out at me with such an intensity that I was paralyzed. I stood not five feet from him, in an immobile, hypnotic stupor, my eyes locked onto his. For an instant he was calm and quiet. Then he twitched and convulsed in an orgy of rage and berserk frenzy. I was shaken out of eye-locking shock and paralysis, and in that scene straight from hell, the wounded, screaming tiger, his eyes on fire with that brilliant, luminescent red and his huge head splattered with foam and blood, leaped straight at me. I fired my second shot point blank at his chest and the Man-Killer of Dalat fell dead at my feet.

Tiger Briefing

Man-eating tigers in South Viet Nam today represent much less of a danger to the peaceful Montagnards than do the Viet Cong and North Vietnamese invaders. What will happen to these kind, quiet people now that North Viet Nam has conquered the South no one can tell—but I fear the time will not soon come when the Montagnards will only have Mr. 30 to fear once again.

Even then, the fear will not be as great as it was—for Ong Bang Mui's ranks, like those of every living thing in South Viet Nam, have been fearfully decimated by war.

Thus, there is little need for you or I to enter these jungles now in search of man-killers. But there are other jungles and other tigers, other remote areas where primitive people live in fear and awe of dangerous and berserk animals.

This briefing, then, represents a departure from the previous three, for we are not going to confine ourselves to the doing of one adventure in one specific place in the world. Rather, we will search out those remote places wherein dwell the most dangerous, the most rare, the most exotic animals in the world, and we will learn to hunt them: with gun and—particularly with the latter two—with camera.

I want to make no apologies, however, for the ancient and noble sport of Big Game Hunting. It is a current vogue to deprecate hunting, to portray all hunters as contemptible killers. But for anyone who is not a vegetarian, to claim this is merely to be guilty of rather shameful hypocrisy.

The hamburger you had for lunch today came from a steer that was bludgeoned to death with a sledgehammer. He innocently followed the Judas goat into the packing house, and in less than five minutes exited in cellophane bags.

Perhaps you enjoyed a Cornish game hen for dinner last night. I hope it doesn't make your stomach queasy to know that your delicious bird was raised in a tiny cage in artificial light, had never seen daylight or enjoyed the freedom of the barnyard for one day, and was killed by having an ice-pick rammed from under its throat to pierce its brain.

I will make no apologies to a vegetarian for these things. I will continue to look upon the eating of steak, and lamb chops, and roast beef, and lobster, and shrimp, and crab, and my mother's fantastic beef Stroganoff (good grief, am I getting hungry!) as among the great pleasures of life.

While there may be no rational conflicts of interest between human beings endowed with reason, there are legitimate conflicts of interest among different species of animals, the species of man among them. I accept this as a fact of reality, and see no reason to attempt to evade it.

I think we have to grant that there is a reasonable justification in the killing of animals for food. Are there other justifications that are much *less* reasonable? Yes, there certainly are.

The hunter who hunts because he loves to kill, the hunter of hides for the coats of women—these men are, truly, contemptible killers.

Yet, hunting for food does not remain hunting's only bona fide justification. One such is the "cropping" procedure of intelligent game management.

Another is the hunting of dangerous animals: a rogue elephant, or a man-eating tiger, lion, or leopard. Unfortunately, often this serves as an excuse for wanton killing. An animal is claimed to be dangerous or branded as "vermin," bounties are even offered, and it is hunted to extinction by bored farmers who get a kick out of shooting an animal for the fun of it.

Sheep and cattle ranchers are notorious for this. Let a coyote or mountain lion try to survive by attacking and eating an occasional young, sick, or dying lamb or cow, and the cry of *"killer!"* is sounded and every shepherd and cowboy around gets to hunt it down.

The Western Sheep Association is responsible for the Government Predator Control Act. Operating under its mandate, professional government poisoners and trappers have killed hundreds of thousands of wolves, bobcats, lynx, foxes, badgers, skunks, beavers, raccoons, opossum, and porcupines, and thousands of mountain lions and bears. A needless slaughter of obscene proportions.

A man-eating lion or tiger is, on the other hand, a different matter. When the choice is live tiger and dead human beings, or dead tiger and live human beings, the choice is simple: You opt for the latter, of course.

I have gotten arguments, though, even here. I once attended a dinner party in Capetown and was seated next to Dr. Christiaan Barnard. Somehow, the conversation drifted into hunting and when I mentioned I had shot a tiger the famed heart specialist exploded. Informing him the tiger was a man-killer only increased his fury. "That's no excuse!" he fumed. "The tiger you murdered was rare, a member of an endangered species. It's just too bad for the villagers if he ate them."

I've often thought it so curious that a renowned doctor of medicine would value human life so callously. No mere animal, no matter how rare or beautiful, is worth a human life. Much less more than a score of human lives, the grisly tally of the Man-Killer of Dalat.

Contrary to Dr. Barnard's claim, no species is endangered by the big-game trophy hunter. No rare animal faces extinction at the end of a sportsman's rifle. The threat comes from two other directions.

Number 1 is the population explosion, resulting in increasingly more land under cultivation. A decade or two ago, if you flew over the hills of Ethiopia, from Addis Ababa to the Danakil Desert, you would note that they were very sparsely inhabited. Now, virtually all these hills are under cultivation. You really have to see it to believe it—and the same thing is happening all over the world. The animal's natural habitat is turned under the plow; with his proper environment gone, he dies. There is no place for him to live. And if he tries, he is shot, poisoned, trapped, and killed by the farmers and herders.

Number 2 is the poacher, the commercial hunter. The native who kills elephants for their ivory, leopards for their pelts, rhinos for their horns (the Chinese frantically buy them in their insatiable search for aphrodisiacs, which may help to explain why there are 900 million of them). A few years ago it was seals for their skins, beavers and buffalo for their hides, snowy egrets and ostriches for their feathers.

In A bert (or Virunga) National Park in the Congo (now called Zaire), anyone seen with a rifle is shot on sight, from low-flying government planes. That is one way to deal with poachers.

Another way is to raise these animals commercially, as are

187

minks. I am told this can be done with leopards. Perhaps with other species as well.

Still another way is for the government to let the local tribe operate a hunting preserve in game-plentiful areas. The monies derived from hunter's fees would be greater than from poaching, in most cases. The tribes would be operating with the government's assistance, not it's forceful oppression, and the fees would go directly to the tribe, not government bureaucrats. In addition, the tribe would have an incentive for keeping less land under cultivation and thus more for the animals, and also for preventing poaching, which it can more effectively do than government forces.

Frankly, approaches based on incentive appeal to me much more than ones based on suppression, such as shooting poachers and banning importation of skins. Almost invariably, they work so much better.

Increasing land under cultivation (along with resultant killing by natives) and poaching: These are the reasons for an animal's being on the endangered species list, not the hunter.

This year, over twenty million Americans will buy hunting licences, and pay 11 percent excise tax on all the guns and ammunition they purchase. It will amount to over $100 million, and it will be spent exclusively (except for the bureaucrat's cut) on game management, game conservation, and hunting safety.

It is the hunter and his dollars that are mostly responsible for there being more deer in the United States today than there were before Columbus.

And of all hunters, the big-game trophy hunter represents the smallest threat to any species.

The reason the big-game trophy hunter does not represent a threat to a rare or endangered species is because he hunts only for the prize bull—the animal of true trophy dimensions who is past his prime, has performed his ecological function of reproducing and continuing his species, and will soon die of old age, disease, or being eaten by predators. Surely, the taking of this animal will not jeopardize the existence of his kind.

I am talking, here, only of the legitimate, experienced trophy hunter, those deserving to be called "sportsmen." Many hunters are inexperienced. They wound and lose an unconscionable amount of game through ignorance and buck fever. Later in the chapter, there will be suggestions on how to overcome these two problems. Some hunters are killers. They enjoy killing animals, for it helps them feel like men, so they can brag about it to others at the country club, or simply because they like to kill.

There is a man in Los Angeles who has an enormous polar bear mounted in his office. He shot that polar bear by chasing the bear down with a helicopter until the bear collapsed with exhaustion. The helicopter then landed a few feet away and our hero stepped forth, walked up to the gigantic bear gasping for breath and unable to move, put a .45 pistol to his head, and blew his brains out. Returning home, our hero boasted of killing a polar bear with a handgun.

Now, this stinks. Fortunately, this type of individual is in the hunting minority. Unfortunately, it is this sort of thing—which the great majority of hunters would condemn as dispicable—that gets the most press.

Hunters of the calibre of C. J. McElroy, Herb Klein, Elgin Gates, Jay Mellon, and Abdorreza Pahlavi will often spend thousands of dollars and weeks of backbreaking effort on a hunt, walk for days through jungle mud and rain, through three-foot-high snow and up steep mountains in a blizzard, in search of one animal that has trophy dimensions. They may see, and have a shot at, hundreds of smaller animals of the same species. But unless they find that one, they will not shoot.

And if they find that one, when they level their sights on him and pull the trigger, it is out of love for that animal, not contempt, out of admiration, not the desire to kill, as a tribute to its beauty and a wish to preserve it, not out of a desire to destroy it.

The true hunter does not kill the animal he hunts. He immortalizes it.

We see a picture of a magnificent Marco Polo ram standing on a ledge of rock and ice high in the Hindu Kush of Afghanistan. He stands there proudly and with the sun glinting off his enormous horns, the picture takes our breath away. Then we see another picture of the same ram, in a crumpled heap at the foot of a smiling man holding a rifle, with a bullet hole in the ram's side, oozing blood. And we get very angry.

What we do not see a picture of is the ram dying a natural death. We do not look into the eyes of the dying ram as he helplessly watches the wolves and the jackals and the wild dogs come and rip out chunks of his still-quivering belly. Later the eagles will come to pluck out and eat those eyes. And later still will come the maggots.

Soon there will be nothing left except the bones, the hooves, the skull with those magnificent horns, and a few shreds of skin, whipped by the never-ceasing winds of the high wastes of Central Asia.

This is what we do not see. And because we do not see it, we call the hunter a killer.

But the hunter does see it, vividly, for it is a familiar spectacle he will see often on a hunt. So he will shoot that Marco Polo ram. With the shock of the bullet, there will be little or no pain, and death will come quickly. Death at the hands of an experienced hunter with a modern rifle is far more merciful than any means dealt out by nature. Then he will have the creature mounted entire, and enshrine him, so that his beauty lives on and does not perish.

Perhaps, after reading this, you will still want to hunt with a camera, and not a rifle. That's fine. I can understand that. But what I hope you can understand are the reasons why that Marco Polo ram is standing in the trophy room of C. J. McElroy.

Mac is quite hospitable, and by writing to him, at 877 S. Alvernon Way, Tucson, Arizona, he may very well issue you an invitation to

189

visit his trophy room. When you run your fingers lightly over the ram's body and around those colossal horns I hope you'll agree with me that this is a far better fate than the wolves and the maggots and the desolate winds.

Death comes to all living things. It is how it comes about that makes the difference.

But if you would prefer to hunt an animal where the only danger he faces at your hands is being overexposed, then a camera is for you.

Hunting with a camera has two significant advantages over hunting with a rifle. One is that for most animals, it will cost a lot less money. Two is, again for most animals (but not all), your chances of bagging a prize trophy—in this case a set of beautiful color photographs—are much higher. For certain of the rarer and more elusive species, the cost and chances of success are about the same. Counter-balancing this is that some of the super-rare (such as Asiatic lion) and fully protected (such as tiger in India) species are found either mostly or exclusively in game parks, where the only shooting allowed is with a camera.

The price of a true hunting safari—we'll call hunting with a camera a camera safari from now on ("safari" means a "journey" in Swahili, the most common language of East Africa)—is often staggering. The average price of a good outfitter can be several hundred dollars per day. And on top of that, for everything you shoot, you normally must pay a fee, ranging from a few dollars to several thousand (e.g., for an elephant or rhino in Kenya) to the government.

A few years ago, safaris cost half of this or less, but with inflation and the devaluation of the dollar, big-game hunting is mostly for the wealthy or the person who saves for a once-in-a-lifetime hunt.

But there are ways to get around this. Do you have any friends from foreign countries? Very often, their families or friends have land that you can hunt on. Foreign students attend most U.S. colleges. If you are a college student, get to know some of them on your campus. Recently, a charming girl was a student of mine at the University of Southern California. She was gracious enough to invite me to stay at her family's plantation on Sumatra, should I ever visit her country. Tiger abound in Sumatra, and Mimi tells me the local villagers would be delighted to help me track and hunt one of them.

Perhaps the company you work for has business contacts in dozens of places where you could hunt—Indonesia, India, West Africa, Brazil, Columbia, South Africa, British Honduras. Find out about these contacts and write them.

If the country won't allow you to bring in a rifle, buy a shotgun and buckshot in a local village. Hunt on the edges of the plantation with the local people. Learn how to skin out an animal expertly and bring your own salt. When it comes time to leave, sell the shotgun, buy a small cheap suitcase, put the salted-down skin in it, and get on your

190

plane. You'll have had a good, adventurous hunt—without the services of a professional outfitter, true—but it will have cost you little more than your plane ticket. One hunter I know collected a rare trophy *bongo* in this manner, in Liberia.

If you will start earnestly looking around you, I think you'll be surprised at the number of hunting opportunities and invitations that will materialize in front of you. So while professional, organized hunts are expensive, they are not the only alternative. You needn't be wealthy to hunt big game.

We'll still discuss outfitters, however, in the *Tiger Particulars* section of this chapter. There, we will talk about where and with whom to hunt throughout Africa and Asia for lion, leopard, elephant, kudu, ibex, Marco Polo ram, Mongolian argali, rhino, bongo, Russian grizzly, and more; where and with whom you can photograph mountain gorillas, white tigers, Asian lion, and over 1,000 species of gorgeous tropical birds around one lake in the jungles of South America. We'll talk about guns and ammo, cameras and lenses, film, guides, equipment, and costs.

First, however, I must help get you in shape, physically and mentally. And then make sure you can shoot straight—with rifle or camera, whichever you choose.

GETTING IN SHAPE

All the physical preparation you need for the average "African Safari" that you see advertised in the travel section of your daily newspaper is to practice a great deal of sitting. These advertised "Safaris" consist in your being driven around to the various large game parks of East Africa in Volkswagen buses painted with zebra-like stripes. You will sit on your duff all day long, for the park regulations do not permit you to get out of the car.

You will sit on your friendly *okole* all evening long too, on the veranda, at the bar, or in the dining room of the modern, luxurious lodges at each game park. You'll get more exercise strolling through the Louvre in Paris than on a "Safari" through the East African game parks.

But if you're on a wild sheep hunt in the Zagros mountains of Iran, or out to photograph the Walia ibex in the Simien wilderness of Ethiopia—ah, that is another matter. For true adventure in hunting with gun and camera, you must develop three things: heart, lungs, and legs. And what exercise develops all three? Right. Jogging and running, once again.

To plod your way through the snow-clogged passes of the Altai Mountains of Mongolia searching for the giant Argali ram, or the knee-deep mud of the Colombian rain forest stalking a jaguar, to walk for days up the steep jungle slopes and bamboo thickets of the Ruwenzori tracking down the lair of the mountain gorilla—you must run, and run, and run some more.

191

Run at least two miles a day for a minimum of two months. Go through all the supplementary leg exercises we talked about for the Matterhorn. I would like to see you run more than two miles, if truth be known. I'd be happier with four or five—which would only take you about forty-five minutes or less, once you get into it. But two miles at least—and remember: *every day!*

You may want to do all kinds of other things—work out in a gym, swim, hike, play tennis—all of which are great, just as long as they are (you've heard this before) *in addition to* and not *instead of* running daily. Don't say, "Well, I took the kids on a five-mile hike today (or perhaps played two sets of tennis, swam for an hour in the pool, etc.), so that makes up for the jogging." Run every day, and no excuses.

I am so insistent because this is really all you need to do to physically prepare for a strenuous big-game hunt. That's all. Just get down to where you can run two miles in fifteen minutes, four to five miles in about forty to forty-five minutes, and do it every day for two months, and you've got it covered. Simple.

A NOTE ON AGE AND SEX

Age is not that important in hunting as long as you're in good condition. The only exception would be the strenuous climbing involved in sheep hunting. And even here, men in their sixties make it with little strain, because they jog every day for months before a hunt, set their own pace, and take it slowly while on a hunt. Once you are in your seventies though, better stay away from the sheep.

There is a picture in Weatherby's catalog of a woman, Claire d'Acquarone of Verona, Italy, who weighs less than 100 pounds. Lying next to her is an elephant with 100-pound tusks that she shot in Kenya with a .460 Weatherby (yes, a .460, the most powerful big-game rifle in the world). The picture is not a fake. She shot the elephant herself. There is no reason in the world why a woman cannot hunt as well as a man.

BEING MENTALLY READY

Where the difficulties begin is when we move into the mental area. All the top big-game trophy hunters of the world are driven by a fierce determination, a surging enthusiasm and love for their sport that enables them to get through those snow-clogged passes and bamboo thickets. Without it, they would stare from their tents at the mountain above, say, "We'll climb it tomorrow," and get back to the booze and the cards. With it, each can say, "I don't care how steep that mountain is, if the snow is five feet high, or there's a blizzard— I'm going to get to the top of that ridge because I think there's a big animal up there."

How one acquires this fiery drive I frankly don't know. Many, if not most, of the top hunters developed a love for hunting, a love for animals, and a love for the outdoors when very young. I think all of us are born with the seeds of these three passions within us. They may grow and prosper or wither and die, but once nurtured in the early years they will bear fruit throughout one's lifetime.

For those whose youth was not so fortunate, these seeds can still be made to spring to life with effort and the proper climate. Step number one is to get outdoors, take Saturday hikes, then weekend backpacking trips. Just by spending time with nature, it won't be long until you hear the horn of the hunter. Whether you answer with rifle or camera, you will hear it.

A love of hunting, a love of animals, and a love of the outdoors: These are among the most necessary components of that most vital of mental assets possessed by the big game trophy hunter— an unbridled incentive.

But hard on its heels is a set of mental virtues without which the hunter has little chance of success. To begin with, nobody digs a griper. Not your guide, not your trackers, not your porters, not your hunting companions. Nobody. So what if you're stuck in a cramped tent, 12,000 feet up in the Koh-i-Baba range, it's snowing outside, and you haven't seen anything worth shooting in a week? You're still having an Adventure you'll tell you're grandchildren about, while everyone else you know is nine-to-fiveing it in the smog of downtown Burbank. Greeting each sunrise with a smile makes those mountains seem less high and less steep than anything else I know. Optimism and cheerfulness on a hunt just can't be beat.

Something else there's no substitute for on a hunt is patience and se f-control: The patience to sit and wait for a tiger or leopard in a flimsy blind for hours in the darkness. The self-control to shoot *only* at the true trophy animal, when you could take a smaller animal with much greater ease, and the self-control to stalk that trophy animal properly and wait until you have the best possible shot.

And finally: courage. The courage to take defeat on a hunt. It takes a person of unusual strength and courage to travel thousands of miles and spend thousands of dollars, venture into a remote wilderness and put forth a gigantic effort, see a great deal of game that he could have shot, but refused to because it was not of trophy caliber—and return home empty-handed. This takes guts.

Perhaps the hunter with a camera has an edge here over the hunter with a rifle, for the former rarely has an unsuccessful hunt. Of course, he may never get a photograph of a trophy bull, either, so it depends on what you term success. It's difficult for one hunter to do both on a hunt: shoot and take pictures. He must concentrate on one only to have a good hunt. Many couples are able to do both, by one hunting and the other photographing.

A fierce determination to succeed, optimism and cheerfulness, patience, self-control, and courage. All are necessary requirements for being a big-game trophy hunter. And, similar to what we saw on the Matterhorn, all are necessary for having a good life in general, right?

It is worth noting that your outfitter should possess these traits as well. One should always choose an outfitter with the utmost care, and this is something you must always check on. The best way is to ask people who have recently been on a hunt with the outfitter in question. How to find these people we'll talk about a little later.

It is also good advice to forget about Rowland Ward while on a hunt. *Rowland Ward's Records of Big Game* is published each year and lists the largest trophies taken for each species of big game. Some hunters are frantically driven to shoot a trophy animal large enough to be listed in "The Book" as they ca l it. If their trophy doesn't make "The Book," they view their hunt as a failure and are often desperately unhappy, even though they got a fine animal.

Forget about this. If your animal makes "The Book," fine. If it doesn't, so what? Your object is to have a good hunt, stalk a trophy-size animal skillfully, and take it with a well-placed shot. That's what counts, not records. Forget about the tape measure.

Before passing on to straight shooting, a word on "buck fever." The word is: Don't worry about it. Most of us have wondered whether we would panic if a lion or wounded Cape buffalo charged us, if we'd go to pieces when the time came to shoot.

Remember the tiger skins on the mayor of Dalat's wall that came from a zoo? The reason they came from the Dalat zoo is because every time Chi took the good mayor hunting, the mayor would freeze. Once a tiger was *three feet* from him and Chi in the mirador. He could not pull the trigger. The poor old guy was scared out of his wits.

The way to get around this is to forget about it. Don't worry about how you're going to react under stress. You'll have enough shooting experience and ability under your belt before you go on the hunt; you and I will see to that. Know you have that experience, know you have the proper rifle, and know that you have confidence in your guide. Your guide will get you close enough to your quarry so that you can place the bullet right. He is there to back you up and will, should anything go wrong. Know these things. Say to yourself: "I'm going to collect this animal. I've got the gun to do it, I've got the ability to do it, and my guide is here to back me up. I'm going to do it and that is the end of the matter."

SHOOTING STRAIGHT

Now, no book is going to teach you how to hunt and shoot properly. All I can hope to do is give you a little worthwhile advice, suggest other books that cover the subject more completely—and leave the rest up to you: practice. Only a great deal of the actual *doing* will make you a good hunter.

But we're not going to practice on African elephants. No, we had better start out with jackrabbits. The rifle you will be hunting big game with is a bolt action, with calibers ranging from .270 to .460. More important than the rifle, however, is the bullet, and more important than the bullet is bullet placement: where you put the bullet. You want to be able to place that bullet exactly where you want, and be able to do so not just when sitting with a rest aiming at a steady target, but with a snap shot at an animal on the run.

To develop that kind of expertise, you need to buy or borrow a .22 rifle. I would prefer a bolt action rather than an autoloading or lever action, and chambered for .22 rimfire magnum cartridges (this is the best cartridge for rabbits, squirrel and other small game; the .22 long rifle is O.K. but *never* use a .22 short). Remington, Winchester, and Marlin all make bolt action .22s. Be sure and have it mounted with an inexpensive 4X scope.

Take this rifle into the field, hunt rabbits with it long enough, and you will turn into an excellent shot on the run, with a fine snap and lead. An added benefit is that rabbit stew is delicious.

Couple this with a copious amount of target practice. Shoot in all three positions: free standing (offhand), sitting, and prone,* all both with and without a rest, at a variety of distances. This practice should be with your big-game rifle, not the .22 magnum. The object here is not to become a champion shot, but to become familiar with your rifle. I want it to be so comfortable and so familiar in your hands that you know its every idiosyncrasy, every range and trajectory of every size bullet it can shoot, intimately.

When hunting big game, your target will almost always be a killing zone of a foot or eighteen inches square, at a distance normally of twenty to thirty yards, sometimes longer, but very rarely over 150 yards. For this, you do not need to be able to hit a half-dollar on edge at 500 yards. You need a confidence in, knowledge of, and secure familiarity with your weapon, and you need to be able to hit animals on the run.

Once you have acquired these virtues, start hunting whenever you can. With your .22 magnum you can hunt all small game and varmints, and your big-game rifle (which can use a variety of different-size bullets) is, of course, adequate for deer and antelope, which is initially what you'll be after.

Perhaps you'll get interested in shotguns, practice at trap and skeet shooting, and give your diet a break from all that rabbit stew with some pheasant, quail, and chukar.

Perhaps you have a friend or two that go deer hunting and will take you with them. Maybe you know someone who's into hunting woodchucks, and will be happy to show you his skills in the field. These opportunities are probably all around you, and you should take advantage of them, sharpening your hunting proficiency.

But it isn't necessary. You may just want to do the required hunting and practice so that you are skilled enough to hunt the one animal you've dreamed of hunting. That's fine. Just stick to the

*Unless your rifle is larger than .30 caliber, as the recoil is too powerful.

195

rabbits and the rifle range and you will be.

Many people do not want to engage in hunting as a sport and pastime. Rather, they have a dream of hunting one particular animal. A lion under the shadow of Mt. Kilimanjaro, a jaguar in the jungles of the Amazon, a polar bear in the white barrenness of the Arctic, an elephant in the deserts of northern Kenya—you see yourself there, stalking that animal, raising your rifle and finding him in your sights, and as the cross-hairs come to rest on his shoulder you smoothly squeeze the trigger. You do not care about hunting in general, you do not want to hunt any other animal except this one, which, because of his beauty and majesty, has taken your breath away. You want to make that beauty and majesty a part of your life, not relinquish it to the buzzards and the maggots, but give it life eternal. And after you do, you may never hunt again.

Perhaps you are one of these people with this dream. It is a noble dream and a noble Adventure, and the lives of the people who dream it are wealthier and more meaningful for it. *The Adventurer's Guide* exists to help those dreams come true.

I encourage you to hunt, as long as you always do so with skill and wisdom. But if you dream of a meeting between you and one animal, and no other, I believe I understand, completely.

No matter what you hunt after moving beyond your base of rabbits and target practice, however, there are a few rules that all sportsmen wishing to hunt competently and humanely should strictly abide by.

The first is to remember that *the most important factor in hunting is bullet placement.* Hit the animal right and he will be quickly dead. Hit him wrong and you have a wounded animal that you may never find, that wanders off to die in slow-motion misery. The make of rifle and caliber of the bullet counts for little compared to this.

Aim for the largest vital area. Aim for either the heart, the shoulder, or the center of the lungs, no matter what the angle of the shot. For dangerous game, aim for the shoulder. If the shot doesn't put him out, it will disable him, most often knock him flat.

Following bullet placement in importance is bullet action: how the bullet penetrates and expands. For thin-skinned big game, you want a bullet with a thin jacket and a soft lead core for even, reliable penetration (mushrooming) and controlled expansion.

For dangerous and thick-skinned big game, you want either a Nosler-type partition bullet, or a solid bullet with a full jacket in steel to smash bone and penetrate that thick skin fast and deep (no mushrooming).

So don't get drawn into an argument with some guy who claims his rifle is better than yours. Mark him down immediately as an ersatz nimrod, for *you* know any one of a score of rifles and calibers are fully sufficient as long as the bullet does its job and you place it right.

(We're talking here of particular brands within a given range of rifles and calibers. Although Eskimos kill polar bears with .222s, don't you try. Always have a powerful enough gun—its better to be overgunned than undergunned.)

The second rule to hunt by is *always shoot from the steadiest position possible*. Never, ever shoot offhand if you can at all help it. Never stand if you can sit, and never sit if you can lie prone* (although that's not too often). If you program yourself for this, it will become second nature for you to instantly drop to a sitting position and squeeze off a steady shot, instead of to remain standing and bang away. Always use a rest whenever you can. It can be a rock, a branch, a jacket on top of a rock, or your guide's shoulder. A good idea is to carry a child's bean bag in your pocket.

There are no exceptions to this. You can always miss. Always take the time to sit or lie prone, get a rest, squeeze off a good shot, even if the animal is standing stock still at twenty paces. Practice getting into these positions and setting up a rest quickly. Do it over and over again until you have it cold.

Third is to *never attempt a medium- or long-range shot at an unwounded animal on the run*. There is small chance you will hit him, and if you do, the chances are you will merely wound and lose him. You should never take that chance. Even short-range running shots are risky, and are to be avoided. But at any running target fifty yards or more away—forget it. There's always another animal, another day, another hunt.

Fourth is to *track all wounded game until you find him or there's no hope of recovery*. Many hunters make a perfunctory effort for a hundred yards or so, then give up in their frantic desire to shoot up something else. Such an action is an obscenity. If you follow thoroughly all the advice offered in these pages, you will wound little game. But If you do, please: Never give up trying to find the animal until you do, or you are *sure* you can't.

And fifth is to *regard* all *long-range shots with suspicion*. A long-range shot is anything much over 150 yards. You should never attempt such a shot if there is a chance of getting closer; always shoot from as close as you can get. You should not try a long-range shot from anything but the steadiest of positions: sitting or prone, with a rest (or sling, maybe). And never, *ever* attempt a long-range shot at a dangerous animal. Wounding such an animal can make for a very nasty recovery operation, in which you stand a solid chance of getting mauled, gored, clawed, ripped open, or otherwise maimed, perhaps fatally. You will not like that I'm sure.

If you follow these rules, and develop your skills on the rifle range and with the rabbits and varmints, you will be a wise and good hunter.

I must admit that I have nothing but disgust and antipathy for the clowns who get out into the forest, the plains, or the hills and start

---

*Except, once again, with the big calibers. Try shooting a Weatherby .460 prone, and you may break your shoulder! One tip on heavy recoil: Stand with most of your weight on your front foot, and rock straight back with the impact.

blasting away at everything that moves. They're so excited about killing, and their hunt won't be successful unless they kill *something*, that they often wind up killing each other. Undoubtedly they thought they were shooting at a deer wearing a bright red cap.

The object of a hunt is not to kill. The object of a hunt is to secure food for yourself or your family, or to secure a trophy, as a tribute to the animal and yourself, to immortalize his beauty and make him a part of your life. If you hunt with calmness, with patience and self - control, always take the time to get into a solid steady position, never take aim at an animal unless you *know* you can hit him well, and never jerk the trigger, but squeeze it smoothly—be assured you will have a good hunt. For even if you do not collect your animal, you will have retained your peace of mind and self-respect.

HUNTING WITH CAMERA

A camera safari can be fully as rewarding as a hunting safari—and, as we have noted, it can be much less expensive. This is especially true if you camera hunt in the game parks. Most are operated by a government agency, have overnight facilities, guides you can hire inexpensively, and small entrance fees. With many, you can fly into a nearby town, rent a car, and drive to and through them yourself.

Another benefit is that since the animals are protected in the park, they are less skittish of humans. The famous lions that sleep in trees at Lake Manyara, in Tanzania, are so used to tourists poking lenses right underneath their noses that it's child's play to take exceptionally good pictures of them.

It is, of course, not always so easy. Quite often, a camera safari can be as fully rigorous and costly as a hunting safari, and with even less chance of success. The hunter has to see his quarry properly for only a few seconds, and he can squeeze off a shot to put an end to the hunt. The man with a camera, however, will rarely be satisfied with those few seconds. He will want to view his quarry for as much time as he can, expose as much film as possible, and often—especially with animals not found in game parks—he will fail while the hunter succeeds.

Probably the most necessary piece of equipment the camera hunter requires is an excellent telephoto lens. It has got to be powerful—300 mm at a minimum—and it has got to have quite good optics.

In the wild, even in game parks, you rarely get close enough to take good pictures with a normal lens (around 50 mm). This applies particularly to animal portraiture; to fill up the entire screen with an animal's head, the only way you're going to make it is with a strong telephoto.

We'll be going over various telephoto and zoom lenses shortly, in the *Tiger Particulars*, as well as all the other equipment you'll be needing. Once you've got it, your first camera safari should be at

198

your local zoo.

The zoo is the ideal place to practice—as well as to test any equipment you're thinking of buying. Many zoos strive to achieve a natural-like habitat for their animals, which makes it easier for you to keep signs of imprisonment out of the picture. The telephoto, with its shallow depth of field, can throw bars, wires, and cage backgrounds out of focus.

We'll use the zoo to gain familiarity with your camera, lenses, and film just as we used the rifle range to gain familiarity with your rifle, scope, and ammunition. Shoot a great deal of film, use different kinds of film, experiment with angles, unusual views, shutter speeds, and exposure. Once again: Become intimately familiar with your equipment.

Now take this newly gained intimacy into the field. Probably your best targets are birds. Trudge out to the seashore, mountain, or forest nearest you and refine all the skills and techniques you've been developing at the zoo.

You don't need to get fancy. Wild bird photography is a science in itself, with special blinds or "hides," silent shutter devices, and the like. All you need is to get out there with a minumum of equipment and start snapping away. You're not after prize-winning photographs, you're after speed—being able to see the shot, set your gear up, focus sharply, and shoot, calmly and quickly. Shooting birds will develop this like nothing else I know of. Besides, they're in great abundance—even in your own backyard.

I can't pretend to offer you anything approaching a complete course in animal and nature photography. Just as with hunting with a rifle, all I can hope to do here is suggest a few good books, offer a little worthwhile advice, and leave the rest up to you. It's not that hard, really, taking good pictures. I am nowhere near a professional or expert in photography, and yet every picture in this book (except those taken *of* me, of course!) I took myself.

By following a few simple rules, I am sure you will have no difficulty taking pictures fully equal, or superior, to any of mine.

The first you already know: the intimate-familiarity-with-your-equipment number. To this I would like to add two appendices: (1) buy only good equipment, nothing cheaply made, but (2) don't overbuy—by that I mean don't purchase anything overly expensive and too fancy for your needs, and buy only the minimum necessary equipment. Don't overload yourself with a whole bunch of extra lenses and gadgets.

Second: Have all your equipment thoroughly checked and cleaned before you leave on your camera safari. Shoot a test roll of film, take everything into your local store and have them test and clean it all. In the field, keep everything in the shade and in the camera bag when not in use. Clean and dust everything at least once a day, and your lens every time before you anticipate shooting. If you're in a very humid climate, check periodically for battery leakage. For very cold climates, have your camera degreased and get special batteries.

Third: Always shoot from the steadiest position possible (heard that before?). Never hand-hold a powerful telephoto: The slightest motion will blur the image (unless you're panning on moving game). Rest the lens on a rock, branch, car door, etc., cushioning it with a bean bag. Preferably, use a tripod and cable release (the stronger the lens, the more this changes to an absolute necessity).

Fourth: Stay off the sauce on a camera (or hunting, for that matter) safari, so you can get up before dawn each morning, and with a clear head.

At dawn, in the early morning, is when the animals are up and about, feeding. This is the best time to take pictures of them. The light is better as well. It is low and soft and fresh. The harsh light of midday makes good picture-taking very difficult. Besides, the animals don't like the noon heat either: They bed down in the brush and disappear from camera view.

Late afternoon is also good. The animals come out once more, and the light is again soft and warm. With a little luck and perseverance, you can get some marvelous silhouette shots of animals, backlighted by the sunset.

Fifth: Always look out for unusual lighting effects on the animals: sunlight coming through the trees, dappling or backlighting an animal, the long shadows and low light of the early morning and late afternoon. Train yourself to constantly watch for these things.

Since most of your better wild-animal pictures are going to be close up and portraiture (using the telephoto), trying for the best and unusual lighting is doubly important. It can make the difference between an average picture and an outstanding one.

Sixth: Try for as much action in your photographs as possible. Unless an animal is striking a particularly regal or dramatic pose, or you catch him in an interesting light, a picture of an animal just standing or lying around can be pretty damn dull. Catch him on the run, stalking, eating, mating, fighting, playing with the young or rolling around in the grass. Get him *doing* something and you have the makings of a good picture.

This is often quite difficult (especially if you're trying for unusual lighting as well, which is ideal). What it takes is a lot of patience, perhaps some good advice about when and where to be from your guide, a little luck, quick reflexes so you can snap the shutter at just the right moment, and a lot more patience still. (Another tip here is when you get an animal in action, take several pictures—don't wait for "the" one shot, but snap away. "The" shot will be among them, somewhere. But by waiting for it, it may slip by you.)

Seventh: Take advantage of your guide's advice. Very often he will know not only where the game is and when, but also the angles for the best pictures. He normally is quite experienced at taking people on camera safaris. He knows the right *kopje* (hill) to stand on to view the migrating herds below, the predictable habits of the birds and animals in the parks and around the lodges. Ask for his suggestions and milk them for all they're worth.

Eighth: Like the Boy Scouts, always be prepared. Never relax in game country. Carry your camera with you even when you walk down to the river from camp to take a bath, or when strolling around the park lodge. Once, I was sunning myself on the lawn near the pool at the Victoria Lodge, right at Victoria Falls. Baboons abound in the nearby scrub and suddenly one came loping across the lawn, to calmly jump into a seat next to a woman eating a piece of cake. With the woman staring aghast and too startled to move or yell, the baboon calmly scooped up her cake, hopped off the seat, and leisurely made it back to the bush. I watched in amazement and laughter—as did everyone else—but also with regret. My camera was safely ensconced in my room. So when *you* sit at that pool next to Victoria Falls. . . .have your camera with you!

Tiger Particulars

Hunting Safaris

Rifles

We've already seen that bullet placement and bullet action is more important than the rifle. There are a number of well-made rifles that will provide excellent accuracy, so when it gets down to the nitty gritty, it's mostly a matter of personal taste.

For example, C. J. McElroy's favorite rifle for the toughest, most dangerous game (elephant, rhino, etc.) is the .458 Browning, and there is no rifle I despise more.

So you're going to have to try a few out, borrow a friend's or rent one from a gun dealer. Don't go by what others say—go by what feels and shoots good for *you*.

It must be a bolt action, one that works smoothly. The wider variety of game it is adequate for and the greater the selection of bullet weights it offers, the better. The best all-around rifle for all but the most dangerous species of big game, from deer to moose to *Ovis poli*, in my opinion, is the .300 Weatherby. I took both the leopard and the tiger with it, although, if truth be known, I should have used a bigger caliber for the tiger.

I must stress, however, that this is only my opinion. You may not care for it, prefer a .270 Winchester, a 7mm Remington Magnum, a .300 or .338 Winchester Magnum, or something else of similar caliber: Your rifle should be in this caliber range. McElroy, Elgin Gates, Herb Klein, for example, all swear by the .300 Weatherby. There are other hunters who wouldn't want it as a gift. (Personally, however, I think they'd be crazy. Roy Weatherby is a true craftsman, and I urge you to read the information in his catalog before you purchase another rifle. He developed a higher velocity bullet to compensate for lack of accurate bullet placement—the shock provided by the tremendous velocity kills the animal even if the bullet is placed poorly. He pioneered this view, and, finally, other manufacturers are agreeing with him.)

For the biggest and most dangerous game, you're going to need a caliber of .375 or above. I used Chi's .378 Weatherby, as you may recall, on the elephant. "Karamojo" Bell, the famous African elephant hunter, had as his favorites a .256 and a .275. But he was the best that ever lived. Some hunters gain excitement by using the smallest calibers possible on dangerous game, like fishermen use the lightest test line they can. What they stand most to gain—and you as well if you try the same stunt—is a tusk through the chest.

If you're after dangerous game, such as gaur, tiger, elephant, rhino, Cape buffalo, and the like, I'd recommend the .378 Weatherby. If you want something bigger, go for the .458 Winchester or .460 Weatherby. They have a lot of kick—although the .460 has a muzzle brake—so if you're confident of your ability, perhaps a smaller caliber would be better (as long as it's .375 or above!). But remember the adage: It's better to be overgunned than under-gunned!*

Whatever rifle you choose, see that it comes equipped with a recoil pad. And in addition to your rifle, you might want to take a shotgun along, for birds. Be sure all your firearms travel in sturdy fiberglass, foam-lined gun cases.

Ammunition

There are several factors involved in the selection of the proper ammo. We've already talked about one: *bullet action*, on page 193. There we found that you want a thin-jacketed, soft-lead core bullet for thin-skinned game, and either a partitioned or a fully jacketed solid bullet for dangerous and thick-skinned big game. Bullet action refers to what the bullet does when it hits the animal. But, of course,

---

*Better for knocking an animal flat. But a rifle with too powerful a kick can, with repeated use, give a hunter a "flinch" that will destroy his accuracy. Thus it is your skill at bullet placement you should learn to depend on, not the size of your bullet.

the bullet has to hit the animal in the first place. So, we have to take *bullet deflection* and *bullet velocity* into consideration.

If you are hunting in the forest, jungle, or heavy bush, your bullet stands a good chance of being deflected by a branch. You need a bullet, then, that has a flat, blunt tip, does not have too great a velocity, and has strong construction so it will stay in one piece.

But if you are hunting in plains or high mountains, where there is little chance of brush deflection and often your only shot is long range, you need just the opposite: a bullet with a sharp point and high velocity, to achieve a flatter trajectory.

Bullet weight is also of key importance. Normally the rule is: the larger or more dangerous the game, the heavier the bullet. The possibility of deflection plays a role here. A heavier bullet stands a smaller chance of being deflected. It also stands a smaller chance of hitting anything at long range—the lighter a bullet, the flatter its trajectory.

Thus, just to give you an idea, many hunters use a 150-grain bullet for sheep and deer, a 220-grain bullet for kudu, elk, and leopard, and a 500-grain solid for the big and bad fellows. With Weatherby ammo, however, you'll use smaller bullets, as their velocity more than compensates for their size in terms of foot-pounds of energy.

Scopes

You definitely should have a scope mounted on your rifle. Leupold, Bushnell, Redfield, Weatherby, and Bausch & Lomb all make fine ones. I'd suggest a 4X Bausch & Lomb, or the 3X-9X variable wide-angle Premier model with the luminous reticle by Weatherby. You may want a swing mount, so you can swing the scope aside to use the iron sights, but often you have to resight the scope when you do this. Griffin and Howe make a mount that slides on and off, and this is probably the best.

Binoculars
and Spotting Scopes

Right behind the rifle in importance to the hunter is his pair of binoculars. You must not scrimp here; it is too important. Get an excellent "roof-prism" pair—they are small and light (very important!), and have extremely good optics. You want a 10X, except for desert game, where an 8X is better due to heat-wave distortion. The best binoculars in the world are made by Leitz, and by Zeiss. They are expensive, but, believe me, either one is worth it. Most binoculars, even cheaper ones, look clear. The *big* difference is how long you can look through them without getting a headache— and on this point Leitz and Zeiss have no competition. Miida makes an 8X56 pair called the Night Owl, for use at night. They're long and heavy, but invaluable for dusk, twilight, and moonlight. Bausch & Lomb probably makes the best spotting scopes. Their Balscope Zoom has 15X to 60X and you don't need to change eye pieces. Miida makes a very good one (15X60X), but you have to change the eye pieces, a real disadvantage.

Some tips on finding and seeing game, which is what your binoculars are so crucial for: (1) Don't look for the whole animal—look for *parts* of the animal—especially in the woods: Look for an ear, a leg that looks like a tree, a little movement (remember the leopard's eye?). (2) Don't scan or sweep an area, like the side of a hill, but study parts of it closely, stare at each part for a while. Animals often stand quite still, and if you look and look at one small area an animal can suddenly materialize right in front of you. (3) Always go over an area with your binoculars first, not your spotting scope. Once you've seen something, *MARK YOUR GAME.* Using a triangle of landmarks with the animal in the center is a good way. After marking it *well*, and only after, then bring out the spotting scope.

Other
Equipment

Generally, all you'll need in addition to the above is your personal gear: clothes, toiletries, camera(s), film, etc.

Normally, all your hunting clothes should be khaki or tan. But for the jungle you may want camouflage clothing, or for the arctic, all-white. It is best to find out from your outfitter, or whoever is taking you hunting, what clothes and boots are most suitable for his terrain.

Where and
with Whom
to Hunt

Choosing an outfitter is something you must do with the utmost care. I would recommend that you follow this schedule:

1. Start by knowing what you're after. Haven't you always dreamed of hunting one particular animal? For me, it was a man-eating tiger. What is it for you? An African elephant with 100-pound tusks? A giant Alaskan brown bear? A Mongolian Argali ram? Whatever animal it is, read all you can about it, its habits, description, distribution, everything. *Rowland Ward's Records of Big Game* is a good place to start.

2. Know how much time and money you can spend. Unfortunately, the more of both, the better—but there are ways to pare this down, as we've seen. Another is to try for only one or two species, not a whole slew of them.

204

3. Once you've got these two steps behind you, ask hunters who have recently hunted for the animals, or in the area, you're interested in. Go to as many of the top trophy hunters you can contact and pick their brains. Often, however, the latter is of little help in choosing a specific outfitter, for you need to talk to someone who has hunted with an outfitter in question *recently*.

The best way I know of to get ahold of these hunters is through organizations like the Safari Club International, Mzuri Safari Club, Shikar-Safari Club, and Game Conservation International (Game Coin).*

By writing to the chapter nearest you, and others as well, the chances are excellent that you will be put in touch with one or more members that have hunted your animal, or at least hunted the area of your animal recently. Ask these members what outfitters they would recommend and why.

Generally, you're looking for an outfitter whose cost is within your budget, who runs a good organized camp, knows what he's doing, and knows where the game is and can get you to it *if* the game is there at all. You want to hunt where the game is, of course, but this can change rapidly. Many outfitters have established a fine reputation over several years, but other good ones develop, or collapse, quickly. That is why the newness of your information is so important.

Ideally you want to get several recent opinions of a given outfitter, for just as there are lousy outfitters, there are also lousy clients. So get as many as you can for a balanced view.

4. Once you have zeroed in on an outfitter, write him a letter. Tell him what animal or animals you are after, have an idea of what size trophy you want—but forget about the records, right?—just strive to take a good mature trophy. And don't be too greedy—by concentrating your hunt on one or two animals you up your chances of a successful hunt.

Tell him how much time, money, and hunting experience you have, your age, and what physical condition you're in (don't bluff; be honest. I, of course, assume your condition will be excellent!). Ask him when he can take you and for how much. Ask him what is included in his price and what is extra, like government hunting fees, licenses, permits, and tags. Ask him what the game situation is, when is the best season, what he thinks your chances are of securing the trophy desired, what equipment you should bring and

*Addresses at end of chapter.

what he has, and supplies. You could also ask him to comment on any negative remarks you may have heard about him.

If you like what the outfitter says in reply, you're in business. If not, find another.

Instead of writing an outfitter direct, perhaps you would prefer going through an agent in the United States. It will cost no more, as the outfitter will pay the agent a commission.

For many areas, using an agent who has contacts already established is virtually the only way to satisfactorily arrange a hunt. Try writing to Sedgochoo Luvsandash, who is in charge of hunting for the National Tourist Office at Ulan Bator, Mongolia, and you will most likely never get an answer. But if you get Roman Hupalowski to write for you, the response will be prompt.

Hupalowski heads up Safari Outfitters, Inc., and writing or calling him at 8 S. Michigan Ave., Chicago, Illinois 60603 (phone 312-346-9631), no doubt is the most efficacious way of booking a hunt in Mongolia, Siberia and the Caucasus in Russia, and Afghanistan. These hunts are expensive because they are run by government hunting agencies with no competition. Mongolia will really sock it to you to hunt *Ovis ammon* (Mongolian Argali ram), and Mongolian ibex in the North Altai, although they lessen the blow to your pocketbook to hunt the smaller *Ovis ammon darweni*, ibex, and gazelle in the Gobi. (Most of the hunters I have talked to who have hunted in Mongolia, by the way, report they had a very successful hunt, and that the Mongols were quite friendly, helpful, and efficient—so they weren't bugged by the price at all.) And in Afghanistan, the Afghanis will want a pound of your flesh to hunt the fabulous *Ovis poli*—the Marco Polo ram—in the Wakhan valley of the Hindu Kush. The best place for *poli* is the Russian Pamirs, but so far, the Russians won't permit it. Roman, however, is working on that too, (The Russians do allow hunting for Tur and brown bear in the Caucasus and Siberian grizzly in Siberia—and their prices are quite reasonable.

Two other agents with excellent reputations that can book a hunt for you anywhere in the world (except for Mongolia and Russia, where Roman is better) are: Bert Klineberger, at 1507 12th Ave., Seattle, Washington 98122 (phone 206-329-1600), and Bob Huskinson, at 3435 Wilshire Boulevard, Suite 504, Los Angeles, California 90010 (phone 213-386-2927 and 545-5459). Bob is especially good for Africa, and is the only safari agent I know who will guarantee the arrangements of your hunt in writing.

To sum up then:
    A. Begin by knowing what you're after (Number one above,

page 204).

B. Explore opportunities with friends, school associates, foreign business contacts to secure an invitation to inexpensively hunt your animal. (Note: Kenya, Rhodesia, and South Africa permit what they call private lands hunting—hunting on privately owned ranches with a professional hunter at about half the price or less of the average hunting safari. In Kenya, you can get a list at the Kenya Tourist Office in Nairobi. Or, if you prowl around enough in the bars or outfitter's offices in Nairobi, Salisbury, or Johannesburg, you might find a ranch-owner who'll invite you hunting on his land "on the cheap," as they say. I met Max this way—Baron Max Von Truntzschler, who has land with fine hunting in Tanzania. He supplied the guns, equipment, everything. Max lives in Europe now, but with a little luck, I'm sure you could find someone as well).

C. Write to the organizations listed on page 220 to get in touch with hunters who have hunted for your animal recently. Pump these hunters for information and advice.

D. Either contact the recommended outfitter(s), or Roman, Bert, or Bob, should this be your preference rather than B.

E. Be well prepared physically, mentally, and in terms of hunting knowledge and ability by following all the suggestions we discussed on pages 191.

To help you get started, here is a sampling of major big-game species and where they may be best hunted today:

Black-maned Lion: Botswana (also Zambia and Kenya*)
Bongo: Southwest Sudan (also Aberdare Mountains of Kenya)
Elephant. Southwest Sudan (best in Africa for 100 lb. tusks; also Northern Kenya when open)
Giant Crocodile: New Guinea
Greater Kudu: Southwest Africa (also Botswana)
Jaguar: Paraguay; Colombia. I have to recommend my good friend Mike Tsalickis here, who lives in Leticia, on the Amazon. Mike can arrange for you to hunt giant jaguar, black panther, ocelot, wild boar, tapir, and alligator in two ways: (1) on a straightforward safari with a professional hunter; or (2) living with Ticuna, Yagua, or Witoto Indians in their villages, and accompanying them on their own hunting excursions. Can you guess which one I prefer? Mike is also the one to contact for Amazon fishing expeditions: 200 kilo giant catfish, 100 kilo pirarucu, all those fish Ralph and I talked about (back on pages 83-85), are

*Contact the East Africa professional Hunter's Association (EAPHA), Nairobi Hilton, Nairobi, Kenya, for the political situation with respect to hunting for Kenya, Tanzania, Uganda, and Ethiopia.

swimming around in the Amazon this very moment—waiting for you. Mike's address: Leticia, Amazonas, Colombia.

Leopard: Zambia

Polar Bear: Canada ** and Spitzbergen

Rhino: Zambia and Kenya (black); South Africa (white, or wide-lipped)

Sable: Zambia (also Rhodesia)

Tiger: Sumatra (Although a tiger is not an endangered species in Sumatra, it still remains illegal to bring the skin into the U.S., no matter where it was taken; the same applies to leopard. One can, however, fly directly to Canada or Mexico where there is no ban, and have the skin prepared by a reputable taxidermist. You can then wait until the ban lifts in the U.S., or take a drive someday across the border, visit the taxidermist, and. . . .drive back).

Camera Safaris

Cameras

You've probably guessed, by reading the section on hunting with a camera, that we're talking about still photographs and not motion pictures. This is because I believe still photography is much more rewarding for the amateur than home movies. There are simply too many problems in taking good motion pictures, then editing them into a cohesive film—it's just too easy for the whole thing to turn out half-fast.

But if your purpose is simply to record your wild animal adventures for personal memories, and you're not going to make your friends and neighbors suffer through watching them, motion pictures can indeed be a unique way of capturing these adventures.

Our purpose here, however, is trophy hunting, and the best way to secure a big game trophy with a camera is through still photography. If you would like both, and are not traveling alone, have your companion shoot the movies while you concentrate on stills—or vice versa. If you are traveling alone, many outfitters can arrange to have a professional motion picture photographer accompany you. They will both shoot and edit your film—but they are expensive. (This service applies, of course, to hunting safaris as well.)

Thus, when discussing equipment, we'll confine ourselves to still cameras. And the first piece of equipment you must select is, naturally, the camera itself.

****

**No planes allowed; dog sled only. Write Travel Arctic, Yellowknife, NWT, Canada.

Unquestionably, your camera should be a 35mm single lens reflex (SLR). There are a number of very fine ones on the market, but the one I would recommend is the Konica Autoreflex. You want a camera you can use very quickly in the field, one that is simple to operate, yet has great versatility and delivers slides or prints of first-rate quality. I've yet to see the camera that beats the Konica in providing all these factors. There are SLRs with more features than the Konica, but besides being more expensive (often twice as expensive, such as a Nikon F 2, or even three times, such as the Leicaflex) they are more complex to operate, and what you need in the field is simplicity.

You know me well enough by now, I think, to know that I'll expect you to try out several SLRs before purchasing one and not to rush right out and buy a Konica on my say so. Honeywell, Canon, Alpa, Minolta, Nikon, Leica, and others all make excellent SLRs. My preference is Konica, but you may like another. That's fine.

But Konica or not, your SLR will come with a built-in light meter. (One thing I like about the Konica, incidentally, is it is "aperture preferred": the meter gives you actual f-stop readings not just a plus or minus sign, as most SLRs do. You can also focus at full aperture, another important feature many SLRs lack. Be sure there are new batteries in the camera to operate the meter before you leave on safari, and that you take an extra pair as well.

Another good idea is to replace the thin strap that comes with the camera case with a wide one. It makes the camera much easier on your shoulder when you're carrying it around all day.

Film

Always shoot in color. Black and white is a complete waste of time in wild animal photography for anyone but the professional.

There are two basic factors in choosing a color film: its speed (shown by its ASA, or in Europe DIN, number) or light sensitivity, and what colors it is sensitive to, as well as how accurately it reproduces those colors.

The different brands of color film—Kodachrome, Ektachrome, Agvacolor, Fujicolor, etc,—all vary in how they reproduce color.* Try them all out in your practice at the zoo or in the field, but I think you'll settle on either Kodachrome or Ektachrome.

The faster a film (the higher its ASA number) the more sensitive it is

*"-chrome" means slides, "-color" means prints. Slides have better reproductive qualities for the amateur than prints.

to light. Thus you need much less light with an ASA 400 film than with an ASA of 64. For this, however, you pay a price: The less acceptable becomes the quality of the picture—it is grainier and less sharp, the colors are not as vivid and there is less contrast.

Some photographers want the sharpest, most color-saturated pictures they can get. Thus they use a film like Kodachrome with an ASA of 25. For this, they are willing to pass up taking pictures in all but very good light (or they hope to compensate by shooting at a lower shutter speed, which often doesn't work with moving animals).

I personally prefer a little more leeway. My favorite film is Ektachrome with an ASA of 64. If the pictures are less sharp and vivid than those of Kodachrome 25, perhaps the picky experts at National Geographic can tell, but I can't. Ektachrome is sensitive to blues, by the way, while Kodachrome is sensitive to reds.

Thus I suggest you normally use Ektachrome 64, or the new Kodachrome 64, whichever are your druthers—and make sure you bring enough of it on your camera safari, for color film is a great deal more expensive overseas. It is also a good idea to take a few rolls of High Speed Ektachrome, which has an ASA of 160 (and which you can boost up to 400 with special processing), with you as well.

Lenses

We already know that you'll be needing a big telephoto. The following factors in choosing one are important:

    1. minimum focus—how many feet away a subject must be before the lens can focus on it.
    2. minimum aperture—the lowest f-stop possible to the lens.
    3. size, both weight and length.
    4. adaptability to your SLR camera body.
    5. having an automatic diaphragm (with a manual override) that can work off your camera's built-in meter.
    6. telescoping lens hood and rotating tripod mount (for vertical shots).
    7. most important of all: *critical sharpness*—you want extremely sharp focus for crisply detailed slides or prints.

This latter, most crucial factor is why you should avoid like the plague doublers and triplers (converters of 2x and 3x). Some amateurs try to economize by buying a telephoto of small focal length (100-135 mm), which is less expensive, then a converter for twenty bucks that doubles or triples their lens' power. What they end up with are photographs that aren't worth the price of the processing. You simply can't get a sharp picture with them, which is what you want more than anything from a lens.

You'll have to choose between two basic kinds: *zoom* telephotos and *straight* telephotos (ones that have a fixed focal length). There are two strikes against zooms: one is that you need a lens of at least 300 to 400 mm, and the zooms that have this much power are pretty costly. Second is that the sharpness of a straight telephoto is generally greater than with a zoom (although with the more expensive ones the difference is very slight).

What zooms have going for them, of course, is their tremendous versatility—with one you can take a wide range of shots on the same subject without moving. With a straight telephoto you have one shot and that's it. In other words, one zoom lens takes the place of an entire battery of straight telephotos. If you can afford it, I would definitely say you should have a zoom as your telephoto for wild animal photography.

What I think is the best, all factors considered, is the 200-500 mm made by Tamron. It has a minimum aperture of f/6.9, which is very fast for a big telephoto, and a minimum focus of 8 feet 6 inches, which is incredible. It weighs six pounds and is fifteen inches long, has items 4 to 6 above (adapters for it, such as its Konica EE adapter, are available) and especially item 7: Its optics are really excellent. If you can come up with around $600 you'll have quite a lens.*

Nikkon makes a 200-600mm zoom, but its minimum aperture is f/9.5, its minimum focus 13 feet, and it is more costly than the Tamron. It is nonetheless superb. Nikkon also makes a f/4.5 50-300mm, while Canon has a nice f/5 85-300mm. You might be interested in Soligor's f/5.6 180-400mm. Its optics and features do not match Tamron's or Nikkon's, but they are still pretty good—and at a price that's attractive.

With straight telephotos, the problems of choosing one multiply rapidly.

You really need a lens of 300 to 400mm. Below that, a telephoto will help, but you'll always be wishing for more power. Above that, the

*A word on camera and lens prices. A dealer's cut is normally about 20 percent, sometimes much more, and since he probably doesn't sell many large telephotos you should be able to bargain with him. Of course, a major part of the cost is government duty. If the duty were to be abolished, as it certainly should be, as well as all other duties and tarriffs—staunch advocate of free trade that I am—the cost of cameras and camera accessories would be drastically lowered. There are ways, incidentally, of buying a camera or lens outside the United States and upon returning getting it past customs without paying any duty at all. You'll have to figure them out for yourself, because I'm not about to list them here.

minimum focus gets to be a problem and you'll be wanting less power on many shots. So, perhaps your best bet again is Tamron. They make a 300mm f/5.6, with a minimum focus of 7 feet, 10 inches. The Konica and the Nikkon 300mm are excellent as well, but they are also twice as expensive. Vivitar makes a good 400mm f/6.3, at a nice price too, but its minimum focus is 24 feet.

Moving into the really big stuff, Konica puts out an 800mm f/6.5 number, with a minimum focus of 65 feet, and a weight of over 12 pounds, with a price tag that's just as heavy. They've also got a 1000mm, f/8., minimum focus 80 feet, weighing in at 18 pounds, 12 ounces. Nikkon has 1200mm f/11, but the top of the Nikkon line is their 2000mm f/11 special. A steal at $4,000. On the other hand, Vivitar makes an acceptable f/8 800mm—and you can get both it and their f/5.6 300mm (or Tamron's which is better quality) for almost a hundred dollars less than the big Tamron zoom. I'd still prefer the zoom, but the choice is yours—not mine.

Besides the telephoto, and the normal lens (around 50 mm) that comes with the camera, you should also get a wide-angle lens somewhere between 25 mm and 35 mm. Lenses much below 25 mm are called "fisheye" lenses, and are used for special effects only. Alpa makes one that, believe it or not, has an angle of view of 360°! Expect to pay $100 or more for a good wide-angle lens.

I must plead with you to always get good lenses. Nothing takes the place of first-class optics. You only really need three lenses, and one of them (the 50mm) comes with the camera. Don't scrimp and get cheap lenses, like Spiratone's. Get top quality lenses, and your pictures will be worth all the effort and cost.

Binoculars
and Spotting
Scopes

What I said in the *HUNTING SAFARIS* section applies here as well. Get a Leitz or Zeiss 10x (8x for the desert), and perhaps the Miida Night Owl for dusk and evening. While binoculars are essential on any kind of camera safari, spotting scopes are not that necessary, especially in the game parks, so I think you can pass on this item.

Other
Equipment

1. Some professionals suggest you take a spare camera body. I don't think it's necessary, especially with a zoom. Even without one, you can learn to change lenses very quickly. Plus, one extra body is a large extra expense.

2. With that big telephoto, you'll definitely need a tripod. Get a

sturdy, light one that collapses to about a foot or a little longer. *Slick* tripods are excellent. Avoid monopods. Always use a cable release with the tripod.

3. A pistol grip is what to have where you can't set up the tripod in time. Use it and bring along a bean bag to cushion the long lens against whatever rest is handy.

4. Vivitar makes an electronic flash unit or strobe that is small, light, and gives a flash so brief most animals don't notice it.

5. Keep a skylight filter on all your lenses to protect them. The only film you'll be using will be daylight color film so keep them on permanently.

6. The best way to protect your camera and lenses during travel (especially when riding in a Land Rover with worn shocks) is an aluminum foam-lined case.

7. Get a gadget bag with a wide strap that you can carry over your shoulder when walking through the bush. Handy items to put in the bag are: an extra cable release, lens-cleaning paper, a light meter (in case the built-in one goes awry), lens hoods for the normal and wide-angle lenses, a set of extension rings for extreme close-ups, a small watchmaker's screwdriver, black masking tape (for light leaks if your camera is damaged), a supply of plastic food-storage bags, and a small tarpaulin (for sitting on wet or dusty ground).

8. Many foreign airports now examine your luggage with fluoroscopes, which can ruin your film. It's a good idea to put your film into small lead-lined bags that hold twenty rolls. If your store doesn't carry them, order them from: Drake Morton, Lomita Pacific Photo, 1945 Lomita Blvd., Lomita, California 90717. $3.98 each.

9. As to clothes: Have your outfitter or tour operator supply you with a list.

Where and
with Whom
to Photograph
Big Game

All that was said in the section on hunting big game about choosing an outfitter applies here as well. (So if you didn't read it because you're only interested in hunting with a camera—go back and read it now!)

Every outfitter you'll contact takes out camera safaris. For some of the areas, however—especially East Africa—it is both easier and cheaper to take a tour through a game park.

East Africa: Most any travel agent can book you on the "milk run" of game parks in Kenya and Tanzania. Leaving Nairobi, you'll be driven to Keekorok Lodge in the Masai Mara park, famous for lion as well as elephant, rhino, leopard, cheetah, and huge herds of plains game. Then on to Lobo and Seronera Lodges in North and South Serengeti to see hundreds of thousands of gnu, zebra, gazelles, and more lion; Ngorongoro Crater with elephant and rhino; Lake Manyara where the lions sleep in trees; Amboseli with a lot more rhino and lion; and return to Nairobi. A longer version bypasses Amboseli; goes under Kilimanjaro to Tsavo, the best place in Kenya for elephant; then up to Nairobi. If you don't want to go with a group in a VW bus, you can hire a car with a driver, or drive yourself. Even here, however, have a tour operator, such as Percival, book the arrangements,* making sure there is space in the lodges.

Avoid the blatant tourist traps such as Treetops, but be sure not to pass up Nairobi National Park, where you can get pictures of all the animals with Nairobi's skyscrapers in the background.

Legendary Ahmed, the world's biggest elephant, finally succumbed in January 1974, in Kenya's Marsabit Forest. But Tony Dyer has found an "immense rival claimant to Ahmed's throne." To photograph him, write Tony, c/o EAPHA at the Nairobi Hilton.

For millions (yes, millions) of flamingo, you can rent a car and drive out from Nairobi to Lake Nakuru, about two hours away.

The best place in the world for photographing wild chimpanzees is at Gombe National Park, in Tanzania. Have Percival get you there via Kigoma. Visiting the haunts of the mountain gorilla near Kisoro in the Mountains of the Moon is among the great thrills East Africa can offer the camera hunter.

There is no doubt that the game parks of East Africa offer the greatest concentration and variety of big game to be seen on earth. For legitimate pictures of the most rare species, an outfitter is best (e.g., Tony Sesmith for bongo in the Aberdare Mountains of Kenya.** I say "legitimate" because the Ark, another tourist trap like Treetops, has a couple of tame ones). But booking a tour through the milk run with your local travel agent is no more difficult and little more expensive than an American Express bus tour through southern France.

*Percival Tours, Ltd., Box 43987, Nairobi, Kenya. One of the best in the United States is: Adventureland Safaris, run by Pierre Verheye, at 735 N. La Brea in Los Angeles.
**Box 61, Njoro, Kenya.

214

Zambia: The Luangwa Valley Park has "Wilderness Trails" that you can walk along, accompanied by an armed guard (this is rare—in most every park in Africa you are not permitted out of your car). You'll see a lot of elephant and black rhino, and have an excellent shot at a leopard. (Note: I'm not listing all the animals in these parks, just the ones each park is best known for.) Fly from Lusaka to Mfuwe.

South Africa: Traveling through South Africa is just as easy and comfortable as traveling through the United States. South Africans are among the friendliest people I've met anywhere. South African Railways has tours going to most all the parks, or you can rent a car and drive quite safely. Hluhluwe (*Shuh-sloo-wee*) and nearby Umfolozi parks have wilderness trails and are famous for both black and white (or wide-lipped) rhino. Best known of all is Kruger, one of the finest game parks in the world. (SA Railways is at 109 Paul Kruger Bldg., Wolmarans St., Johannesburg.)

Congo: In a futile attempt to abolish its history, the former Belgian Congo is renaming everything. It now calls itself Zaire (*Zah-ear*).* It is a law here that every tourist must spend $40 every single day while in the country, and is required to prove it with receipts upon departure (please allow at least three hours for customs formalities).

The Congo has three rare animals in its eastern jungles: the bongo, the super-rare okapi (an unevolved giraffe), and the mountain gorilla. There is an okapi catching-station, run by a chap named Medina, at Epulu. Drive there from the Mambasa airstrip. This is Ituri Forest pygmy country, and M. Medina has the pygmies track and catch both okapi and bongo. Arrange with him for you to accompany the pygmies on such a search through the jungle and you'll have one hell of an experience.

At the Kahuzi-Biega national park near Bukavu, the Belgian game warden, M. de Schryver, will guarantee your photographing wild mountain gorillas within two to three days.

Incidentally, I'd suggest that you have Pierre Verheye make your travel arrangements for the Congo-Zaire.** If you want to wing it yourself, it may be a little dicey.

Albert, or Virunga, national park is also famous for its gorillas. Fly from Kinsasha to Goma, rent a four-wheel drive Land

*"Zaire" is a Portuguese term, by the way.

**See note, page 214.

Rover and drive to Rwindi. At Rwindi there is a small hostel and you can hire a Belgian park employee to guide you. The Rwindi River, by the way, has the largest concentration of hippos in the world—over 25,000.

Ethiopia: The mountain nyala, in the Mendebo mountains, and the Walia ibex, in the Simien wildness, are two of the rarest and most beautiful animals on earth. To photograph them calls for an expedition to each area for at least a week. You can hire horses, mules, bearers, and guides at Goba for the mountain nyala, and at Debarek for the Walia ibex, but it would be better to have Bob Huskinson arrange the expedition for you.

India: When you think of India, you think of tigers. Tigers are becoming rare in India due to native poaching and increasing land under cultivation. But there are several game parks where they can be seen and photographed. By far the best is Corbett National Park, named after the famous hunter of tigers, Jim Corbett.

You can easily drive there from New Delhi, about three hours away. At the rest house at Dhikala, hire an elephant and a mahout (for $2) to take you tiger-viewing through the forested foothills of the Himalayas.

Not many people know there are lion in India as well as tiger. In the Kathiawar peninsula north of Bombay there is the Gir Wildlife Sanctuary, wherein dwell several hundred Asian lion. Fly to Kestod from Bombay or Delhi. By writing to the Forestry Department, Gir Division, Junagadh, Gujarat, India, you can arrange to be picked up at Kestod and driven to Sasan, where you will stay at the forest rest house, have trackers locate the lions, and be guided to view them on elephant—all for about $50.

If not many have heard of Asian lions, even fewer know about the one-horned Asian rhinoceros. There are several small pockets of them throughout Southeast Asia, but where you stand the best chance of capturing them on film is at Kaziranga, Assam. It is flat, swampy land on the south bank of the Bramaputra river, and the rhinos are easily seen from atop an elephant. Fly to Gauhati from Calcutta, then take a bus to Kaziranga (sixty miles) where there is a tourist bungalow and trained elephant waiting for you.

You know, of course, what a tiger looks like: orange with black stripes. In the forests near Rewa, however, there are tigers that look dramatically different. White tigers. Not orange, but white, with baby blue eyes. How about that? This forest is halfway between Delhi and Calcutta, about eighty miles south of Allahbad. If you write to the Maharajah of Rewa, Rewa, Madhya Pradesh, India, he may extend an invitation for you to visit his forest and photograph one of the most exotic and gorgeous creatures there is.

Sumatra and Borneo: We're going to visit these jungles in the next *AG* in search of the Sumatran tiger, one-horned rhinoceros, and the only Great Ape found outside Africa, the orang-utan. But if you want to beat me to it, ask Burhan Pranatio, at Priangan Tours, Djalan Surjopranato 55, Djakarta, Indonesia, to put together an expedition for you. Burhan can get you to Komodo as well, in the Lesser Sunda Islands east of Java, to snap away at the Dragon Lizard.

You will also stand a good chance of seeing orang-utan, rhino, and gibbon apes by tramping through the Kinabalu National Park in Malaysian Borneo (Sabah). There's a daily Land Rover service from the capital, Kota Kinabalu, to Renau, the park headquarters. Also in the park is Southeast Asia's highest peak, Mt. Kinabalu (13,450), which we'll be climbing someday. For reserving hostel accommodations and procuring guides, write to: Park Warden, Box 626, Kota Kinabalu, Sabah, Malaysia.

Australia: No doubt, here are many of the strangest animals to be found anywhere. There are a very large number of game parks, refuges, and sanctuaries throughout Australia. One of the best is the Sir Colin McKenzie Sanctuary, which is only forty miles from Melbourne, at Healesville. You get to wa k through—no cars are allowed, and you will have an opportunity to photograph koala bears, kangaroos, duck-billed platypuses, emu, wallabies, and many other unusual animals and birds.

Russia: To see a giant Siberian tiger in the wild is going to take some doing. You'll need more than a machete to cut your way through the gnarled and paranoid Russian red tape (pun intended). Up the coast almost 400 miles from Vladivostok, on Russia's Pacific Coast, there is a village called Terney (or Ternyei). Near it is the abode of the Amur or Siberian tiger, long-haired and argest of his species. Much of this area is enveloped by the Sikhote-Alin game reserve.

There are Mongolian Argali rams and Siberian ibex in the Altai reserve near Biysk. In the mountains and valleys above the village of Ust'Barguzin, on the eastern shore of Lake Baikal roam thousands of huge Russian bears. And in the Tien Shan and Pamirs, there are snow leopard, Asiatic lynx, and *Ovis Poli*—the Marco Polo ram. To get to them, I can think of only

217

two ways. One is to see what Hupolowski can do. His contacts in Russia are good and numerous. Second, get some kind of official-sounding *GROUP* together. Communists traditionally hold the individual in contempt—it is collectives or groups they revere. Further, they all have the bureaucrat's awe of officials and titles. Form your own Burbank or Yonkers Wildlife Preservation Society, or some such. Get some stationery printed up, perhaps a letter of recommendation from a museum or zoo. Then write Professor A. G. Bannikov of the Soviet Academy of Sciences in Moscow, and possibly he can do something. He is a good man and will help. Best of luck!

Mongolia and Afghanistan: Once again, friendly Roman is the one to turn to here. He should be able to get the Mongols and the Afghans to cut their monopoly prices a little for camera safaris to photograph the *Ovis ammon* and the *Poli*.

Iran: Have Massih Kia* take you through the Tandurek National Park in the Elburz mountains. There are thousands of urial sheep and ibex, and it is overrun with leopards.

Colombia: In the remotest forests of Colombia, there is a group of small lakes around which flock the most incredible collection of tropical birds in the world. There is probably close to a thousand species of brilliantly plumaged birds on the shores and waters of El Dorado lakes, and in the forest surrounding them. Moreover, there is not only a small resort with modern amenities at the lakes, but air service as well. $225 will buy you six days and five nights accommodations, all your meals, and a guided expedition every day. Write: El Dorado Lodge, Miraflores, Colombia.

My *compadre* Mike Tsalickis** is again the person to see for photographing big game in the Amazon. Besides hunting for jaguar, ocelot, giant anteaters, and black panthers, he can organize an Amazon safari to the Peru-Brazil border. In this remote jungle lives one of the largest, rarest, and strangest-looking monkeys on earth: the red uakari. A picture of him in the wild is a trophy to be proud of.

Galapagos: Probably the only place on earth you can get fantastic pictures of wild animals and birds without a telephoto is the Galapagos. Furseals, penguins, giant land tortoises, huge iguanas, and astoundingly large numbers of birds (over a million storm petrels just on Tower Island a one)—all with little

*Iran Shikar, Ltd. Box 11/1934 Tehan, Iran.

**See page 207.

or no fear of man: If there is a photographer's paradise, the Galapagos Islands is *it*.

Metropolitan Touring (Casi la 2542, Quito, Ecuador) has a fine cruise ship that offers four-, five-, and eight-day excursions through the islands. You fly from Guayaquil, Ecuador, to Baltra, then get on board. By chartering a yacht you can set your own schedule and itinerary—and with a group, it's much cheaper. Quest 4 (Ashton Wold, Peterborough PE8 5LD, England) has a nice sloop available that sleeps six, and a ketch that sleeps eight. If you write them, please tell Roger Balsom you read about it in the *AG*!

Well, that is about it. This has been not only a long chapter, but also a frustrating one for me, because so much is only an outline and very incomplete. There are so many other places to hunt and photograph wild, dangerous, beautiful, rare, and exotic animals that I haven't touched on, and those that I have I could give only a sketch. But there's always the next *Adventurer's Guide*!

And whether you hunt with camera or rifle, my friend—good hunting. May the Goddess of the Chase smile upon you.

Books

1. *Animals of East Africa*, by C.A. Spinage. Life histories, unusual observations, and little-known facts about East African wildlife. ($7.50)
2. *Complete Book of Shooting*, by Jack O'Connor. Fundamentals on shooting with rifle, shotgun, and handgun, in the field and on the range, by the Grand Old Man of America's hunters. ($5.95)
3. *The Great Arc of the Wild Sheep*, by James L. Clark. The source book for sheep hunters: Every classified variety in the world is discussed. ($8.95)
4. *Great Game Animals of the World*, by Russell Aitken. A history of man's hunting big game throughout the world, with many excellent pictures. ($22.50)
5. *Guide to Safaris*, by Burk H. Steizner. A highly informative discussion of different African regions, types of safaris, costs, etc. ($6.95)
6. *Home Book of Taxidermy and Tanning*, by G.J. Grantz. A primer on skinning, tanning, and mounting fish, birds, and animals. Must reading for the trophy big-game hunter, so that he is able to prepare his trophies himself when necessary, *and* so that he may knowledgeably oversee his outfitter's handling of his trophies, as well as the work of his taxidermist. (As for your choice of taxidermist, utilize the advice of your nearest Safari Club.) ($7.95)

7. *Hunting with Camera and Binocular*, by Francis E. Sell. Excellent advice on both. ($2.50)
8. *LIFE Library of Photography*. Undoubtedly the finest series on photography, it covers every aspect: cameras, film, lenses, light, color—you name it. There are fourteen in the series.(at $7.95 each), and well worth every one, especially, for our purposes, the volume on *Photographing Nature*.
9. *Man Eaters of India*, by J.L. Corbett. Two of the most famous stories by Corbett, India's greatest hunter: "The Man Eaters of Kumaon," and "The Man-Eating Leopard of Rudraprayag." ($8.50)
10. *Rowland Ward's Records of Big Game*, fourteenth edition, compiled by G.A. Best. $45 and worth every dime.
11. *Safari*, by Elmer Keith. One of the best guides ever written on big-game hunting in Africa. ($7.95)
12. *The World Wildlife Guide*, edited by Malcolm Ross-Macdonald. A complete handbook covering all the world's outstanding wildlife preserves and sanctuaries. ($8.95)
13. *The Wanderings of an Elephant Hunter*, by W.D.M. Bell. The classic work by the greatest elephant hunter who ever lived.
14. *Trophy Hunter in Asia*, by Elgin Gates. Hunting Asia's rarest animals. Gates' accounts are thoroughly fascinating, and include his bagging the world's record Marco Polo ram.

Safari
and Hunting
Conservation
Organizations

1. Safari Club International. 877 S. Alvernon Way, Tucson, Arizona 85711. Associate Memberships are $10 per year and certainly worth it.
2. Mzuri Safari Club. 11 Columbus Ave, San Francisco, California 94111
3. Shikar-Safari Club. Box 1328, Racine, Wisconsin 53403.
4. Game Conservation International. 324 Milam Building, San Antonio, Texas 78205. This organization has several outstanding game conservation projects throughout the world. I urge you to write them, finding out how you can participate.

5

EXPLORING
OUTER MONGOLIA

The Gobi Desert. My eyes were fixed upon my boots, for underneath them lay the sands of the Gobi.

Outer Mongolia. The ultimate for the remote, the vast, the hidden, the mysterious. How many times in my youth did I dream of digging up dinosaur eggs with Roy Chapman Andrews, or mounting a Bactrian camel with Sven Hedin, off to explore the ruins of Karakorum, city of Genghis Khan? It did not matter how many times, for here I was, in Mongolia, in the Gobi, now.

The Land of the Blue Sky. Six hundred thousand square miles of wild beauty, landlocked and sandwiched between Russia and China. To the west rose the towering Altai, the beautiful Kobdo valley dotted with alpine lakes, and the *khangai*, the prairie highlands with fast-flowing clear streams and patches of forest. To the east lay the Khingan hills of Manchuria; to the north, the *taiga* forest jungle of larch, pine, and tamarack; in the center, the immense, rolling grasslands that look so much like Wyoming—and in the south there is the Gobi.

The wind, howling out of Siberia, was at my back. I stood facing an immense, flat sea of clay, sand, and gravel, sprinkled with groups of small pink flowers and patches of "white grass," the favorite of camels and gazelles. Beyond the horizon, the gravel sea stretched into the dreaded Alashan, sand wasteland of Inner Mongolia, ruled by Red China.

Behind me were the foothills of the Gurban Sayhan, with its naked main peaks rising in the distant background. I spotted a

221

patch of white against the foothills. It was a *ger*, the home of a Gobi nomad. Dorlig beckoned for me to get in the jeep.

Dorlig was my guide from Zhuulchin, the Mongolian government tourist agency, and he was puzzled. Why did I travel halfway around the world to visit a desert, he wondered. If I had come to witness the marvels of Mongolian Communism, to sit at the feet of some bureaucrat and write down the statistics showing how he had met his quota for the five-year plan, he would have understood. But to drive through these trackless barrens in a Russian jeep with no shock absorbers to live with a poor desert herdsman—this he thought a mite odd.

It was obvious to him, however, that I was enormously excited to be in his country, and this made him happy. With a smile that split his round, red face in half, he said: "We will visit the *arat* [nomad herdsman] who lives in that *ger*, yes?"

I smiled and nodded in return. Pointing to the white patch, I yelled "Charge!" Soon we were at the *ger*'s doorstep. A two-humped Bactrian camel munching grass nearby looked up to regard us without interest, them ambled away.

Out stepped a short, stocky, *del*-clad man, oval of face and gold of skin, with cheeks the color of bright red apples. His hair was a thatch of coal black, he had an eagle's beak that any American Indian would be proud of, and his face was not yet engraved with the onslaughts of harsh Gobi winters and the fearful *burans*, black wind and sand storms that attack without warning from China to envelop the Gobi in daylight darkness.

"*Sain bainu,*" I asked of the Mongol: Hello, how are you?

"*Morilamu*": You are welcome, was the reply.

Dorlig and I then asked the three other questions required by custom: "Is your family well?. . . .Are your animals fat?. . . .Is the grass good this year?" To each he nodded in assent, then bid us enter his felt home.

A Mongol *ger* (or *yurt* in Turki and Russian) is a round, conical tent of felt with a white canvas sheathing. Its skeleton is a circular lattice of wooden laths, around which the canvas and felt are stretched. The roof is formed by rods along the top of the lattice extending to a wooden ring. More canvas and felt are placed over the rods, with the ring at the apex left open for air and sunshine (there's a flap in case of rain). The *ger* has been the traditional Mongol home for tens of centuries. A nomad family can set it up or break it down, place it on two camels, and be on the move within an hour.

As we stepped through the three-foot high wooden door and entered, I was startled at the *ger*'s roominess. With a diameter of at least twenty-five feet and a height of eight, maybe ten, it was quite spacious. A thick *shirdik* (mat of wool) lay on the floor, and in turn was covered with carpets of many colors, richly designed. The rods and the *toono* (wooden circle at apex) were painted a shiny red, and someone had spent many hours decorating them with flowers of pink, purple, blue, and green.

Along the wall were cots laden with heavy quilts; lacquered wooden chests, their tops adorned with a radio, family photo, graphs (together with an annoying portrait of Lenin), and a statue of Buddha; a washstand with an aluminum pitcher; and three large goatskin sacks filled with fermenting mare's milk. A young woman stood at one of the sacks, churning with a large wooden pole. She also was wearing a *del*, the high-collared, full-length tunic, belted at the waist, that is the traditional Mongol dress for both men and women. Hers was pale blue, but they come in all colors of the rainbow.

A muzzle-loading shotgun lay across one chest; above it hung two bows and bamboo quivers. Four low stools were on the carpet, with two low tables littered with aluminum pots, china bowls, and other items. A small wood-burning stove commanded the center, its pipe jutting up through the *toono*. Only the stove did not burn wood: It burned dried camel dung. Feeding the fire was an exceedingly old woman. I noticed with a start that her head had been shaved. She was a *chabgants*, a "female lama," something like a nun who continues to live with her family.

As we sat down the girl stopped stirring, produced a brick of Chinese tea, broke off a bit, ground it in a wooden bowl with a pestle, put it in a pot of cold water, and set the pot on the fire. While the water boiled, we learned we were guests in the tent of Garghel, his wife, and his grandmother. Garghel's three children were out with relatives tending the horses, sheep, goats, and camels.

Shiri, Garghel's wife, let the water boil for several minutes. Taking it off the fire, she added milk, salt, and a rather liberal dose of butter. At the prompting of grandmother, Shiri took a ladleful outside and sprinkled it on the ground.

"To appease the spirits of the steppe," Dorlig responded to my upraised eyebrows. "The old woman, being a *chabgants*, still holds on to the ancient ways."

Shiri then served us the *tsai* (Mongol tea) in small Chinese bowls. It was thick, a tea-soup really, but it tasted good and warm after the long jeep ride. With a second bowl served, Shiri set about laying a table full of delights: bowls of *tareg* (yogurt made from camel's milk), platters of *besleg* (a rubbery, tasteless cheese I didn't much care for), and *orum* (wholly delicious strips of solid cream). And, of course, tureens of *kumiss*, fermented mare's milk. To the Mongol, *kumiss* (also called *airag*) is the elixir of life, the healthiest and best-tasting beverage in the world. About as potent as beer, it tastes marvelous, like milk laced with champagne. After three or four bowlsful of *kumiss* everyone was feeling just fine.

The Mongols are undoubtedly among the earth's most friendly and hospitable people. They are not Chinese but Tungusic aborigines (the Tungu are an ancient people of Siberia), with a heavy Turkish admixture. The anthropologists call the race Ural-altaic; the Greeks of Aristotle's time knew them as Scythians.

They were just a bunch of nomadic tribes continually feuding with each other until, in the early 1200s, a Yakka Mongol named Temujin ("the finest steel") welded them together into a maniacal horde that conquered all of China, Central Asia, Russia, Persia, the Middle East, and Eastern Europe. The Mongols called him *Genghis Kha Khan*, the Emperor of All Men. He was the bloodiest butcher that ever lived.

The entire population of Herat (in what is now western Afghanistan) of over *one million* people was slaughtered at his command. Passing by the ruins of Balkh, where Alexander had married Roxanne centuries before, two weeks after the Mongols had attacked the thriving city, Yei Lu Chutsai—the Khan's Chinese scribe and counsel—recorded surprise at seeing a cat in the smoking rubble. He was amazed to find a single living thing not killed by the Mongols.

An old chronicle tells of the time the Khan asked one of his guards what could best bring the greatest happiness. After musing awhile, the guard replied: "To be on the open steppe on a clear day, to have a swift horse under you, with a falcon on your wrist to start up hares."

Genghis Khan disagreed. "No," he said. "To crush your enemies, to see them fall at your feet, to take their horses and goods, to hear the crying and see the tears of their women: that is best."

Just as there are no memorials to Adolph Hitler in Germany, there are no memorials to Genghis Khan in Mongolia today.

In 1368 the Chinese overthrew the Yüan dynasty established by

Genghis and Kublai, his grandson. They razed the old capitol, Karakorum, to the ground. All that is left now of Karakorum is a single stone tortoise, staring blindly out over the empty grassland. For the next 300 years the Mongols feuded and raided—one Oirat chieftain, Essen Khan, almost captured Peking again. But in 1691 the Manchus, having toppled the Ming dynasty, slammed into Mongolia and then made sure the Mongols would cause no further trouble by introducing Lama Buddhism to pacify the nomad warriors.

Pacify them it did—as well as bleed off their wealth and riddle them with disease. Explorers like Prjevalsky (1870) viewed the religion as "the most frightful curse of the country." The Manchus preferred it that way: Keeping Mongolia a poor, stagnant, cultural backwater was their policy, making sure it would be no danger.

Thus, in 1921, there was a "revolution" wherein Mongolia again changed hands and religions. It ceased being a Chinese colony and, instead, became a colony of the Soviet Union. Lamaism was removed, and in its place another religion was forcibly substituted: Communism.

An earlier Mongol revolution, however, took place in 1911. With Sun Yat Sen throwing out the Manchus and their Ching dynasty from China, the Mongols decided that was an excellent idea for Mongolia as well. A free and independent political union of all Mongol tribes was the dream: not just for the Khalkhas and Oirats of "Outer" Mongolia, but for the Ordos banners of "Inner" Mongolia,* the Däde Mongols of Koko Nor, Khoshuts of northern Tibet, Torguts of the Tien Shan and Dzungaria, and the Buriats east of Lake Baikal. The capital was Urga, the chosen ruler was the Khutuku, eighth "Living Buddha" of the Mongols, Bogdo Gegen.

But it was little more than a dream. Soon the Russians and Chinese had gobbled everything back except Khalkha territory. When civil war erupted in Russia, a Chinese general, Hsu Shu-Ching—known as "Little Hsu"—invaded the Khalkha's land as well, captured Urga, and claimed Outer Mongolia to be part of China.

Enter the Mad Baron.

The leader of a small army of White Russians in Siberia,**

---

*"Outer" and "Inner" Mongolia were administrative districts set up by the Manchus.

**The "Whites" were those in Russia's civil war who fought against the "Reds," the Communists. The bitter struggle between them lasted for years.

Baron Ungern von Sternberg, was asked by the Khutuku to help the Mongols fight Little Hsu. In return, Gegen would give him sanctuary from the Bolsheviks. With his band of 800 men quickly gaining 10,000 Mongol volunteers, the Baron defeated Little Hsu on February 3, 1921, and the Living Buddha was back on the throne once again. A free Mongolia at last? Not quite. The Mad Baron, as Sternberg became known, was as much a despot as Hsu.

The Communists could little tolerate an army of rebels just across the border. The Red Army attacked and defeated the Baron at Urga on the eighth of July. The Communists allowed the Khutuku to remain, but with no power. They installed Sukhe Bator, who had helped lead them into Mongolia, as ruler of the "Mongolian People's Government," which declared independence on July 11, 1921, Outer Mongolia becoming the Mongolian People's Republic. It was the founding of the first Soviet satellite. (If it were not for China going Communist, Russia would probably have formally annexed Mongolia during the Second World War, as it did with its colony of Tannu Tuva, or Urianghai, adjacent to Mongolia.)

As Haslund, who accompanied Sven Hedin's Central Asia expeditions in the 1920s, saw, "the proud times were past when free men galloped over the steppes with silver trappings jingling and peacock feathers fluttering in the breeze. The four Khanates had been abolished and the whole of the Grass Country was ruled by a pack of ignorant young fellows who just danced to the *Oros'* [Russians'] pipes."

When several Mongol leaders started demanding actual independence in 1922, Soviet state security agents came in, demanded their arrest from Sukhe on phony charges, and had fifteen shot. With Sukhe's death from tuberculosis in 1923 and Gegen's the year following, and after a short period of semifreedom under a leader named Dambadorj, an admirer of Stalin named Choibalsan took over and the terror began in earnest. Finally civil war erupted in 1932 and thousands of Mongols fled into Inner Mongolia, taking with them seven million livestock. In that year the Mongolian People's Revolutionary Party had 42,000 members. Two years later it had 8,000. There were 34,000 ordered shot by Choibalsan. In one year (1935), he had killed 17,000 children of Revsomol, the Red youth organization.

Thankfully, a program of "de-Choibalsanization" was set up after the tyrant's death in 1952, like "de Stalinization" in Russia. Ever since, Mongolia has made strides in liberalization and modernization. Where fifty years ago the Mongols neither bathed nor washed their clothes and appalled travelers with their filth, now they have a passion for cleanliness. Illiteracy is virtually abolished and there is even a Mongolian Academy of Sciences. Premier Tsedenbal, who has reigned since 1952, still enforces a totalitarian rule over the Mongols, but it is nonetheless a great improvement over the horror of Choibalsan, and, in many respects, the feudal theocracy of the lamas as well.*

I wondered, however, if Garghel's grandmother would agree with the latter estimation. With Dorlig doing the translating, I wasn't about to ask. Instead, we talked of life in the Gobi, and one of my favorite subjects, hunting.

Garghel told us of hunting gazelle and antelope with his old muzzle-loader, and once bringing down a Gobi argali (*Ovis ammon darweni*) with his bow and arrow.

Shiri was obviously proud of her husband's prowess. With great animation she described how Garghel hunts wolves on horseback with a whip.

"Garghel rides after a wolf until the wolf, he is very tired. Then Garghel has the horse go to the wolf slowly, slowly, and the wolf attacks! But my husband is ready! The whip, she has a piece of lead on the tip, and when the wolf jumps"—she flung back her arm, then shot it forward—"*Crack!* the tip of lead hits right between the wolf's eyes, and there is one dead wolf." She laughed, her bright red cheeks glowed; I shook my head in wonder, and asked for another bowl of *kumiss*.

Garghel, Dorlig, and I went for a ride to check up on the children. The sun was warm, not a cloud was to be seen, and the sky was so blue it looked like a huge inverted bowl of lapis lazuli. Two hawks circled above to check us out, then winged away. As we trotted along on the shaggy Mongol ponies, Garghel pointed to the high ridges of the Gurban Sayhan: "Soon we will be moving our herds up there for the summer, in the high meadows where the air is cool and the grass is green. The *tengri* [spirits of the mountains, of rain, thunder, and lightning] have been happy with us this year, for there has been much rain."

Bureaucrats dislike nomads because they don't stay put and mess up filing systems. But the *arats* persist in the nomadic life they love, for they are *nüütel uls*, people on horseback, on the move.

*Re Mongolian history, I highly recommend an objective and scholarly work by C. R. Bowden entitled *The Modern History of Mongolia*.

Even though the government forces them to join herding cooperatives and has abolished private ownership of animals (except for a small personal-use allotment), they continue to move their sheep, camels, and goats in seasonal migrations, as they have for centuries.

I thought I saw something move in a nearby bush. I had Dorlig ask Garghel what it was. *"Almas,"* was the reply. "Almas?" "Yes, Almas—the wild man of the steppe," Dorlig explained. "He is short, covered with fur, and is rarely seen. The same as the *Yeti* in Tibet, no?"

"Yes," I answered, staring hard at the bush and seeing nothing. Another element in the mystique of Mongolia: the Snowman of the Gobi.

A group of *gers* came into view and we had a race to them. I must admit I finished a rather poor third—my sisters are the brilliant ones of the family with horses, not I.

Introductions to relatives and more bowls of *kumiss* were in order. In one *ger*, a young man plucked on a *morin khur*—a two-stringed violin with a long fingerboard that has a carved horse's head at the end—and sang a plaintive song about harsh life during the Gobi winter.

The children were off on a fifteen-mile horse race, Garghel's horse among them. Someone gave a shout and we walked outside to see them charging toward us across the steppe—Garghel spotted his daughter in the lead and was beaming.

As she pulled up first in front of us she remained mounted, and Garghel proudly handed her the traditional prize: a bowl of *kumiss*. She drank a sip or two, then poured the rest over the derrière of her pony, as custom requires.

Soon we were saying our good-byes and galloping back over the plain, Garghel and the children to Shiri, Dorlig and I to the sumptuous dinner Shiri had promised on our return.

And sumptuous it was. The entire head of a lamb was presented first. Being the guest, I had the carving honors. All the head required was slicing off the gristle on either side of the jaw. Then came the saddle, which I carved up in thin slices. It was so good I couldn't begin to describe it. Dorlig claimed it was the wild garlic, onions, and other wild herbs that the sheep eat in browsing that gave the meat its fantastic flavor. Shiri also produced a *drofa* (wild turkey) that was delicious. With all the *tarag, besleg, orum*, and *kumiss* as well, I was stuffed—and with my appetite, that takes some doing!

It was dark now, and the light from the small butter lamps cast waving shadows on the felt walls. Grandmother served cups of *arkhi*, a vodka of distilled *kumiss*. Garghel was astounded to learn from Dorlig that the population of Ulan Bator* was 275,000 now—but grandmother snorted in indignation upon hearing that they lived not in *gers* but in concrete apartment buildings and wore not *dels* but baggy Russian suits like Dorlig's!

Dorlig extolled the virtues of modern Mongolia for over an hour. He told of all the schools and hospitals, the modern equipment and technology used in the cities and farms. I added how impressed I was with Ulan Bator. The beautiful new hotel, attractive shops and stores, wide streets (complete with street lights and traffic signals!)—and the entire city was spotless, the buildings (characterized, however, by that stodgy architectural style of unrelenting monotony I call Dreary Greco-Russian), the streets, the parks, everything. Garghel, Shiri, and the children listened intently. Grandmother still preferred, as she put it, "the freedom of the steppe."

"Our freedom is running away from us as fast as the *saiga* [antelope] flees from the hunter," she said angrily. "But my mother was of the Tsagachin Baile tribe and I know this: Some day Dambin Jansang will come again out of the Black Gobi and the *niuutel uls* will be free once more!"

Dorlig's face turned ashen. As he translated the old woman's words he was clearly frightened and embarrassed. For a while there was utter silence. Then I quietly asked Dorlig who was Dambin Jansang. "Just an old woman's words," he replied with a nervous laugh. "Undoubtedly," I said, "but I would like to hear her story. Could you ask her to tell it to us?"

He did, she consented, and the tale that was told in that Mongol tent while the butter lamps falteringly pushed away the Gobi night turned out to be one of the most incredible I had ever heard—and later verified as completely true by my own researches.

Dambin Jansang—Tushe Gun Lama, the Avenging Lama—was a Durbet Mongol born in the Altais around 1870. All those who met him bore witness to his gigantic force of will and hypnotic power. His early years were spent studying in Tibetan Lamaseries, with fakirs in India, and Chinese mystics in Peking. Upon his travels through Mongolia in the early 1900s the conviction spread

---

*The capital city's name was changed from Urga to Ulan Bator ("Red Hero") in 1925. The total population of Mongolia is a little over one million people.

through the nomads that he was the reincarnation of Amursana, hero of the western Mongols who fought against the Manchus in the mid-eighteenth century.

Worshipped now as a divine warrior, he became the leader of the 1911 revolution. His horde captured and sacked the Chinese garrison at Kobdo, Dambin emerging untouched but his clothes in shreds from bullet holes.

The grateful *Khutuku* in Urga appointed him *Kung* (Governor) of the West where his riches and power grew until it alarmed the Russians who, with the Chinese, were busily putting an end to the new-born free Mongolia.

In 1914, Russian Cossacks attacked Kobdo by surprise. They found Dambin sitting on a throne covered with human hides— from Chinese he had flayed alive. He languished in a Russian prison until the civil war broke out and he was able to escape. It was he who raised the 10,000 Mongols to fight against Little Hsu with the Mad Baron. Again he was worshipped as the Savior, the Mongol Messiah to whom all tribes looked as their champion for liberty.

He fought the invading Red Army just as fiercely as he had fought the Chinese. Branded as the most dangerous public enemy by the Communists, he escaped to an unknown oasis in the Black Gobi, an area so desolate even the Mongols dread it, and just two day's hard ride to the southwest from where we were right now.

There, the Avenging Lama built a fortress stronghold he called Bayang Bulak, and the warriors of many tribes, the Tsagechin Baile tribe among them, came to fight the Communists under his banner. Late in 1922, a force of 600 Russians and Mongols set out from Urga with orders to assassinate Dambin at all costs.

I'd like you to listen with me now as the old woman tells what happened.

"Baldan Dorje, the leader of the attackers, had his men stop several miles from Bayang Bulak. Then he, and two others, disguised themselves as high lamas and went on alone. They told the guards they were on a mission from the Khutuku, Bogdo Gegen, in Urga, who was requesting Tushe Gun Lama's aid in a revolt against the red *Oros* [Russians].

"Dambin welcomed them, and for days they planned with him on how to free Mongolia. Baldan Dorje then pretended to fall ill; he lay in bed for two days and said he was dying. He sent for Dambin, saying that his last wish was to receive the blessing of Tushe Gun Lama before he died.

"Dambin came, and bent over Baldan Dorje to give the blessing and say the sacred words. As he did, Baldan Dorje drew a revolver from his yellow lama's robe, put it against Dambin's chest, and fired.

"Grabbing a knife nearby, Dambin's murderer cut off his victim's head, and before the guards could reach the door, flung it out to land and roll through the dust of the courtyard. Baldan Dorje plunged the knife into Dambin's chest and ripped out the heart. He stepped outside to face the warriors with the heart held high in the air. As all were in panic and watching with great fear, Baldan Dorje swallowed the bloody heart of Dambin Jansang.

"All were convinced that by devouring the heart, Baldan Dorje became invincible, as was their leader. They fled, into the Black Gobi, and Baldan Dorje took the head of Tushe Gun Lama to Urga. The *Oros* put the head on the point of a lance and had it carried throughout Mongolia to show all the tribes that the Divine Warrior was truly dead and that revolt was hopeless.

"But to this day, no Mongol goes to Bayang Bulak, for there the ghost of Dambin Jansang still dwells. My Uncle knows this, for he was there the day Dambin's severed head lay in the dust. But when he and others once returned to Bayan Bulak, they saw Dambin, whole again and dressed in robes of silk and gold, riding through the ruins on his black, lightning-swift stallion. They called to him but he did not answer. Instead, the savage watchdogs that used to guard Dambin's tent appeared, growling horribly and ready to attack. Afraid, they left. They swear, and many Mongols believe them, that one day Dambin Jansang will ride out of his Black Gobi fortress, the tribes will come again to his banner, and old Mongolia will live once more."

The butter-lamp beside Grandmother had gone out, leaving that part of the *ger* in darkness, so that as she talked in her deep, ancient voice, these last words came rumbling out of the shadows.

Dorlig was thoroughly shaken and sweating immensely. The rest of us sat unmoving, and all that could be heard was our breathing and the muted crackle of the camel dung in the stove.

Finally, I asked Dorlig to thank the old woman for sharing part of her life and memories with us. I finished the last of my *arkhi* and stepped outside into the Gobi night.

The sky was cloudless, with no moon. The Gobi shone with an eerie, soft phosphoresence under the starlight. Above me, I made out the Big Dipper; to the Mongols, it is the Seven Giants. Beyond it, the North Star—to them, the Golden Nail.

231

All of high, inner Asia lay before me. The Chinese hate and fear this land. On the other side of the Alashan desert was the Gate of Sighs—the western portal of the Great Wall. There is a fortress at the Gate of Sighs that China calls her "mouth." It is of great shame for a Chinese to be spat "outside the mouth," to live and wander in that great and mysterious waste called the Gobi.

Yet no land on earth holds such fascination for me as does this. I was now in the Gobi of Outer Mongolia. But I longed to start walking and not stop until I reached Tibet. Inner Mongolia, Dzungaria, the Takla Makan Desert and its oases of Kashgar, Yarkand, and Khotan, the Wandering Lake of Lop Nor, the Tsaidam Swamp and Koko Nor, Tunwhang and the Cave of the Ten Thousand Buddhas, the Chang Tang of Northern Tibet—all of these remote and hidden places beckoned to me with a force that was overwhelming.

Why do such lost parts of the world call me so? I frankly do not know. But go to them I must. Today—Mongolia. Tomorrow— when the Bamboo Curtain lifts—Chinese Turkestan and Tibet. There is always another Adventure.

Errol Flynn walked through the door. A shock of hair, stygian black, combed straight back. A white shirt with ballooning sleeves and unbuttoned in the front. A wide sash of red silk, black trousers tucked into calf-high leather boots. With those flashing eyes and Barrymore profile, if it wasn't Errol Flynn it was his Central Asian double—for I was in Alma Ata, Kazakhistan, having a beer with a Russian engineer named Oleg Petrovich.

Errol walked up and asked to sit at our table. I said, "Sure," with a smile, and he looked at me incredulously. "Are you an American?" he asked. "I certainly am." He broke into a huge grin. "Why that is, how you say, fantastic! My name is Toktar, and I teach English at my village in the distant north called Ust Kamenogorsk!"

Soon the table was littered with beer bottles. (The Russians make undoubtedly the world's lousiest beer, or *piva*, but here in Kazakhistan, for some reason, it was quite good.) Toktar was the son of a Kazakh chieftain, and, since tourists didn't often get to this neck of the Asian woods, I was the first American (or native English-speaker) he had ever met.

He told me much of the Kazakh traditions and way of life, of the days he spent hunting with his father on the steppe and in the Russian Altais. I, in turn, told him, and Oleg, of living in

Garghel's *yurt*, and of Sasha, a red-haired, freckle-faced young boy in Moscow who took off his clothes in Red Square.

"I listen to Voice of America and know all about your country," Sasha informed me. "They," pointing a finger derisively at the Kremlin behind him, "try to jam the waves, but I know how to tune my radio just right. You know Chuck Berry? He is our favorite. We know you have many dances of rock and roll in America—but we have our own: It is called 'the Medicine,' " and he starts going into a series of rhythmic jerking motions.

"How many rubles do you want for your shoes?" he asked of my $14.95 loafers. "I will give you forty rubles." ($44 U.S.*—he could have sold them for $60). "No? Well, how about your shirt? Everything I have on is made in your country. Here, see?" He had me look at the inside of his shirt collar. Sure enough, there was an American label.

"Yes, everything. . . .look, I will prove it!" And right in the courtyard of Saint Basil's Church on Red Square, in the shadow of the Kremlin, Sasha unzips his pants and proudly displays the label on his underwear: They were a pair of Jockey shorts! I met dozens of kids like him in Moscow, all with the same passion for knowledge of, and products from, America.

Alma Ata means "Father of Apples," and with its vast orchards, tree-shaded canals on every street where the Kazakh children swim, and the noble Tien Shan mountains rearing their snowy heads fifteen to twenty thousand feet high as a backdrop, there are few places on earth more beautiful.

Tien Shan is Chinese for "The Celestial Mountains," and heavenly their beauty certainly is. So often had I walked through the passes of these legendary peaks with Marco Polo, hunted for *Ovis poli* among their slopes with Sir George Littledale, or led my own camel caravan slowly along the edge of the Tarim basin under their lofty shadow—so often, in my romantic young dreams.

Now, with a car secured from Intourist, Toktar, Oleg, and I were driving up into them. We got out and hiked for miles through forests of fir, spruce, and juniper, across alpine pastures of green grass, strewn with flowers of an intense blue, and the yellow, white, and red blossoms of saxifrage, following fast, icy, and clear streams up to quiet pools to go for a frosty swim, then lie in the warm sun.

*The official exchange rate was then one ruble = $1.10 (now $1.30), but outside the Soviet Union, the ruble is worth about fifteen cents—which is why the Russians won't permit their currency outside the country.

We met a group of young Russian hikers and they shared with us some bread and cheese. Again I was impressed with the genuine friendliness and hospitality of the Russian people, whether in Moscow, Siberia, or here, just as I was with the Kazaks' and Mongols'. What terrible thing happens to Russians when they become bureaucrats and rulers?

We looked down upon small lakes of glacial melt, with the color of light jade, the most gorgeous pale green. From one ridge we could make out the Ili river through desert haze on its winding way across the plain below to empty into Lake Balkash. Beyond Balkash lay the dreary Bet Pak Dala—the Famine Steppe.

As the Tien Shan continue to the southwest, they provide high retreats for the Kirghiz, a fierce and independent Central Asian people who continue to fight against the Russians for their freedom. First the Czars, and now the Reds—they've been at war with Russia for over one hundred years, and haven't been conquered to this day.

Farther south, the Celestial Mountains give birth to two west-flowing rivers that have sustained countless ancient empires: the Syr Darya and the Oxus, or Amu Darya. The oasis of Kwarezm, fabled cities with the magical names of Khiva, Tashkent, Samar-kand (the city of Tamerlane), and Bukhara, all are on or between their banks.

Somewhere north of the Oxus was the Sogdian Rock, so steep and impregnable that the King of Sogdiana, entrenched with his army in caves near the top, laughed at Alexander's demand to surrender. "Find soldiers with wings," read his message flung down from above, "for no one else can touch us!"

That night, three hundred Macedonians crept up the Rock, using pitons and ropes. At dawn, Alexander the Great called up to the King: "Come out and see my flying soldiers!" When the King did, he surrendered without a fight. Among the prisoners was the King's daughter, the beautiful Roxanne. So beautiful that Alex-ander married her at Balkh.

Today, no one knows the location of the Sogdian Rock. It's suspected to be somewhere near the village of Derbent. The adventure of discovering it is open to anyone—including yourself.

I would soon be on my way to Samarkand and Bukhara, but my eyes were fixed on the high peaks to the east. On the other side lay Chinese Turkestan. Again I was so close to the land of my greatest fascination. There was Khan Tegri, the Lord of the Sky, over

22,000 feet high. From its peak one could look down upon the Takla Makan. Perhaps it is because Sinkiang (Chinese Turkestan) is to me the essence, the epitome of wild, remote adventure and exploration that the yearning and frustration welled up inside me so powerfully. But then I looked at all the beauty around me. I smiled at my two new-found friends, turned, and started to walk back down the valley.

Her name was Barbara. With auburn hair and a very acceptable figure, she was strolling around Srinigar, in the Vale of Kashmir when we met. We discovered that we shared a dream common to many romantics—to live on a houseboat floating on a lake in legendary Kashmir. Since we also shared an evidently mutual attraction, we pooled our meager resources and rented one together. Our landlord was a fine Moslem gentleman named Ramzan Dongola, and while his servants waited on us hand and foot and stuffed us full of Kashmirian delicacies, the days passed luxuriously, languidly, and indistinguishably by.

I asked Barbara how it was that a twenty-two-year-old girl from Mill Valley, California, seemed to be quite easily prowling around northern India all by her lonesome.

"Well, to begin with, I prefer traveling alone because there's more freedom—I don't have to get anyone else's approval to go where I want—and I meet more people, it seems, and make friends quicker and easier when I'm on my own."

Now, here was a girl after my own heart! These were precisely the same reasons why I have always gone alone in my wanderings. Barbara, it turned out, had become speedily bored with secretarial jobs in San Francisco, applied for an embassy job with the State Department, and was now working for the United States Embassy in Tokyo. She was spending her month's vacation (yes, a whole month) trekking around Sikkim, Nepal, and the Kashmir, having spent earlier ones in Borneo, Hong Kong, Thailand, and southern India. Adventure to her was a way of life.

I told her of two young sisters-in-spirit of hers with whom I sang "The Star-Spangled Banner" on July Fourth in the lobby of the Hotel Tashkent (and rather loudly, I must admit!). They were teachers working for Aramco, the Arabian-American Oil Company, in Riyadh, Saudi Arabia. Oil companies will bring an employee's entire family to live with him on a foreign assignment. They set up schools for the children, and Sue and Kathy had taught in these schools in Morocco, Tunisia, Libya, Aden, and, now, in

Arabia. They were tooting around Russian Central Asia on vacation when I met them.

I told her also of Christine Paul whom I met in Samarkand. A woman of sixty-five, whose enormous energy and *joi de vivre* exceeded even her massive bulk (she weighed at least 300 pounds), she had travelled to more places than anyone I had ever known.

Age. . . .sex. . . .money. . . .physical handicaps. . . .none deterred these women. If they did not deter them, why should they deter you?

I once met a doctor from New York. He was seventy-two years old, and his legs were so crippled from poor circulation that he could walk only with crutches. I met him in Timbuktu. He and his wife were traveling through the Sahara Desert, and doing just fine.

The good doctor happened to be well-off financially, but you need not be wealthy to have Adventure as *a way of life*. Take Clay and Jackie Francisco.

I met them in Bukhara, and a nicer, more charming couple you couldn't possibly meet. They had taken every dime of their savings accumulated from working two jobs apiece for over three years and invested it in camera equipment, film, and a trip through Russia. They were planning on setting up a lecture tour with the film when they got back to America. Hopefully, the lecture tour would be successful enough to finance another trip and launch them into the travelog business.

"I know it's a gamble, Jack," Clay said with so much conviction there was a slight tremor in his voice. "But, damnit, Jackie and I are going to make the most of our lives together—we've *got* to make our dream come true."

I am happy to say that it certainly has. And if their dreams of Adventure come true, why can't yours?

How much does it cost you to live for two months? More than $730, I'll bet. For that much, you can join an expedition from London to India, overland. The expedition is led and staffed by experienced professionals, lasts ten weeks, and the price includes everything: transport in the expedition vehicles, all ferry and road tolls, all your food and accommodations. You bring only personal articles and a sleeping bag. They furnish everything else. Across Europe to Istanbul, past Troy and the Hellespont, through Turkey and Persia to Afghanistan, and the Dasht-i-Margo (the Desert of Death), over the Khyber Pass to Kashmir, India, and the Taj Mahal, up steep mountain roads in the foothills of the Himalaya to the expedition's end in Kathmandu, Nepal. Ten weeks, seventy days, $730, inclusive.

What are you waiting for?

In Chapter One, I made the claim that "the average person is able to see, and go, and do, far more today than at any other period in human existence—more than the richest of the rich but fifty years ago." Now, I'm going to prove it.

I'm going to show you how you can venture to many of the World's remotest and most exotic places—trek in the Himalayas; journey overland from Tangiers to Capetown, from London to Calcutta; spend an afternoon at the North Pole; live with nomads in the Gobi—as easily as taking an American Express bus tour of southern France. For each of these, as well as the many more we'll shortly be talking about, are all offered by professional expedition outfitters.

Before we begin, I'd like to recall two other statements from that same chapter: "Age is no barrier to walk the highway of High Adventure. Nor is the fatness of your bank account."

Average good health is all that is required for most of the expeditions and adventures we're about to discuss. I'm not going to make you jog, or swim, or work out all day long for any of them (well, maybe for some!). And for the majority of them, physical handicaps present no difficulties—remember the seventy-two-year-old crippled doctor in Timbuktu.

You will not need much money, either. The London to Kathmandu junket for $730 mentioned above is just an example. You're going to see prices for these expeditions that I think will astound you.

There are, of course, well-known tour operators that specialize in exotic travel—and at a very high price. The best of these is Lindblad Travel in New York. I have a great deal of admiration for Lars Eric Lindblad; his tours and cruises are absolutely first-rate. But they are still formal, organized, *group tours*, even if they are to the Australian Outback instead of southern France. They are geared for the wealthy (and mostly elderly) tourist, each tour or cruise costing several thousand dollars. This is not what you and I are really after in the World of Adventure. Besides, information on this sort of thing you can get at the office of any travel agent.

One thing you are going to need is time. Many of these expeditions take several weeks, even months. I'll be listing quite a few that you can squeeze into a two or three week vacation, don't worry. But, if truth be known, I'd like to see you can the nine-to-five number. If you'll take a hard look at your talents, interests, and abilities, use your imagination, and examine all the alternative life-styles available or possible to you, I'm sure you can come up with one much more compatible with a life of Adventure than a nine-to-five, fifty weeks a year treadmill. Take my Mongolian expedition, for example. I knew how to handle a 16mm camera reasonably well, and how to get into Mongolia when no one else could. So, in exchange for my filming the Mongolian and Gobi countryside (for use as background shots in motion pictures), I found a stock film company in Hollywood that agreed to pick up the expedition tab. Now, if a 19-year-old kid can engineer something like that, I'm sure that if you put your mind to it, you can too.

OVERLAND TO INDIA

There are several companies offering expeditions from London to India, either terminating in Calcutta or Kathmandu, Nepal. Most can arrange for you to fly back to London on a group charter flight. Some have extensions of the expedition continuing on to Singapore and Sydney, Australia.

They vary, of course, in quality and price. The best way to find out about them is by writing to an amazing outfit called *Trailfinders*, at 48 Earls Court Road, London W8 6EJ, England (phone 01-937-9631). They will send you, free of charge*, the latest issue of their news›aper, the *Trail Finder*, which is loaded with articles on "overlanding," and with ads placed by expedition outfitters. The one I outlined above for $730 is, I feel, just about the best. It is run by *Exodus Expeditions*, next door to Trailfinders at 52 Earls Court Road.**

It is important to stress that theirs is not a group tour, but an expedition, and you participate in it as an expedition member, not as a pampered tourist. You help set up and break down camp, purchase food in native bazaars, help with cooking and camp chores. You spend most nights in a tent, not a hotel (although for

*Include $1 if you wish it sent airmail.

**By writing to Exodus, or any of the companies listed in the *Trail Finder*, they will send you an illustrated dossier on the expedition, with detailed itineraries, costs, departure dates, and specifics on what transport, accommodations, food, and equipment they provide.

238

four days you live on a houseboat in Kashmir!), and travel very much "off the beaten track" in four-wheel-drive Bedford trucks. As Exodus puts it:

> An expedition is the only way to make the most of travel. You don't do much exploration in a 45-seater coach, or need much pioneering zeal in the Tehran Hilton—but fording a swollen river in India, drinking tea with the Kurdish nomads, or bartering for carpets in an Afghan village is, we think, something more like what real travel is all about.

I couldn't agree more.

All the "overlanders" you'll be getting in touch with leave from London and follow the same general itinerary: Europe—Belgium, southern Germany, Austria, Yugoslavia, Bulgaria to Istanbul; Turkey—along the Black Sea coast, or (more frequent and more interesting) to the Hellespont, down the Ionian coast, across to the Goreme valley, meeting the northern route at Mt. Ararat and crossing into Persia; Iran (Persia)—to Tabriz and Tehran (the good ones, like Exodus, Intertrek, and Encounter Overland make a side trip to Isfahan and Persepolis at this point), over the Elburz mountains to the Caspian Sea, across to Meshed and the Afghan border; Afghanistan—from Herat to Kandahar,* skirting the Dasht-i-Margo, up to Kabul (with a side-trip to Bamyan on the better ones), and over the Khyber Pass; Pakistan—straight to Lahore and the Indian border; India—Amritsar, up to Kashmir and the houseboats, down to Delhi, Agra (the Taj Mahal), and the Ganges River, then turning north to end in Kathmandu.

Once in Nepal, you can go on a friendly Himalayan trek—book one in advance through Trailfinders, or check in on Col. Jimmy Roberts and Mike Cheney at their Mountain Travel office in Kathmandu to see what they have going—buzz around India, or continue on to Singapore and Sydney.

Driving down from Kathmandu to Calcutta, then south to Madras, India, you board a steamer for a six-day voyage across the Bay of Bengal to Penang, Malaya. From there it's up to Bangkok, then back down the Malayan peninsula all the way to Singapore. A seven-day cruise, passing between Sumatra and Java, ends at Freemantle, on the west coast of Australia, and a two-week drive

---

*Another reason I like Exodus: They take, weather and roads permitting, the northern route to Kabul via Mazar-i-Sharif, and visit Turcoman nomad encampments.

across the entire length of the Australian continent brings you at last to Sydney. Fourteen thousand miles. From London to Sydney: overland.

Certainly this is one of the great journeys you can make across the face of the earth. Most of those who make it are between seventeen and forty years of age, but as overlanders say: "It is the right attitude to life, rather than years, that counts."

Should you wish to take the overland-to-India route all by your lonesome, as I did recently, using the local transport of buses and trains, look into the Asian Rover ticket that Trailfinders offers. And if you'd like to hook up with someone who is making the journey in his own four-wheel-drive vehicle, check the travel section of the Sunday London *Times* for a few weeks (your local library should have it). Very often, these independent overlanders place classified ads in the Sunday Times inquiring for people to share expedition expenses.

TRANS-AFRICA

Sixteen thousand miles across the entire length and breadth of Africa. From the coast of Morocco to the sand seas and oases of the Sahara, to see prehistoric cave paintings and visit "The People of the Veil," Toureg nomads in a lost mountain range named Hoggar. Out of the sands, through savannah grasslands, and into the jungles of the Central African Republic and the Congo, following muddy tracks, fording rivers on makeshift rafts, and staying in pygmy villages. Camping at the foot of Mount Kilimanjaro, touring the famous game parks of East Africa like Serengeti and Ngorongoro, lying on the white, sandy beaches of Mombasa. Heading south on the route known as the Hell Run, through Tanzania and Zambia to Victoria Falls, pressing on toward the mysterious ruins of Zimbabwe, past Johannesburg to Durban, along the "garden route" finally to arrive in beautiful Capetown, South Africa. From London to Capetown, 16,000 miles, thirteen weeks, ninety-one days. Cost, all inclusive? About $1,000.

Once again, this is no group tour, strictly an expedition, using four-wheel-drive Bedford trucks and Land Rovers. It is run by a group of adventurous young lads calling themselves *The Great African Adventure Company*, because that's just what they offer. They're at 233 Station Road, Leigh-on-Sea Essex, England. Both Exodus and *Encounter Overland*, at 280 Old Brampton Road, London, SW5, offer similar expeditions, at slightly higher prices.

For other trans-Sahara and trans-Africa expeditions, write to Trail-finders.

EXPLORING OUTER MONGOLIA

Today, the thought of a lone individual traveling freely throughout Mongolia, going where he wants and talking to whomever he'd like, strikes terror into the heart of every bureaucrat with a baggy Russian suit in Ulan Bator. Why this is, I don't know. I was able to get in through a travel agent who was a personal friend of Khrushchev (remember him?) when he was still in power. Now that fat old butcher is dead and gone, so I can no longer exploit that angle.

There are a few very expensive group package tours, designed for the wealthy, jaded tourist, that include one week in Mongolia. For each of them, the Mongolian itinerary is exactly the same (in some of the brochures, even the wording describing the itinerary is the same, word for word). Flying in from Irkutsk, Siberia, the first two days are in Ulan Bator, the next two are at a special tourist encampment in the Gobi, the following two at the site of Karakorum (all that's left is one stone tortoise, as you know), and the nearby Erdeni-tsu monastery, built in 1586. The last day is again in Ulan Bator, and then it's back to Irkutsk. It is the same for everyone, no matter if they are with Travcoa, Travelworld, World Travel, Lindblad, or whomever. Since the week in Mongolia is always plugged into an extensive Russian or Asian tour, the total price hovers around five grand.

The only tour operator I know of who sells the week in Mongolia separately is *Afton Tours*, 1776 Broadway, New York, NY 10019 (phone 212/757-9595). It costs $775 out of Irkutsk, and you can get to Irkutsk, on the shores of Lake Baikal, any way you like. The best, without question, to my way of thinking, is an adventure in itself: via the Trans-Siberian railway.

You start by taking a boat from Yokohama (the port of Tokyo) to Nahodkha in the Russian Far East. You then board a train that follows the Ussuri River (on the other side is China), to Khabarovsk, crosses the "Jewish Autonomous Region" (yes, that's right—Stalin sent them all to Siberia once), and Buriat Mongolia, to Baikal and Irkutsk. You then join your group making the friendly Mongolian junket, and, upon returning to Irkutsk, resume your Siberian train ride to Novosibersk, Omsk, Sverdlovsk, over the Urals, and on to Moscow. The boat takes two days, the train to Irkutsk three and a half, from Irkutsk to Moscow six. Once in Moscow, you can fly to any number of cities in Europe—or you can disembark in Novosibersk and fly to the fabled cities of Russian Central Asia: Alma Ata, Tashkent, Samarkand, Bukhara, and Khiva. (For details, write to *Intourist*, 45 E. 49th St., New York, NY 10017.)

Now, you may ask: "Yes, Jack, that's fine for pre-packaged group tourist shows, but what about *real* travel and adventure in Mongolia?"

Well, for that, we turn again to Roman Hupalowski (see page 206). Since hunting requires the hunter to travel on an independent and exploratory basis, no matter what country he is hunting in, this is the way a big game hunter travels in Mongolia: independently and individually. And, since Roman is the official American representative for Mongolian Argali Safaris, annointed by Zhuulchin, he is in a position to arrange independent and individual travel throughout Mongolia for non-hunters as well.

Roman is the only one I know of who can do this. It will be expensive. Communists have a great habit of socking it to us rich capitalists, with their noncapitalistic (read noncompetitive and monopolistic) prices. But bear in mind that their price will include everything: all air fares in Mongolia, camping equipment, meals, guides, porters, interpreters, jeep transport, everything (it's much cheaper, by the way, if you can get at least two others as expedition companions).

Zhuulchin will ask $1,345 of you to explore the Gobi Desert for eight days (additional days at $100 per). They'll hit you up for $1,745 for two weeks of fishing and roaming about the environs of the Uburkhangai and Arhangai regions of beautiful western Mongolia. You'll be staying in *yurts*, no hotels, and travel via jeep, horse, and camel, going where you want to. You'll camp in rolling Mongol grasslands, high Altai forests, and Gobi wastelands, and sleep beneath the Seven Giants and the Golden Nail. You'll visit the *gers* of Gobi nomads—and might even meet Garghel and Shiri.

Personally, I think the prices are well worth it. Remember, you'll be traveling in *Mongolia*, exploring the bloody *Gobi Desert*, the land of all adventurers' dreams.

JOINING A SCIENTIFIC EXPEDITION

Between the Himalayan giants of Everest and Kanchenjunga in northeastern Nepal, there is a mysterious valley. It was carved out by the Arun River millions of years ago, while the Himalayas were still rising. Remaining unchanged all these eons, it has provided isolation and protection for many of Asia's strangest and rarest creatures—snow leopard, ibex, bearded vultures, langur and macaque monkeys, marbled cats, leaf birds, sun birds, ghoral, bharal, lesser panda—and, possibly, unknown species, yet to be discovered. It is uninhabited, and largely unexplored.

To reach this valley you must walk near the Tibetan border, pass through and live in villages of over twenty different cultures—Sherpas, Bhotias, Rais, Limbus, Gurungs, and others—most over 8,000 feet high.

To accompany scientists doing conservation research on an Arun Valley Wildlife Expedition, you must contact a most unique organization: *Educational Expeditions International*, at 68 Leonard Street, Belmont, Massachusetts 01218 (phone 617/489-3030).

EEI is a non-profit organization that sponsors research projects for scientists from all over the world. The projects are funded by non-scientists who participate in them as staff and research assistants. Participants may be women and men of all ages, and need no scientific background. You will receive your training right in the field. As EEI puts it:

> EEI expeditions are not tours or educational outings. They are working experiences designed to meet the needs and requirements of professional scientists. As a member of a team you will share the life-style of scientists whose research often takes place in remote environments. Rugged topography, extremes of climate, and isolation are not uncommon. You will be challenged intellectually, culturally, and physically.

On an EEI expedition, you may survey an ancient shipwreck off the coast of Mallorca, study the strange stone monuments of Bronze Age man in the Lake District of Scotland, excavate for mammoth bones and those of other prehistoric creatures deep in natural caves in Wyoming, or investigate the behavior of the whistling jungle dog in southwestern India. Ready to go? Good.

TO THE HERMIT KINGDOM
OF THE HIMALAYAS

East of Sikkim, north of Assam, and south of Tibet, there is a country of mountains and mystery that only a handful of Westerners have visited in the entire twentieth century. It is the

Kingdom of Bhutan, and it has recently opened its doors—ever so slightly—to wanderers in search of the remote and exotic.

Travel Corporation of India (TCI)* can arrange for you to accompany a small group visiting the Land of the Peaceful Dragon. Should you wish to avoid the mark-up (TCI's is lower than most others) and can put together a small group—no individual travel is permitted—write directly to the Bhutan Mission to the United Nations in New York.

From out of the jungles of west Bengal you'll enter a ravine where the village of Phuntsoling, a concoction of Tibetans, Mongolians, Bhutanese, and Indians, marks the gateway to Bhutan. A spectacularly precipitous road takes you up into the mountainous center of the Hermit Kingdom, and its capital, Thimphu. You'll visit medieval palaces, religious shrines or *chortens*, and fortresslike monasteries or *dzongs*. You'll climb high above the Paro Valley to enter the Tiger's Nest—the Taktsang monastery suspended on a vertical cliff. And then you will ride a yak from the monastery of Phajoding to Dongtsho-La. Here is a high pass where snowy Himalayan giants seem close enough to touch, where beneath you lie crystal lakes, frothy streams, countless millions of alpine flowers, and sudden glimpses of blue sheep and fluttering silver pheasants. Everything—the sky, the mountains, the meadows, and forests—is clear, open, and spacious, and there is a distant tinkling of yak bells. It is as close to Shangri-la as you will ever get.

ACROSS THE WESTERN HEMISPHERE

You are in Anchorage, Alaska. In your hand you hold a bus ticket. You are about to board a small "minibus" with a few friendly and adventurous people from several different places in the world. Where are you bound for? Rio de Janeiro.

From Anchorage past Mt. McKinley to Fairbanks, Whitehorse, Edmonton, Banff, and Vancouver; across to Yellowstone, Chicago, Montreal, and New York; down to Washington, Miami, New Orleans, Mexico City, Guatemala, Honduras, and Panama; a quick flight over the swamp of the Darien Gap to Bogota; then to Quito, Lima, and Cuzco, over the Andes to La Paz, Bolivia, and down the length of Chile to the beautiful Lake District; through the Andes for the fourth time and across the pampas of Argentina

*Their U. S. office is at 20 E. 53rd St., New York, NY 10022 (phone 212/371-8080).

to Buenos Aires; past Iguacu Falls to Asuncion, Paraguay; into the Amazon jungles to Brasilia, and finally, at last—Rio. You'll be camping about 75 percent of the time, with the rest in budget hotels, and be on the road for five months. Interested? Then contact *Hughes Overland/Intertrek* at 62 Battersea High Street, London, SW11 3HX, England.

You can book either half of the trip separately (halfway is Panama). Both take about seventy-five days and cost about $1,100 (allow around $450 for food and accommodations).

New York to Rio, Caracas to Buenos Aires, Bogota to Brasilia, Alaska to Brasil—these and other incredible journeys across the face of the Western Hemisphere are all out there, waiting for you to join in and jump on. To find out about all of them? Right. Contact Trailfinders.

SAILING AROUND THE WORLD

Owner of 96 foot Schooner leaving on 18 month around the world cruise. Crew wanted. Experience not needed. Investment required which is to be made back by the end of the cruise. Write owner for details.

Owner-skipper of 50 foot Alden Offshore Ketch requires 4 crew to cruise from Rhodes, in the Greek Islands, to the Canaries. Stops in Malta, Algiers, Tangier, Las Palmas, and others. Chance to stay on for two more months. Owner pays all expenses on trip, crew must be responsible for own transportation to Med and from Canaries. Write owner.

Owner of 56 foot motorsailer seeking couples to leave from California area to cruise to Amazon Basin. Share expenses and work. Please write for details.

These ads—and many more like them—are to be found in a very unique monthly newsletter, the *World Cruise News*. I say unique, because it is the *only* regularly published source of berth and employment information on private sailing yachts.

The newsletter is put out by an old Florida salt named Phil Beach. In putting together a sailing project of his own, Phil discovered that there are a lot of "big wind machines" tied to docks all over the world that are in need of crew. So he formed a "Sail Crew Clearing House" to act as a pool for crew of all ages and degrees of experience—including no experience at all—connecting them with various owners, skippers, and marine opportunities worldwide.

It should be stressed that this is for crewing on sail-powered ships only—no stinkpots. And while many owner skippers are requesting "all-girl crews" (one for a 130-foot Schooner) and female First Mates, there's a lady with a forty-five foot Ketch wanting an all-male crew for a cruise to South America. Now how about that?

It's true that experience is sometimes not needed—but, let's face it, experience and training will make you a lot more marketable to a skipper. If you take a course in celestial navigation (at your local college, or through ads in magazines like *Sea* and *Yachting*), you'll be a wanted asset on any ship. Look into whatever sailing opportunities and courses there are in your area. Acquire all the sailing experience you can get your hands on—then send $10 for a year's subscription to the SCCH *World Cruise News*, Box 1976, Orlando, Florida 32802.

I know that you, just like me and all the rest of us, have dreamed of presenting your medical extremity to the smog and bandicoot-race of the cattle car culture, clambering onto the polished wooden deck of a big schooner, hoisting the white sails up that tall mast, and gliding off into the sunsets of the Greek Islands, the Caribbean, and the South Pacific. Write to Phil, and that beautiful vision may very well become reality.

DIVING FOR SUNKEN TREASURE

Carved out of the jungle coast of Quintana Roo is a small cove called Xelha. By swimming through Xelha's clear turquoise water you can reach a grotto that leads to a subterranean cavern. The entrance to the cave is blocked, but you can look through a hole in the cave's roof. The Caribbean sunlight sparkles through the water, and one beam enters the hole to shine directly upon a Mayan sacrificial altar.

Inland lie hundreds of unexplored *cenotes*, the sacred wells of the Mayas, into which they threw, for thousands of years, their treasures of jade, gold, turquoise, and ebony, which lie on the bottoms now, together with the bones of countless human sacrifices.

One hundred miles to the north, a crescent of coral lurks just beneath the waters of the Caribbean Sea. It is Scorpion Reef, and along its submerged, multicolored flanks lie the encrusted wrecks of sixteenth- and seventeenth-century galleons, and their remains: cannons, cannonballs, glass bottles, flasks of mercury, flintlock pistols, silver plates—with the hallmarks still legible—gold doubloons, and silver eight reale coins, or "pieces of eight."

Would you like to join an underwater expedition to unblock the entrance to Xelha's cavern, enter the dark waters of a sacred *cenote*, or search for sunken treasure among the Scorpion's prey? Then contact Paul Bush Romero.

Paul is one of the key people behind an extraordinary organization: CEDAM International, a unique combination of professional marine archaeologists and amateur SCUBA divers. In cooperation with museums and universities throughout the world, CEDAM operates several major underwater archaeological expeditions every year.

By inviting amateur divers to participate in these expeditions, not only are some of the expeditions' costs defrayed, but the serious problem of souvenir scavaging and vandalism of important underwater sites may be alleviated by training divers in professional underwater exploration techniques, and by developing in them a desire to preserve these sites, to gain from them knowledge rather than mere souvenirs. And if you are interested in professional marine treasure salvage, here is the place to learn the skills required.

To join CEDAM International, write to Paul at: 5820 Burning Tree Drive, El Paso, Texas 79912; or to Dr. Andreas B. Rechnitzer at: 6368 Dockser Terrace, Falls Church, Virginia 22041. If you are not SCUBA certified, contact your nearest YMCA or dive shop for course and instruction information.

Several of CEDAM's leaders are convinced that there is an entire sunken city, built by the Mayas when the sea was lower, lying hidden in the waters off Mexico's Yucatan Peninsula. They will soon be conducting a search for it—the first sunken city found in the Western Hemisphere. Perhaps you will be diving with the expedition that discovers it.

TO THE NORTH POLE

Near the North Magnetic Pole, on Cornwallis Island in Canada's High Arctic, there lives a man named Eric Rowan. Early next spring, and each spring thereafter, Eric will be organizing one or two airborne expeditions that will have as their destination the end of the earth: the geographic North Pole.

As the experienced base manager of Kenting Aviation, the only privately owned commercial aviation service in this distant part of the world, Eric is in a unique position for leading such an expedition. And if you have saved up about three grand for a once-in-a-lifetime adventure, take the Nordair flight from Montreal to Resolute Bay, on Cornwallis Island, and give it to him, here is what he will do for you:

He first must prepare by placing fuel caches, equipped with radio beacons, far out on the pack ice. When all the many preparations are completed, upon your arrival Eric will have you clamber aboard a Twin Otter, loaded with sophisticated navigational equipment, with a skilled Kenting bush pilot at the controls. Your first stop will be Lake Hazen, on Ellesmere Island. At Lake Hazen is the base camp for your expedition to the Pole.

You'll be staying in a cabin with electric lights, a real bed, and blackout curtains—for Lake Hazen is more than a thousand miles north of the Arctic Circle, and the sun shines twenty-four hours a day.

It is an eerie feeling to know that the North Pole is only 600 miles away—and soon the time will come when Eric tells you the weather is clear, and to get aboard the Otter. As you pass over Cape Colombia, northern tip of Ellesmere, the frozen white ice sea of the Arctic Ocean will stretch out blindingly in front of you. Somewhere in all that whiteness is a mathematically calculated point exactly 90 degrees north.

When your pilot finds that point, using all his navigational skill, he will land on it. The skis (not wheels) will touch down on the ice, the plane will come to a stop, Eric will whip out the picnic basket, and you'll step out to have lunch on the top of the world.

A few days and 3,000 miles later, you'll be in Montreal, catching a plane back home and imagining the look on a friend's face when he asks you, "Where'd you spend your vacation?" and you tell him: "At the North Pole."

You can write to Eric c/o Kenting Aviation, Ltd., Resolute Bay, North West Territories, Canada (tel: 819/252-3849, via the Ottawa operator, area code 613).

WITH LOST TRIBES IN NEW GUINEA

One of my best friends is a tall, lean Yugoslav named Sava Maksic. Many of his other friends, however, call him Masta Pukpuk—for they speak no English, only Pidgin; they are the headhunters and cannibals of the Upper Sepik headwaters, and in Pidgin, Masta Pukpuk means Mr. Crocodile.

248

As a teen-age refugee from Yugoslavia, Sava ended up on a freighter bound for Australia. There he found he could make more money hunting crocodiles in northern Queensland than as a taxi driver in Sydney. It's just a short way across the Torres Strait from the tip of Cape York to Papua-New Guinea, and soon Sava found himself hunting crocs with primitive tribesmen in the remotest parts of the worlds's largest island.

So remote, in fact, that many of the areas had never been explored, and for many of the tribesmen that he lived with, alone, he was the first white man they had ever seen. He learned Pidgin and several tribal languages, lived their way of life, as one of them, and, over the years, became more knowledgeable in the whys and hows of their wild and beautiful primitive art—their masks, shields, drums, weapons, sculpture, costumes, and decorated human skulls—than most anyone on earth.

Today, Sava is a consultant and supplier of primitive art to various museums here in the United States. But, ever so often, he can be induced to lead a group of adventurous souls into the deepest, most remote regions of New Guinea, to visit and live with primitive tribes still living in the Stone Age, and still practicing, to some degree, headhunting and cannibalism.

You'll see rites and rituals seldom witnessed by outsiders, if ever. And, more importantly, you'll learn of their meaning. You'll hear their legends, eat their food, live in their villages, and, at night, sitting by a fire in their spirit houses, get inside their minds.

For exploration into the life and soul of New Guinea's Stone Age peoples, you can have no better guide than Sava. To accompany him on such an exploration, write to him at: 62 West 56th Street, New York, NY 10019 (phone 212/581-0079). Don't be surprised if you return home with a collection of primitive art worth enough to pay for your adventure.

RUNNING REMOTE RIVERS

The expeditions do involve a fair amount of risk, including encounters with wild and dangerous animals, local tribes who may be hostile, as well as bandits, the risks of some extremely hazardous rapids on the rivers, and risks on land involving cliffs, ravines, etc. . . . .

What are you waiting for?

This matter-of-fact description is to be found in the expedition dossier sent to applicants wishing to join river expeditions down the Omo and the Blue Nile in Ethiopia. They are run by a group of young yet very experienced white water explorer-adventurers called *Sobek Expeditions* at Box 67, Angels Camp, California 95222 (phone 209/736-2924).

These fellows were the first to explore and descend the Omo River. One of their discoveries was that of innumerable hidden waterfalls—up to 1,000 feet high—up adjoining ravines. Another was the fishing. Are you ready for 200-pound perch? They report it is almost impossible not to catch a ten-to-twenty-pound fish with but an hour's patience.

If dugout canoe voyages down tributaries of the Amazon near Iquitos, Peru, and staying in Yagua Indian villages appeals to you, contact *ARTA* (American River Touring Association), at 1016 Jackson St., Oakland, California 94607 (phone 415/465-9355). They are among the best river people in the business, and even though I must express strong disagreement with their views on the morality of private profit, I recommend them highly for any river trip in the West you may have in mind, from the Grand Canyon to the Middle Fork of the Salmon.

(Note: A listing of most river trips available, both foreign and domestic, is to be found in the "Special Interest Tours" section of the *Worldwide Tour Guide*, published by the Official Airline Guide. Any good travel agent has a copy.)

WILDERNESS EXPEDITIONS

Exploring northern Pakistan and the Valley of Swat; joining a camel expedition through the Hoggar mountains of the Sahara; trekking in Patagonia, the Himalayas, and the Karakorum; backpacking in Greenland and Iceland; climbing and hiking in the Soviet Alps, the Peruvian Andes, and the Mountains of the Moon; sailing to the forgotten islands of French Polynesia. . . .one organization offers all of these, and many more.

It is Mountain Travel, and it is unique in the world of adventure.

Mountain Travel, at 1398 Solano Ave., Albany, California 94706 (phone 415/527-8100), is operated by three amiable fellows—Leo Le Bon, Allen Steck, and Alla Schmitz—whom I had the pleasure of meeting one sunny spring afternoon, and I frankly became convinced that at what they have to offer—"expeditions

250

and outings to remote wilderness areas of the world"—they are the best there is.

They do not engage in long overland expeditions, but rather in-depth wilderness experiences in particular remote areas lasting, on the average, from twenty to thirty days.

While Leo's favorite spot is the Sahara, and is happiest roaming around the Tassili n'Ajjer astride a camel, and Allen loves to organize mountaineering expeditions to such giants as McKinley and Aconcagua, the real specialty of Mountain Travel is Nepal. Treks to Annapurna and Dhaulagiri, Mansalu, and the base camp of Mount Everest are all waiting for you.

One I like especially is through the Karnali district of remote western Nepal, hiking through the forests surrounding beautiful Rara Lake, and uninhabited valleys—except for the pandas, bears, monkeys, and leopards—to the hidden fortress-city of Tibrikot, where women kneel over wooden troughs making their cooking oil from the seeds of the *Cannibis sativa* plant.

You'll have to be in good physical condition. No riding around in a Land Rover or Bedford truck in Nepal; you must go it on foot, and trod the same narrow, steep trails and paths as the hill people. You do not have to backpack—porters will carry everything for you, as well as set up and break down camp, and cook all your meals besides. No technical mountain climbing experience is required, either (except on those specifically designed for mountaineering). You just have to be able to walk and hike about ten miles a day at high altitudes.

The ultimate in Himalayan trekking is, of course, a trek to the base of Mount Everest, the highest mountain on earth. It takes eighteen days and it is tough. You'll walk over 50,000 feet uphill in those eighteen days, so you'd better be pretty fit. Thankfully, you only have to walk part way back, to an airstrip and a chartered plane to Kathmandu.

Someday—although Leo is doing his best to talk me out of it—you and I are going to climb this sacred mountain, to stand on its crest 29,028 feet in the sky. But until we do, getting 18,000 feet up its flanks to Everest Base Camp will suffice as a first-class adventure by itself.

Write to Mountain Travel and you will receive an illustrated dossier outlining all their expeditions and outings. Their prices should pleasantly surprise you, but merely by looking at where they go, I guarantee: You will be astounded.

Another outfit I'm quite impressed with is *Earth Explorers*, at

1560 Sandburg Terrace, Chicago, Illinois 60610 (phone 312/787-5290). They run, among others, 4-wheel-drive expeditions in Kurdistan, Afghanistan, and Yemen, trekking expeditions in Borneo and Ladakh (the part of western Tibet in the Indian Himalayas), and—this is realy impressive—a mountaineering expedition to Tirich Mir, the highest peak of the Hindu Kush (25,282'). The prices are more reasonable than even Mountain Travel's: the Afghanistan and Kurdistan expeditions, for example, last 20 days and cost only $500 complete. The person to contact at Earth Explorers is a friendly and capable chap named Chris Wegelin. Contact Chris, and he'll make it his business to get you into "the remote, the untouched, and the unknown."

LEADING YOUR OWN EXPEDITION

In the remotest center of the Sahara there is a range of mountains called the Tibesti. A strange tribe lives in the Tibesti whose racial origins are very obscure: the *Tibu*, the "rock people," Aborigines of the Sahara. Past expeditions to the Tibesti have found crocodiles in hidden grotto pools, throwbacks to prehistoric days when the Sahara teemed with life as a grassland, and stunted from thousands of years of isolation. The highest mountain of the Tibesti (and of the entire Sahara as well) is Emi Koussi, at 11,004 feet—and in the winter, believe it or not, in the middle of the Sahara, there is snow on its peak.

If you want to beat me to the Tibesti, and climb Emi Koussi before I do, get in touch with Roger Balsom at Quest 4. You may remember Roger and Quest 4 from our discussion of the Galapagos (page 218).

Roger can custom-tailor an expedition for you—at a wonderfully low price—that will get you to just about any place in the world. Quest 4 (of which he is Controller of Operations) does not operate any fixed schedule of expeditions. They are, rather, "Expedition Consultants." They organize and conduct expeditions for museums, universities, and scientific institutions. They have advised the United Nations on the construction of the Trans-Sahara Highway, done African ritual mask research for Le Musée de l'Homme in Paris, and were in charge of the Smithsonian's expedition to witness the Total Solar Eclipse in Mauritania.

I met Roger in the most unlikely place of Nueva Rocafuerte, a jungle town on the Napo River just before it flows into Peru. Now with Quest 4, he lives in a cottage built in 1753, near the Rothschild Forest Reserve at Ashton Wold. It is there that he and his charming wife, Gillian, compile a register of people who are interested in, or are putting together, various expeditions. He calls it, with a touch of whimsey, B.E.R. (Balsom's Expedition Register).

Let me ask you a question. Sit back, relax, and just let the answer come without any effort. OK? Here it is: What is the one place in the world that, for you, is the ultimate in remote, exotic adventure?

If the *AG* hasn't told you already how to get there, Roger and Quest 4 will.

Mountain Travel can also help you organize your own expedition, particularly for most any place in Nepal, northern Pakistan (Hunza, Baltit, Karakorum, etc.), and Afghanistan.

For Australia, and expeditions to the Outback, visiting groups of traditional Aborigines—there are still some small groups of Abos in the Great Sandy Desert that have never seen a white man—or perhaps visiting the primitive islanders of the Torres Strait, I highly recommend Warwick Deacock, who heads up *Ausventure*, at Box 54, Mosman, N.S.W. 2088, Australia.

And then, once again, there is Trailfinders. They have an independent expedition service, specializing in long "overlanders."

ADVENTURE IN NORTH AMERICA

We have already talked about overlanders across our continent, and thence on to that of our Latin neighbors'. We also touched upon river float trips as well.

I'd like to turn you on now to an extraordinary publication. It is *The Explorer's Ltd. Source Book*, by an enterprising group calling themselves the Explorers Ltd. (Harper & Row, $4.95). With a style and format patterned after the *Last Whole Earth Catalog*, it provides information on an amazing variety of outdoor activities, from aerial photography and meteorology to survival schools, climbing schools, rock-climbing and mountaineering equipment, river touring, winter bivouacking, wilderness living, caving (spelunking), and even—are you ready?—dog-sledding and falconry.

It will give you detailed information—costs, equipment, schools, clubs, publications—on four of my favorite sports: rock-

253

climbing, sky-diving, SCUBA-diving, and ballooning. One they left out, however, is hang-gliding. For information on what is one of the most thrilling sports in the world, contact: *The United States Hang Gliding Association*, box 66306, Los Angeles, California 90066 (phone 213/390-3065); dues are $10 per year, which includes a subscription to their excellent monthly publication, *Ground Skimmer*.

So much of the World of Adventure is right here in America—and *The Explorer's Ltd. Source Book* is a good place to begin looking for it.

Another is that "Special Interest Tours" section of the OAG's *Worldwide Tour Guide* we briefly discussed back on page 250. A perusal of it will discover junkets for those into archaeology, bicycling, geology, snowmobiling, wine-tasting, covered wagons, and nude Caribbean cruises.

Braniff Airlines publishes a pamphlet listing a number of action trips for sportsmen, naturalists, archaeologists—and sun-and-fun seekers too—from Alaska and Canada to Mexico and South America. Send $1 to Braniff Outdoor Adventures, Room 1033, Box 35001, Dallas, Texas 75235.

If the Far North calls you as it does me, then Mountain Travel will tantalize you with their expedition to the unclimbed peaks and unexplored valleys of the Romanzof Mountains in extreme north-east Alaska. You'll fly from Fairbanks to Barter Island on the Arctic Ocean, then by bush-flight to base camp in the Romanzofs, for eighteen days of backpacking through incredibly beautiful terrain. I should, however, repeat the warning Leo and his friendly gang issue to all expedition applicants: "Caution: Mountain Travel trips can be habit-forming!"

Above the sixtieth parallel lies Canada's North West Territories. Here is the haunt of the Eskimo, the polar bear, Dall sheep, and grizzly bear in the majestic Mackensie Mountains, unending miles of untamed wildness, the midnight sun, *aurora borealis*, and some of the greatest fishing in the world. To find out how you can absorb the adventure of this land into your system, write to *Travel Arctic*, Yellowknife, North West Territories, Canada.

CONCLUSION
THE ADVENTUROUS ATTITUDE

The sea beneath me is one hundred feet straight down. The huge swells are rolling in from the Molokai Channel to crash against the cliff, sending spray fifty, sixty feet into the air. As the surf rebounds off the rock wall, it washes over two gigantic coral heads, turning the narrow space between them into a seething, churning mass of foam and white water. It is into that narrow, frothing space that I am about to jump. My heart is pounding so it seems I can hear it over the strong sea-wind blowing in my face and the loud *ka-WHUMP* of another wave pounding into the cliff. I give myself a pep talk. It does no good. I make several false starts. They do no good. One almost unbalances me, and I very nearly tumble off backwards. Finally I realize there is only one way: Look down at the ocean, say to hell with it, and go. I push out with my legs and take off into space.

That cliff is on the island of Oahu in Hawaii, between Koko Head and Makapuu, just south of Eternity Cove. It is waiting there, right now, for you. That cliff is the world of Adventure— and Life itself. For that is what Adventure and Life are all about. You must look them straight in the eye, say to hell with it and go. How many years do you think you have left to live? What are you going to do with them? Waste them, fritter them away? Keep on plugging at the old nine-to-five, reading about *me* climbing the Matterhorn and living with headhunters while *you* sit on your butt and do little but dream?

I've given you the tools, the information on how to live a life of Adventure. The rest, as they say, is up to you. You've made a good start: You bought and read this book. Now keep on going. That cliff, that mountain, that jungle—the whole beautiful world of Adventure—is out there, right now, waiting for you.

I once had a student from Mexico. Her name was Marina, and we spent one afternoon sitting by the fountain in the courtyard of the Philosophy building at USC, talking of her climb up Popocatepetl. Popo, at 17,888 feet, is the most famous—and most beautiful—mountain in Mexico. While Marina talked, she was looking off into the distance, and her blue eyes had such a shine that I knew she wasn't sitting next to me by the fountain but was up there, on her mountain, once again. When she reached the top, she put her hand on mine and said: "There is such a purity—a purity of joy—in accomplishing such a thing. Standing on the top of Popo I felt a happiness that was so clean, so pure."

It is Marina's "purity of joy" that I want *you* to achieve for yourself. It cannot be achieved by doing something for others. It can only be achieved by doing something for yourself. By yourself. Alone.

I'm not asking you to become greatly skilled, technically, or to be in the physical condition of an Olympic gold-medal champion. I'm not asking you to do anything foolish, or overly risky because of inadequate preparation and training. I had jumped off seventy- and eighty-foot cliffs dozens of times—but never off one of one hundred feet, never into a frothing ocean, just smooth ponds.* My problem was that while I knew I could do it, my will was not up to snuff. So I simply had to say to hell with it and go.

The skiers have an expression that sums up in three words this attitude towards life. You're at the top of a run, a steep run, and you're wondering that maybe it's a little *too* steep. Noticing your hesitation, they will turn to you, smile, and yell: *Go for it!*

Basically, then, and quite frankly, what it takes most for you to be an adventurer is for you to get off your *okole. Go for it!*

This is particularly true for women. Every Adventure in the *AG* is for a woman just as much as it is for a man. There is *not one* of them that women cannot do as easily as men.

What is un-feminine about climbing a mountain, living with headhunters, or exploring the Sahara? Not a damn thing.

For every reader of the *AG*, man and woman, boy and girl, I want *adventure to be a part of your life.* I want you to be *excited about*

---

*To prepare for your jumping off this cliff, practice at Waimea Falls on the north shore of Oahu, Kapena Falls in Pali Valley above Honolulu, and at the smaller cliffs just to the Koko Head side of the cliff itself.

life, life in general and especially *your* life in particular. Get excited about ideas, knowledge, history, philosophy, art, music, the marvelous beauty of the world, and the infinite number of things you can accomplish, of wild, romantic, wacked-out and exotic places you can go to. Far from being a "vale of tears," I think life on this earth is fantastic. I'm in love with it—and I want you to be too.

But, of course, I may be very presumptuous here—because, perhaps, you already are.

We've traveled a long ways together since we took that first step up the Matterhorn, haven't we? And in the years to come, we'll be traveling much, much farther than we have now.

We'll climb Kilimanjaro and, someday, even Mount Everest. We'll learn how to drive a Formula One race car, stunt a biplane, fly a hot-air balloon and get shot out of a cannon. We'll live with cannibals and pygmies, explore the Sahara, Arabia, and the Antarctic, and search for hidden jungle temples. All these, and many more, we will do together, in future editions of *The Adventurer's Guide*.

From now on, Adventure will be a part of *both* of our lives, right?

I don't think you need to ask me now why I jumped off that cliff. I jumped because—as I suspect you already know—it is in doing things like that that I feel so *alive*. As I spread out my arms, pushed off that ledge, and hurtled down toward that foaming water, I felt that free, joyous purity once again, when an overwhelming love for life surges through my body like an electric shock. And when *you* jump off that cliff, you will feel the same.